Dialogues in Academia I:
Introduction to a
New Faith for Mankind

Dialogues in Academia I:

Introduction to a New Faith for Mankind

Kathryn E. Ruggles

Kanehoe, Oahu, Hawaii

Contents

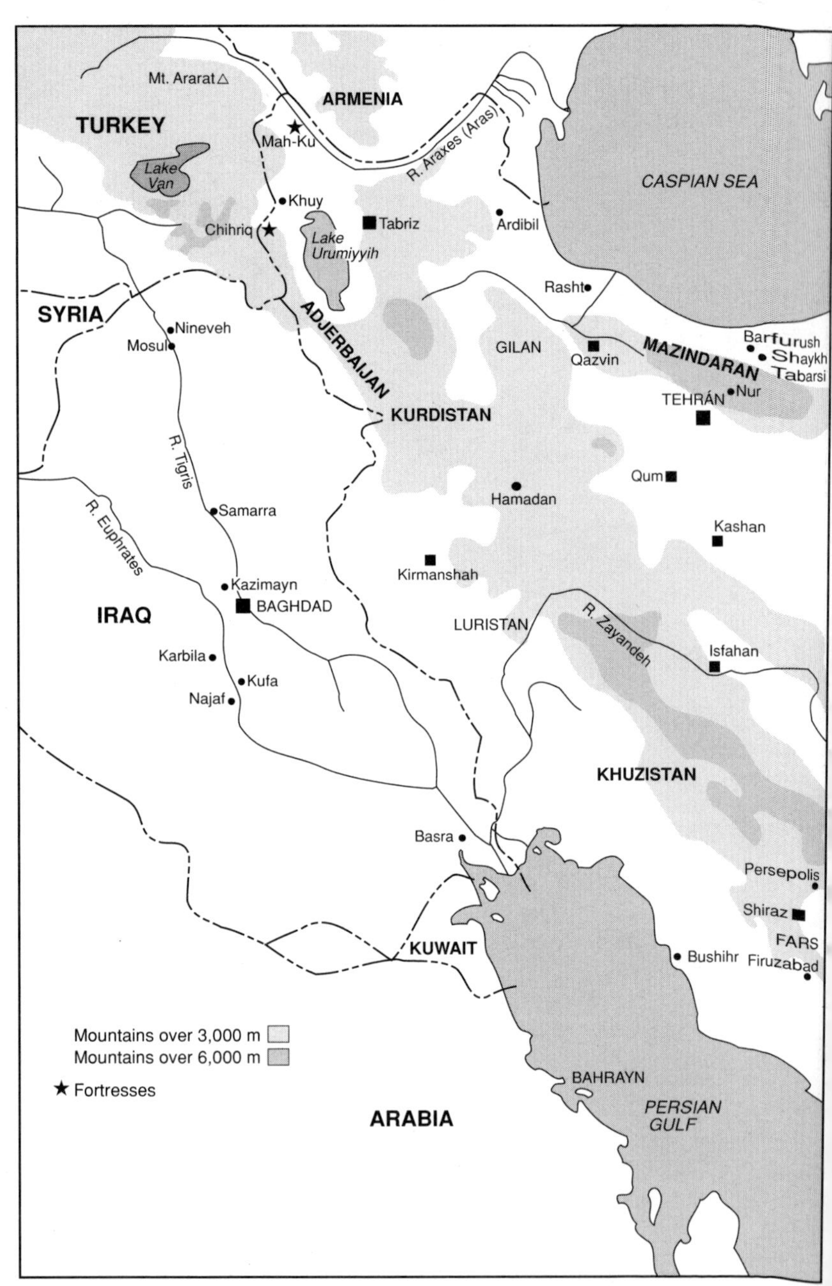

TURKEY
Mt. Ararat △
ARMENIA
Mah-Ku
Lake Van
Khuy
Chihriq
Tabriz
Lake Urumiyyih
Ardibil
CASPIAN SEA
R. Araxes (Aras)
ADJERBAIJAN
SYRIA
Nineveh
Mosul
Rasht
GILAN
Qazvin
MAZINDARAN
Barfurush
Shaykh Tabarsi
KURDISTAN
TEHRÁN
Nur
R. Tigris
Qum
R. Euphrates
Samarra
Hamadan
Kashan
Kirmanshah
Kazimayn
BAGHDAD
IRAQ
LURISTAN
R. Zayandeh
Isfahan
Karbila
Kufa
Najaf
KHUZISTAN
Basra
Persepolis
Shiraz
KUWAIT
FARS
Bushihr
Firuzabad
Mountains over 3,000 m
Mountains over 6,000 m
★ Fortresses
BAHRAYN
PERSIAN GULF
ARABIA

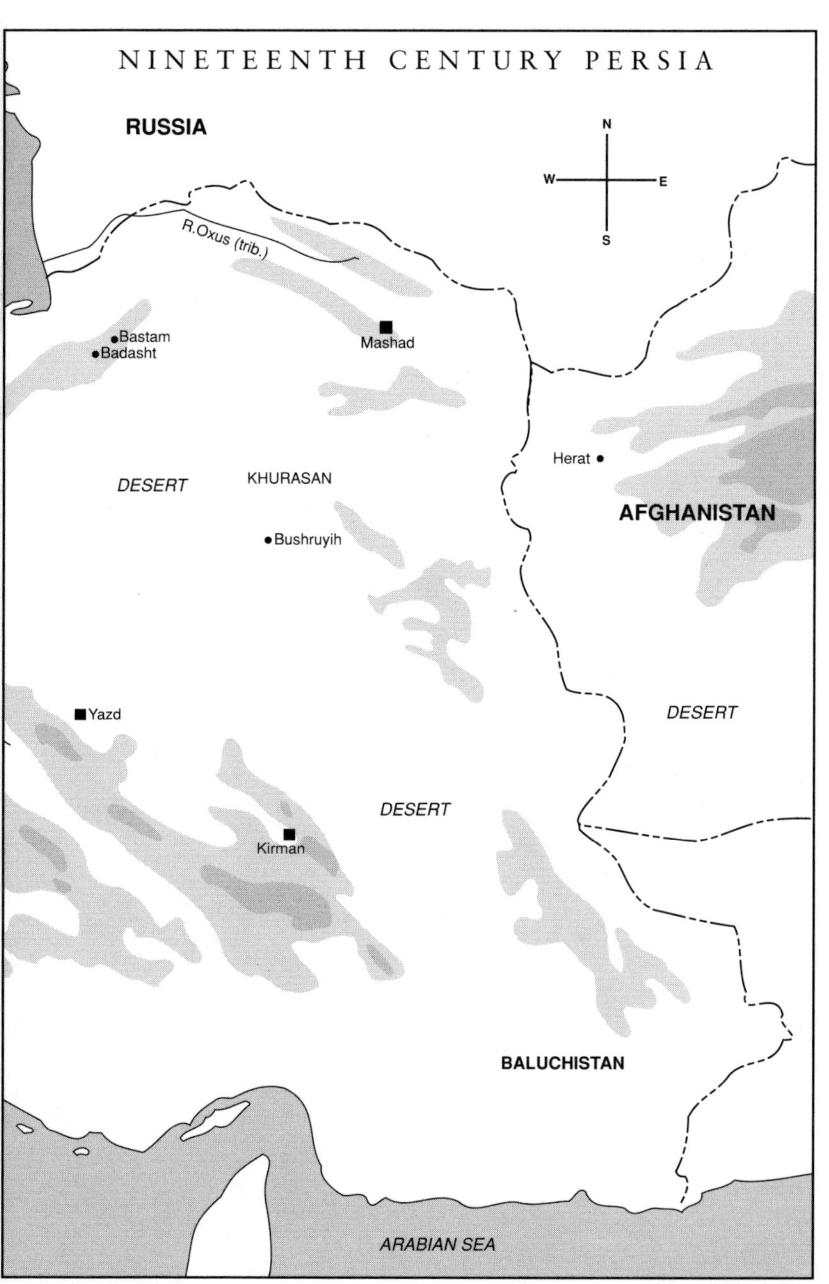

NINETEENTH CENTURY PERSIA
RUSSIA
N
W E
S
R.Oxus (trib.)
Bastam
Badasht
Mashad
DESERT
KHURASAN
Herat
AFGHANISTAN
Bushruyih
Yazd
DESERT
DESERT
Kirman
BALUCHISTAN
ARABIAN SEA

Foreword by the Author

The characters involved in the opening Introduction to this presentation, as well as the speakers in the ensuing dialogues, are fictitious. The basic subject matter, however, is not only factual but has produced in the last one hundred years a global movement unprecedented in its scope and speed. A list of both the historical and imaginary characters in the dialogues, including the persons portrayed in the scenes and conversations in the Shaykhi school in Iraq, can be found in the Appendix, along with grateful acknowledgment of preliminary material that has made possible the writing of this first series of academic discussions.

The stage will be set for the dialogues in the Introduction, a necessary prelude to the understanding of a nineteenth century phenomenon in the Middle East so little known to an unheeding, materialistic world that its potential for religious and political peace has been almost entirely ignored. The repercussions from this stirring drama, whose initial events are presented herein by two fictional professors in a midwestern university, are still resounding throughout the world and have come to two major consequences in our day: an emerging higher religion of global proportions and an almost incredible series of religious persecutions, deprivations and executions in Iran.

In the midst of disintegrating cultures and theological dissensions there exists in our time a blueprint for world peace, encompassing at the same time and from the same source the solutions to the major problems, reverberating from crisis to crisis, which plague every nation on earth. Political harmony is considered by and large a matter for governments, summit meetings, secular efforts for the cessation of war, and changes in temporal institutions, but without a religious accommodation to accompany such a desired achievement it can only be a lesser peace that is still vulnerable to the centuries-old disagreements and war-producing animosities of the world's still-living religions.

This is the final conclusion of a group of university professors, a Unitarian minister and a poetess, who gathered off campus every two weeks to discuss the affairs of an ailing world from the standpoint of a new approach to science and technology, art and poetry, mysticism and the levels of consciousness, politics and corruption, and the long cyclical sweep of the higher religions as a civilizing force in the life of mankind. In the friendly and informal setting of the dialogues, these subjects as well as others are far from an intellectual exercise for its own sake, and arise spontaneously as two of our professors, in whose home the discussions are conducted, introduce to the group a new religion they had brought back with them from the Middle East. The tapes of these first meetings during three months of the academic year of 1985-1986 will allow us to sit in with a number of scholars in academia, hitherto absorbed in their own expertise, as they respond to the history and tenets of a new faith.

Because of the desire on the part of our two host professors to impart the details of a new religion in as chronological a form as possible, the name by which this global faith is now known to the world has been kept in abeyance in Dialogues I. For the same reason the full acknowledgments that are due to the volumes of reading and research engaged in by the author have been reserved for the second series of meetings, in order that the titles and subtitles of these books do not carry us beyond the limits of the taped discussions presented here. Certain publications and their authors, however, are listed in the Appendix, as the general nature of their titles will not expose the mystery—for those who are not yet acquainted with his name—of that towering figure who declared himself in 1863 to be the Qayyúm, the Great Announcement prophesied by Muhammad, and the Spirit of Truth foretold by the Christ, whose story is revealed in many hundreds of volumes now spread around the globe.

The Forerunners of the Qayyúm, their beliefs and their rank in this historic movement, appear in the following pages. As for the so-called Qaim or Hidden Imam, the Promised One of Islam, the immediate Herald of that prophesied Spirit of Truth, his short and tragic life is presented in the final chapter of these first dialogues—a life sacrificed for the One whom he proclaimed to both East and West as the imminent Universal Prophet expected in the latter days by all the higher religions of the world.

Considering the extraordinary claims recorded here, as well as the magnitude of the loss of lives which occurred in the Middle East in the nineteenth century and still continues in relation to such claims, it is not surprising that our professors and their friends should find these matters a fruitful subject for discussion. The author wishes to emphasize in this respect that the viewpoints expressed by the speakers in these dialogues reflect opinions and attitudes during three months in the mid-1980s, and are therefore unaffected as yet by world events taking place from that period and onward, through 1989 and 1990. Unable to meet again due to commitments or changes of location, certain members of the group portrayed in this presentation will be replaced by others when further meetings in the same setting will hopefully be held in 1991.

And finally, I must stress that certain scenes and details in Dialogues I, as well as the conversations reported by

Mustafa's fictional journal as taking place within the Shaykhi school, are purely imaginative, though they are nevertheless deduced from and reflect as closely as possible contemporary accounts of the teachings and beliefs of the founders and scholars of the school. Historical events, however, are presented in as straightforward a manner as the author's research could ascertain; but in both areas, fictional and historical, she takes full responsibility for the way in which these extraordinary religious developments are portrayed, including the various interpretations, theological or otherwise, which show up in the dialogues.

Kathryn E. Ruggles
30 December 1990
Kaneohe, Oahu, Hawaii

Introduction

Before proceeding, in conjunction with my wife, to offer the following tapes in written form, I must first of all introduce myself.

My name is Hamilton Adams, a name part Anglican and part American Protestant, reflecting my family ancestry in the city of Boston. A graduate of Harvard, I hold a professorship at a well-known university situated in the midwest; am married to Professor Julia Livingston Adams, whose degree was obtained at Wellesley; and we live off-campus in a leafy part of our college town. My wife and I have written the requisite number of books in the respective areas of our scholarship, and are fortunate that our specialties, grounded in political history and religion, are interwoven in such a natural process that we have been able to give assistance to one another in any number of important ways.

In the fall of 1978 we began a year's sabbatical to be spent in several Near and Middle East countries in search of further material for our mutual interests. As Senior Professor in the Department of Middle East Studies I was well aware of the unstable conditions in that area, and both of us were anxious to make the journey before any further disturbances occurred. As far as our visit to Iran was concerned, we had been lulled, along with the rest of the country, by President Carter's declaration in 1977 when he toasted Iran as "an island of stability in one of the more troubled areas of the world." How wrong he was we have all discovered since the revolution unseated the Shah in January of 1979, and a subsequent reign of terrorism began on an ever-increasing world-wide scale.

Before we departed on sabbatical, Julia, as Professor of Comparative Religion, had felt extremely remiss that she had not yet unearthed any information about a new world faith initially generated in a holy city in the Ottoman province of Iraq in the last century. She had always prided herself on a thoroughly egalitarian approach to religious beliefs wherever they might be found, and was deeply versed in the various sectarian divisions among the Muslims, the Christians and the Jews, as well as the Buddhists and the Hindus. The divisive character of these various segments of religion had left both of us with a somewhat agnostic view of the subject, but Julia was conscientious in her scholarship and was bent on pursuing the tenets of the new faith for exposition in the classroom. She had ascertained that there were at that time many thousands of followers in the United States, but most of the population, though they may have heard or seen its name in one place or another, knew little of its history and principles, and looked upon it as some sort of Eastern cult quite out of the mainstream of the independent religions of the world.

Our first stop on sabbatical found us in mid-September in Egypt, where encounters in Cairo would provide me with a good deal of material for an upcoming book. But our stay in that country turned out to be short-lived. Rumors were rife that the Shah was in serious trouble in Tehran, and we thought it best to go there before the country closed itself to foreign passports. Julia was anxious to question the Iranian authorities at first hand, for in spite of its early beginnings in the so-called Shaykhi school in the holy city of Karbila in the Turkish province of Iraq, the meteoric rise of the new faith in the bordering country of Iran from 1844 to the present day has associated the religion with Persia and the Persians. We found out, of course, that such questioning would have been totally inadvisable, if not a dangerous mistake, and with an almost incredible stroke of good fortune it turned out to be unnecessary as well. If we had not taken our providential flight to the capital of the Shah at that particular time, and on that particular plane, the following dialogues in their present form would not have been produced.

To this very day we marvel at the windfall that came to us on that flight to Tehran, the extraordinary synchronization of events that found Doctor Ibrahim Varqa sitting beside us on the aisle seat. Buried in magazines we were uncommunicative for some time, but when Julia took from her bag a small volume on the differences between Sunni and Shia doctrines, the handsome gentleman, obviously an Iranian, who had been reading with such concentration beside her, glanced down at the title of the book. Tapping the article he had been so absorbed in, he addressed us with a warm smile.

"A good deal is being written lately about my country," he said. "I have been away in England, but felt that I ought to return if a revolution against the Shah's regime is imminent."

He paused and looked down at the book in Julia's hand. "It is a rare experience to see a Westerner so interested in the doctrines of Islam. May I ask if you are visitors to Tehran for the first time? If so, I may be able to assist you during your stay in the city. There is much to learn at this crucial period, if one is careful to talk with the right people."

We thanked him for his gracious offer, remarking that it was a fine example of the well-known hospitality of the Persians. At that point we introduced ourselves as university professors, and learned that our seat-mate was a practicing physician whose patients included certain members of the royal family; their possible fate at the moment deeply concerned him. We talked at some length of the parlous state of world politics and the sad decline of morals and ethics everywhere. When we finally enlightened the doctor on the respective areas of our scholarship he looked at us sharply, his dark eyes alert with interest. We had come to his country, we said, to update our information on political and religious affairs; that we were writers as well as scholars, and hoped to find the right people he had mentioned to whom we might address our questions.

"As far as political conditions are concerned in Iran," he told us, "they are fairly evident—a state of chaos bordering on insanity, and there is no doubt in my mind that blood will be shed if the fundamentalist clergy gain control in the capital. In our country, as you know, religion and politics go hand in hand—at least they have always done so in Islamic lands until the Pahlavi regime and especially the present Shah proceeded to Westernize the nation and throw aside the centuries-old customs of Islam."

The doctor turned and glanced around the plane. It had been obvious from the start, from the lowered tone of his voice, that he did not wish our conversation to be overheard. The flight had been undersold, due, no doubt, to the precarious state of affairs in Tehran, and the seats around us were unoccupied; indeed it had seemed strange to me that the three of us were put together in adjoining accommodations. Apparently satisfied that no one was paying us the slightest attention, the doctor leaned toward us once again.

"The reaction to all this modernizing has been brewing for some time, and the orthodox radicals are now bent on ousting the Shah and returning the country to the old ways. Unfortunately this kind of revolution by extremists will not correct the brutalities of the Savak police or the lack of observance of human rights, but on the contrary will produce a government far worse, and far more brutal, than any we have known in this country since the days when the Qajars ruled the land in the nineteenth century."

"As a matter of fact," he said, his voice carefully diminished, "the final demise of the Shah's regime is something I am not looking forward to. My fellow religionists and I will be far more at risk under the fundamentalists than under the rule of the Shah, however corrupt. I had thought of remaining in England but finally decided I could not desert my fellow believers in Iran—there are some three hundred and fifty thousand or so still resident in my country. You will not be able to extract any true facts about us from either government or religious authorities now in power, but I can aid you with certain information if you will trust me to do so."

Julia and I were both aware at that point that something unusual was taking place there in the skies, and that we had linked up in that plane, incredible as it may seem, with exactly the right person to interview on religious and political affairs in Iran. Julia in particular was in a state of complete amazement at finding beside her, without a doubt, a member of the faith which she had come to the Middle East to explore. She had been informed of their large numbers in Iran, and the more than one hundred years they had struggled amidst Islamic hostility to maintain their dignity, their institutions and their way of life. The doctor was a good example, according to what we'd been told, of the men in high positions in Iran who belonged to the faith; he appeared to be extremely well-balanced, socially at ease, and manifestly well-educated; there were no signs whatever of fanaticism or bitterness. I judged him to be in his early forties and a person of considerable affluence. As a court physician he could advise us how to conduct ourselves in a country in apparent turmoil and when, if necessary, we should pick up our passports and depart. Julia was now determined to settle the matter, and clasping her hands with enthusiasm she turned to our new acquaintance.

"Doctor Varqa, you are most kind. May we invite you to dine with us tomorrow evening at our hotel? It is evident to me that you belong to the one religion that is missing from my books, and I intend to make amends for this oversight as soon as my university work will allow. The meeting with you is quite providential, a most wonderful coincidence. I have not yet encountered the faith at first hand in America and have read none of the books on the subject—clearly an omission of the worst kind on my part. Perhaps it is just as well, as you may be able to give me information not yet available in the West. If you are willing, we might have a series of meetings —"

"Professor Adams—there is no doubt whatever in my mind that this is not a matter of coincidence. In the first place I am not in the habit of speaking of my religion to Western visitors, who might be offended by such an intrusion, but something told me that here was an opportunity, in the company of two eminent writers and scholars, to inform the Western world that my faith does not consist in my country of fanatical Persians devoted to the arts of martyrdom as a free pass to heaven, that we are not an off-beat sect of Islam, but a quite independent religion which holds no hostility toward any of the former faiths of the world, including Islam."

He glanced once more around the plane. It was obvious he wished to protect us as well as himself.

"In order to cover the history and the theological aspects of the faith," he said, "we will need more than a few meetings in a hotel dining room—a public display of mutual interest that might cause some trouble for the three of us. I have a rather nice house in the northern section of the city. My wife died three years ago and my son and his wife live in London. I suggest that you come to dinner with me instead tomorrow evening, and if you like the place you are more than welcome to stay as long as you wish as my house-guests. If this is agreeable I will send my car for you after sunset, and return you to your hotel to make a decision on the matter. I can promise you some good Persian meals, if you like them, and I hope some absorbing conversation on a subject that long before this should have aroused the interest of the world."

It will suffice to sum up here that we spent three active and informative months in Iran, dividing our time between observing the intensifying political developments and spending long evenings and sometimes the weekends in the home of Doctor Varqa, our notebooks in hand. We paid the requisite visits by plane to Qum, Isfahan, Shiraz and Tabriz, remaining reluctantly for too short a period in each city in case some sort of political explosion occurred in the capital. In Tehran we accepted invitations from a number of families of the more modern elite, who seemed to us—the men in expensive business suits and the charming and well-groomed women without the customary veils—to be very much like our own well-to-do friends in the West. Although disturbed by the possibility of revolutionary changes in their country, they were unable to envision the loss of their wealth or prestige or to imagine their civilized and up-to-date city without the glamor and majesty of the Shah and his beautiful wife, who had done so much to return the monarchy to the brilliance of the ancient Empire.

But the doctor knew better. He was aware of conditions at court, the precarious health of the Shah, and the long-prepared plans of the Ayatollah Khomeini, in exile in Paris. In mid-December he became concerned that we might be caught in a situation uncomfortable or even dangerous for foreigners, and at his urging we decided to fly to Baghdad, and from there to visit the town of Karbila some miles to the southwest on the river Euphrates, where anticipations and prophecies in relation to a coming Apocalypse were taught in the Shaykhi school from 1821 to 1844. These were not the first teachings, however, on the imminent Advent of that sacred figure who was known by the Shia Muslims as the Hidden Imam, the Qaim, the Promised One of Islam, and sometimes the Mihdi or the Mahdi, the Lord of the Age. We will deal later in the dialogues with the earliest Forerunner of the faith, Shaykh Ahmad-i-Ahsai, who established the school in Iraq with his closest disciple, Siyyid Kazim, after years of teaching and proclamation in Persia.

We were anxious to see the one-time holy city from where a new religion had eventually spread to every corner of the world, and to visit the tomb of the Imam Husayn, the grandson and the most revered of the Shia descendants of the House of Muhammad. But when we reached Karbila we found the present population self-absorbed and unfriendly, and unwilling, it seemed, to talk to two foreigners about the past. Nevertheless Julia conjured up in her imagination the remarkable events that occurred there a hundred and forty-odd years ago, and declared that the ghosts of Shaykh Ahmad and Siyyid Kazim would see to it that she presented the facts of these Forerunners in the way they deserved.

As for Baghdad, it featured prominently in the history of the faith from 1853 to 1863, and we were able to pinpoint certain locations where the exiled followers from Persia would gather in their weakened numbers and carry on the teachings under conditions which almost wiped them out. But such a demise was not to be. In 1863 a startling announcement was made in Baghdad in a large garden on the banks of the Tigris river, and this momentous happening, a turning point in religious history, brought about a change in the name of the faith. In our second series of dialogues we will discuss how the initial belief in the Advent of the Promised One of Islam, the Qaim, in 1844, rose slowly to a new beginning under the Universal Prophet, the Qayyúm, and in

1863 began its long journey through Ottoman Turkey to the Holy Land. In September of 1893, through the World Parliament of Religions in Chicago, it reached the United States, and in the following year the first American believers came into the faith.

Before our departure from Tehran we had spent a last weekend at the doctor's home, polishing up our notes and going over the many books and manuscripts in his comprehensive library. Two days later we said farewell to a man whom we now looked upon as a close friend, esteemed not only for his brilliant intellect but for the wonderful warmth of his personality. Julia and I were by this time captivated by the potentialities of the new religion, and indeed its already proven capacity, to bring about the unity of large numbers of people from all walks of life and from all races, classes and creeds, to establish justice within its ranks and an almost total regeneration of morals not yet seen in the cultures of our world—a world that had lost its way amidst the overwhelming distractions of materialism and the profligate liberty of the individual to do as he or she desired regardless of society at large. Contrary to much of our experience in life, we had soon discovered in Doctor Varqa a complete devotion to the service of his fellow-man, and a mind and a heart which reserved the right to judge the defective systems and institutions of the world, but never the persons who brought them about. Under any and all circumstances, he said, he would leave the individual soul to God.

At the end of our visit to Baghdad, where we were told of the downfall of the Shah, we made our way back to Egypt through Syria, Lebanon and Israel, dropping notes to the doctor as we moved through those countries for the next few months. In Cairo we found a letter awaiting us which disturbed us greatly: the doctor's house had been recently ransacked, his books and manuscripts slashed and thrown on the floor, and red ink—intended no doubt to be symbolic—was poured on his carpets, his furniture and other prized possessions. He himself, he wrote, had no longer any connection with his former patients at court, and his service was now of necessity restricted to his fellow believers, a number of whom were receiving the full force of the fundamentalist revolution and its hatred of a non-Islamic faith in its midst. We answered immediately, urging him to leave Iran and come to us in America. We had now spent eight months in the Near and Middle East, and were ready, we said, to return home, where a place in my department would be found for him at the university. We waited anxiously in Cairo for the following week, fearing without saying so the possibilities inherent in a dangerous and death-dealing situation.

When the news finally arrived we were overcome with such genuine grief that we cancelled a stop-over in Geneva, unable to extract any further pleasure from our journey. The letter came from the doctor's chauffeur, an undeclared believer, who had driven us around the city on many occasions. The doctor, it said, had been dragged from his home, and imprisoned in a cell so deliberately narrow that he was unable to stretch out for a decent night's sleep. His adamant refusal to recant his faith had so angered his jailers that he had been tortured on several occasions, bearing up with the greatest heroism and without a word of retaliation against his tormentors. His servants were forbidden to take him the proper food, and no one could tell what his fate might be. He himself, the chauffeur wrote, would soon attempt to leave Iran for another country, as so many of the Persian believers and the Westernized subjects of the Shah, both wealthy and otherwise, were continuing to do day by day. He would give this letter to a trusted confidant who was flying to Cairo, and it was unlikely that any further information could be sent to us in the future.

Feeling that we must make a last effort to receive further news of our new friend in Tehran, we went the next morning to the American Embassy, hoping they could advise us on how this could be accomplished. The Ambassador was away in Aswan, but one of the young secretaries came from behind her desk to talk with us. In the course of explaining our reason for the visit, we noticed that the girl's eyes widened suddenly with surprise, and she led us to an empty corner of the room.

"I am a Persian," she said, "and I knew Doctor Varqa well—a wonderful man. He was chairman of our Spiritual Assembly when my family lived in Tehran." She looked at us sadly, her eyes brimming with tears. "We were told last night that he was executed a week ago and his body thrown outside the prison walls. For one reason, the authorities said, because he was an underling and spy of the Shah—but secondly and even more important he would not withdraw his membership in a blasphemous movement whose intention was to undermine the true Islamic faith. It is all lies, of course—they are dedicated, as they were in the nineteenth century, to wiping us out completely in Iran."

We thanked her, wished her and her community well, and in our sorrow walked silently from the Embassy. On the ride to the hotel we reached mutually for a sympathetic hand, and without a word between us, suffered the loss of our friend.

Once in our hotel room Julia unearthed the copy of certain portions of a manuscript written by an ancestor of Doctor Varqa, a Mulla Mustafa of Kashan in Persia, a member in his youth of the Shaykhi school. She looked it over for some time, and finally packed it away with our notes.

"Ham," she said at last, "we possess all that is now left of the doctor's library. I cannot help but believe that providence has blessed us with all this material, fresh from an honored martyr for what we have come to accept as a culmination for our time of all the religions of the past. And I can hear the doctor saying that none of this is a matter of coincidence, not our meeting in the plane, nor our acceptance of his hospitality, and not our meeting with the secretary at the Embassy. He is still with us in spirit, Ham, and we must do all that we can to present his faith in the proper light."

Back in America we decided to visit relatives in Maine and Cape Cod, and to round out the summer by taking in a number of university conferences in New England. Nowhere did we find the slightest interest in a new religion that had come out of the Near or Middle East, where horrors untold were being performed in the name of the God of Islam. Slowly and reluctantly we realized that our enthusiasm, under the existing circumstances, was not to be shared by relatives who were ardent Protestants or professors absorbed in their own interests. Returning to the midwest we found ourselves overwhelmed with preparations for the fall semester. In October the Shah, suffering with cancer, was given asylum in America, and on November the fourth the revolutionaries entered our Embassy in Tehran and initiated the long and humiliating ordeal of American hostages in the hands of the Ayatollah. It was no time to talk of an alien religion, or so at least we concluded.

Perhaps it was just as well. In the following five years the plight of mankind in both East and West became so obvious to every thinking man and woman that it once again seemed possible—aside from the never-ceasing ministry of the television evangelists who constantly warned the world of the impending Advent of the Christ—to speak of a return to the Revelations of the Prophets of God in various lands, those Founders of religion whose personal teachings, so similar in their spiritual content, had been thrown to the winds in the interests of religious prejudice, political rivalry and national hatreds. It was time to recall the statement of that creative thinker and inventor, Buckminster Fuller, that planetary affairs were now in such a dangerous condition that nothing less than Utopia could save us.

Was the new religion from the East a step to that end? In November of 1985 we redeemed our promise to Doctor Varqa and invited a number of friends to share a review of our sabbatical material. Miraculously, it turned out to fulfill the plans we had long had in mind, and for three months of the academic year we met biweekly in our home off campus, exchanging our views on the state of the world from the standpoint of our respective interests. As time went on in these meetings the orientation toward the new faith became more and more pronounced, and Julia and I were able to present an almost complete account of what we had learned in Iran of its early beginnings. In doing so we dedicated our thoughts and our words to the memory of Doctor Varqa.

As a prelude to the tapes it seemed to me that Julia should present an informative exposition, however brief, of the Muslim background into which the new religion was born, and she readily agreed to do so. But brevity is not Julia's style where religious history is concerned, and she felt that any such prelude should not only acquaint the reader with the differences between the Sunnis and the Shias and the tragic condition of Persia in the nineteenth century, but should include as well a condensation of the course of Islam over the centuries, a subject in its fullness of such vast and complex proportions that the West has remained almost totally ignorant of its former impact on the world and its many and detailed ramifications from the time of Muhammad to the present day. By this means also, many of the names and places later encountered in the dialogues would become familiar, and the continuity and cyclical character of religious development, as well as its rise and fall, would become apparent. No religion arises in a vacuum, as a study of the world's faiths will easily prove; like a phoenix they build upon the burnt-out fires of what has gone before. And this has almost invariably taken place in the area in which the last extant religion has lost its dynamic life and where nothing of its creative spirit remains.

It is obvious that we have had to make a choice from the various spellings of names and places in the Middle East, and we have made a decision at the same time to drop the many traditional marks usually accompanying these names in order to simplify matters for the Western reader. The meaning of certain titles and other designations will also be included in the Prelude, as well as the names and personal appearance of the colleagues who met with us in our home. The preliminary knowledge contained in both the Introduction and the Prelude will enable the reader, we hope, to understand more fully the human figures, both Eastern and Western, embodied in the dialogues.

Julia's Prelude to the Tapes

In order to better comprehend the period in the Middle East which gave birth to a new faith in nineteenth-century Persia, a number of important things need to be said.

A religious historian, Stanwood Cobb, has written that "to understand a people we must try to feel as they do. And to understand an epoch we need to imagine ourselves as living in it." This is a difficult thing to do in a world divided into neat categories of who is right and who is wrong, and we can hardly expect a Christian, for example, to put himself into the shoes of a zealous Muslim in the most downtrodden nation on earth a hundred or more years ago. Nevertheless we must make the attempt if the following dialogues are to have any meaning for either biased or receptive minds.

For a fuller understanding, however, of what occurred in Persia in the nineteenth century, we must look back a long way into the past. To begin with, Persia has been almost totally a Shiite nation since the Savafid regime in the sixteenth century declared the Shia beliefs to be the state religion. But these beliefs, out of which our new religion emerged, had their origin in Medina in Arabia in the first days succeeding Muhammad's death in 632 A.D., and should be properly clarified if we are to apprehend the tenacious continuity of the Shia convictions for over a thousand years.

Although differences and complexities abound, two major facts should be known about these convictions in contradistinction to those of the Sunni sect, a far larger division of Islam. In Medina, a town to the north of Mecca that was chosen by the Prophet as his home and burial place, a minority of believers, who later came to be known as Shias or Shiites, maintained at Muhammad's demise that the male members of his family and their descendants should rule over the spiritual and administrative life of the faith. And secondly, they further maintained that Ali, the cousin and son-in-law of the Prophet, the husband of Muhammad's daughter Fatima, had been designated by his father-in-law to succeed him in governing the affairs of Islam, both religious and political.

On the contrary, the early Sunnis, activated by the well-to-do merchants of the Qoraysh tribe in Mecca, firmly asserted that nothing had been written down to that effect and that elections should therefore be held to choose a successor among the older companions of the Prophet. They contended that Ali was too young and inexperienced to rule, that he was under the thumb of the women in the Prophet's household and would not be an aggressive force in spreading the faith to other lands, both pagan and otherwise. The election of an older Caliph, they declared, would combine in a balanced manner the political and religious power so well displayed by Muhammad. For the time being they won the argument. That the Sunnis later put aside such elections, however, and passed on their authority in the conquered lands to their progeny, their relatives or their favorites at court, is a well-established fact. But the great schism that divided the Muslim faith on the death of Muhammad in 632 and the subsequent division between the Caliphate and the Imamate has left its devastating mark on the faith of Islam to the present day.

An important point to be remembered pertains to the twelve successive Imams of the House of the Prophet, beginning with Ali in 632 and ending with the lost or Hidden Imam in 874. Except for the delayed and tragically aborted rule of

Ali as the fourth Caliph, no other Imam of Medina was allowed by the Sunni descendants of the Meccan overlords, the autocratic Umayyads of Damascus, or by fanatical sub-sects such as the Kharijites, to attain to any real power. One by one, including Ali, and excepting only the child Imam lost in a cave in Samarra in 874, they were murdered in a variety of violent and stealthy ways—by the sword, by daggers, by beheading or by lethal poisons. Edward Gibbon has written that the Meccans, the persecutors of Muhammad, "usurped the inheritance of his children, and the Champions of idolatry became the supreme heads of his religion and empire." But in spite of the sufferings they endured the descendants and the offshoots of the Prophet's household maintained the spiritual integrity of the Imamate, and became for the Shias a sacred focus of loyalty and dedication, remaining the center of their devotion down to our own day.

One must note here, however, that the Sunni House of Umayya carried the banner of Islam throughout the Middle and Near East, and opened the portals to North Africa, Sicily and Spain, to Central Asia and India. Usurpers they no doubt were, but the force of the initial Sunni explosion, carrying with it the Qoran and the oral traditions of the days of the Prophet, and mingling the faith with the cultures of the conquered lands, established the foundations of a civilization unsurpassed in its creativity—in prose and poetry, in art and architecture, in philosophy, scholarship and history, in geography, astronomy, mathematics, medicine and music, in reactivating the learning and wisdom of the Greeks and in building splendid libraries, schools and universities. And last but not least it bound many lands together in the pageantry of its synchronized rituals and the vast unifying system, carried from one region to another, of its code of laws and patterns of behavior, the Sharia and the Sunna.

As a result of the enormous success of the early spread of Islam, the spiritual teachings and the prophecies of the Imams in Medina became a matter of indifference to the Sunnis, who in many instances, though cleaving to the Qoran and Traditions in their laws and political behavior, were personally tyrannical, unscrupulous and dissolute, following in the footsteps of their Caliphs. In the eighth century, after close to a hundred years of detested rule from Damascus by the Umayyads, a group of largely non-Arab Muslims in the province of Khurasan in Persia plotted a revolt and raised an army to march against the hated enemy. Led by descendants of Abbas of Mecca, an uncle of Muhammad and a prominent member of the Prophet's clan, the Bani-Hashim, this Hashimite uprising, flying the black standard of the House of Abbas, defeated the Umayyads in a battle eighty miles south of Mosul in Iraq, and proceeded to dislodge them from power in all areas of the Near and Middle East.

The establishment of the Abbasid Caliphate in a new and resplendent capital, the city of Baghdad, was a turning point not only for the Persians but for other non-Arab peoples within the fold of Islam; the Umayyads, autocratic in their racial attitude of superiority as Arabians, had allowed no one but Arabs to hold the reins of government. Baghdad on the other hand, and despite the shortcomings and often deplorable behavior of individual Abbasid Caliphs, became the hub of a liberal policy which brought many hitherto unwelcome races into the administrative area of the Caliphate, and opened the doors as well to those whose accomplishments and heritage could contribute to a new period of grandeur in the life of Islam. The reputation of the new city on the Tigris, traveling by word of mouth to all corners of the empire, attracted the very cream of the literary, artistic, political and ecclesiastical segments of the faith of Muhammad, and began slowly, and over the next few centuries, to change the face of the Middle and Near East and influence the backward countries of Europe.

As a consequence of the new policies a Golden Age ensued under the reigns of Haroun-al-Rashid and his son Mamún whose magnificence has come down to us in the records of history and in the tales and anecdotes of such compositions as "The Thousand And One Nights." Unfortunately the hostility of the Caliphs against the House of Ali in Medina did not abate under the new regime. Ruling from 750 to 861, the House of Abbas, originally allied in Khurasan with supporters of the Shia claims, was equally as guilty as the Umayyads in their subsequent persecution and cold-blooded treatment of the last remaining Imams. It is a black page to be shared with the House of Umayya in an otherwise remarkable and indeed incredible civilization—a burgeoning of human potentialities stemming from one lone man amidst the idolatry and the desert wastes of the Hijaz, whose teachings and consequent brilliance of the empire he inspired are so little known and understood by the West that the reader's necessity to be informed of some of its salient points has caused me to spend more than a brief time in outlining the major developments in the interest of certain conclusions in the dialogues.

In reporting the histories of our great religions, it is necessary in the name of honesty and justice to expose the deficiencies of their followers—ugly warts and all—which can be found in every living religion on earth. But hitherto the phenomenal flowering of the creative power of the civilizations which have followed the Advent of a major Founder of religion has balanced matters in such a way that the evils—the corruption, the cruelties, the immoralities and devastating wars of the last five to six thousand years—have not as yet threatened to wipe mankind off the face of our planet. But we are no longer able to count on our nonvulnerability to catastrophic extinction by looking to the past and declaring optimistically that "that is the way it has always been, and will always continue to be." We are inclined to a false sense of safety by ignoring the differences and the technological developments of our modern civilizations—the threat of nuclear warfare, the pollution of the planet, the overpopulation of the world's cities, the introduction of an overwhelming drug culture in several countries of the world. And above all we have had the audacity, for the first time, to declare that God, and therefore the relevance of religion itself, are no longer necessary to the life of mankind.

So far, in spite of the evils and hostilities of our civilizations, we have managed to continue our progressive evolution in the usual cyclical fashion, and Islam has been no exception; it was destined to last as a creative force for at least a thousand years, at which time, in keeping with all our higher religions, its dynamism was reversed and it started its visible decline. But in the eighth century the religious fires were still burning brightly, and we find that the Umayyads, who had streamed into southern Spain on their expulsion from the East, were aroused there to renewed efforts and soon became as fecund as the Abbasids. Setting up a new Emirate in Andalusia to continue the Caliphate they had lost in Damascus, they proceeded to produce some of the world's greatest treasures in conjunction with their Moorish converts, embellishing the land with mosques of exquisite beauty, with great universities and well-stocked libraries, and with splendid gardens, parks and architectural marvels in the cities of Seville, Toledo, Cordova, Saragossa, Valencia and Murcia. Scientists, historians, philosophers, theologians and writers of belles lettres abounded—the names, including those from the highly respected Jewish colonies in the large cities, are too numerous to declare here, but the genius engendered in Andalusia would pass over the borders of

Spain into the population centers of Europe, bringing with it the books of such intellectual giants as Ibn-Khaldun, Averroes and Avicenna, and contributing to the eventual breakdown of the feudal system of the Dark Ages and the reflowering of the Christian civilization.

The Umayyads retained their power in Spain until the eleventh century. By that time the encroaching Christians from the north had begun their gradual reconquest of the Spanish peninsula, and in 1096 entered upon the First Crusade to recapture Jerusalem from the Saracens. At the same time Andalusia was harried by rival Muslims from North Africa and broke up into a number of principalities and petty kingdoms, bringing about the final extinction of the Umayyad rule. By 1250 the Christians of Leon, Castile, Aragon and Navarre had won over most of Andalusia, and the Muslims who remained had gathered in the enclave of Granada, a Moorish kingdom to the west of Seville. Here they pursued their way of life in the lush surroundings of colorful gardens and splashing fountains, worshipping in the splendor of the Alhambra, and holding off the Christian armies. But in 1492 King Ferdinand and his Queen, Isabella, ardent Roman Catholics unable to view any part of Islam as anything but satanic, attacked and overran Granada, expelled the two hundred thousand Jews of Andalusia, and prepared the country for the Inquisition. In the same year Isabella sponsored the voyage of Christopher Columbus across the Atlantic and changed the course of history in the Western world.

Meanwhile in the Middle East the power of the Abbasids in Baghdad had weakened in the ninth century and the rule over their subjects had come under the domination of rival families; the House of Abbas, however, retained its right to the complimentary title of Caliph. During the tenth to the thirteenth centuries the strain of the Crusades in the Near

East and the massive attacks of the Mongols in the north and northeast under Ghengis Khan and his descendants kept the forces of Islam at bay. The end for the city of Baghdad came in 1258 when the Mongol hordes under the leadership of Hulagu, a grandson of Ghengis Khan, swept through Iran and Iraq, demolishing everything in sight and putting Baghdad to the torch. It seemed as though the Dispensation of Muhammad and the glorious civilization produced in his name had received a final deathblow in the Middle East.

But this, as we know, was not the case. The conversion of the Seljuk Turks from Central Asia and the Ottoman Turks from beyond the Caucasus who successively had conquered the lands from the Near East to the borders of Iraq, as well as the acceptance of Islam by the Mongol conquerors in Iran and Iraq, had reinstated the faith from the shores of the Holy Land to the two-hundred-year-old Mughal Empire in India, which produced, under the Muslim Shah Jahan, the Taj Mahal. The British won power from the Mughals in India in the 1790s, and the mixture of the age-old Hindu beliefs reasserted themselves as the prevalent religion in that ancient land. We will deal later in the dialogues with the assumptions of Hinduism and how they evolved from 1500 B.C. to the present day, with necessary emphasis on what brought about the basic belief in reincarnation, a stumbling block to the other Scriptural religions of the world which needs to be addressed.

From the fourteenth and fifteenth centuries onward—after the great Gothic cathedrals had risen in western Europe, the Black Death had ravaged that continent as well as Russia and eastern Asia, and the Renaissance in Italy, influenced by the intellectual and material achievements within Islam, had taken place independently of the Church—the civilization of Islam began its serious decline and never again regained its former glory throughout the Middle East. Under the despotic rule of the Ottoman Sultans in Constantinople and the long string of Seljuk, Mongol and even Buddhist dynasties in Persia, the faith of Muhammad had lost its spiritual momentum, while the combination of a reestablished church in Europe and the great leap forward in the Renaissance through new aspects of civilized life—the discovery of printing, the humanization of the arts, and the initial stirrings of the Reformation in Germany—marked, in the view of many scholars, the beginnings of our modern age and the rise of Western dominance.

Islam in Persia, however, underwent a last and remarkable efflorescence in the sixteenth and early seventeenth centuries, largely due to the Savafid family. A mixture of the many blood strains existing on the Persian plateau, but basically Turkish, the Savafids rose to power in the Mongol capital of Tabriz in the northern province of Iranian Adjerbaijan, a region dominated by the Sunnis; indeed Iran at that time had lost its Shia predominence. The cities of Kashan, Qum and Qazvin, and much of the province of Khurasan, were still active areas of Shiism, but otherwise the sect held a primary place only in certain centers in Asia Minor, Syria and eastern Iraq, in northern Arabia and the island of Bahrayn.

It remained for the Savafids to change this situation and to bring about a totally new religious and architectural environment to the whole plateau. Under the leadership of the youthful Savafid Shah Ismail in Tabriz and his successor Tahmasp in Qazvin, both converts to Shiism, the process began which eventually united the people of Persia as a nation, and through a series of both losses and conquests in military encounters with the Ottoman ruler, Suleyman the Magnificent, brought the holy cities of Karbila, Najaf, Samarra and Kazimayn in Iraq, the sites of the sacred shrines of revered Shia saints, once more under Persian control. Ismail, a pupil of Sufism, had declared himself a Shia early in his reign in Tabriz; the stubborn resistance of the Sunni hierarchy was handled by the young Shah through harsh measures and judicial blood-letting, and by 1508 the country had been almost entirely converted to a Shia state.

It was not until the ascension to the throne in 1588 of the sixteen-year-old grandson of Tahmasp, however, that the shattered face of Iran regained a semblance of its former opulence and architectural beauty. For centuries successive armies on horseback, including the most recent hordes under Tamerlaine, had washed back and forth over the land of the Persians; it was now due to the extraordinary talents of Shah Abbas the First, later known to the world as Abbas the Great, that the new nation began the long-delayed task of restoring the public structures, the damaged caravanseries, the ruined houses and burnt-out lands, and renewing the artistic expression of the people. The young Shah personally supervised the transfer of the capital from Qazvin to a site adjoining the ancient town of Isfahan on the Zayandeh river to the south, and built in that lush and fruitful region a city of such artistry, such magnificence, that it became known as Isfahan-nisf-i-jahan—Half the World. In spite of the devastating attack of the Afghans in the eighteenth century and the city's near submission through starvation and decimation, volumes continued to be written by artists and travelers extolling the beauty and grandeur of what has remained to the present day one of the great cities of the world.

Shah Abbas was a genius as well in his role as politician. Both wise and wily in his dealings with foreign countries, he opened the doors to western visitors, accepted the aid and advice of two Englishmen, Sir Anthony and Sir Robert Shirley, who remained with him as friends and envoys for a protracted period of time, and received the first British diplomatic representative to Iran, Sir Dodmore Cotton, in

1628. To counteract continuing depredations on his country the Shah built up a disciplined army recruited from Georgia and Armenia, converted them to Islam, combined them with the fighters from the mountain tribes of Iran, and succeeded in regaining most of the territory from the Caspian Sea to the Persian Gulf and northeast to the Oxus river and Afghanistan. Early in his reign Christian artisans and builders had been imported from Armenia and settled in a Christian suburb of Isfahan known as Julfa; up to the nineteenth century and beyond the citizens of Julfa maintained an independent history of their own. At the same time the Shah had brought to Isfahan a large group of Circassian beauties from beyond the Caucasus to add to his huge harem, and provided young eunuchs, undisturbed by female wiles, to watch over them. Making a final peace with the Ottoman Empire before his death at forty-one, he guaranteed the autonomy of the holy cities of the Shias in Iraq.

This is but a short résumé of the talents and accomplishments of a most extraordinary man, without whose reconstruction of the country the future history of Iran might very well have degenerated into almost irretrievable chaos. But there was a dark and even barbaric side to Shah Abbas which cropped up in full force in his Savafid successors in the seventeenth and eighteenth centuries and continued on in the cruel and unscrupulous monarchs of the Qajar regime in the nineteen hundreds. Abbas, for all his democratic behavior with the people and his generous provision of spectacular entertainment for local residents and visitors alike in the Maydan—the huge square adjoining the palace in Isfahan, unparalleled anywhere in the Middle East—lived a private life that was unsavory, immoral, at times sadistic, and even murderous to those who crossed him, including his own kin. To those who were his intimates he was known as a wine-bibber and as given to pederasty, suspicious of any one of his courtiers or sons who might be capable of taking power. It was the written view of Sir Robert Shirley, who looked upon the Shah in his last years as a friend and an enemy at the same time, that "in this court there is no gentleman but the king; the rest are but shadows which move with his body"—in other words an oriental despot in the Turkish mode whose darker characteristics have not often been mentioned in the history books. That such men, flawed and at times engaged in activities that betray their greatness, can nevertheless produce material marvels in their thrust for power and prestige, is one of the mysteries of life on earth known only to God.

As a consequence of the self-centered policies of the Shah in his final years and of those of his heirs and the rival regimes, both Turkish and non-Turkish, that followed him in the next century and a half, the intellectual development of Iran, never of primal interest to the Savafid court, came gradually to a standstill. Religion lost its philosophic content, and aside from continuing dabbling in Sufism, became a matter mainly of ritualistic repetitions of Shia holidays pertaining to Ali and his sons, of pilgrimages to the shrines of the Imams in Iraq and Mashad, and the build-up of a Shia hierarchy, the ulama, whose control over the many religious colleges built by the Savafids was not only absolute but the source of a total rejection of Western customs and beliefs—a complete reversal of the tolerance taught by Muhammad for peoples of other faiths. In time this brought about a state of ignorance, fanatically egotistical and immovable, of all but the Qoran and Traditions according to the interpretation of the Shia sect. Isfahan itself became so rigidly orthodox that even the Jews and Christians within its confines were looked upon as undesirable infidels, a prejudice that spread to the rest of the country. Creativity had dried up almost entirely, and cruel forms of persecution, including bodily torture, took its place. By the time the powerful Turkish tribe of the Qajars installed themselves on the throne of Iran in a new capital in Tehran, the land was far gone in corruption and moral decay. It was during the period of the almost total self-interest of the Shia regimes which preceded the Qajars that the Ottoman Sultanate in Constantinople, Sunni to the core, reasserted its political control over the holy cities of the Persians in Iraq, a circumstance that later brought about an unparalleled massacre in the holy city of Karbila.

The Qajars settled into this situation with no idea whatever of reform, religious or otherwise. They instituted no secular laws and established no rights for the people; and although they maintained the existing social structure of wealthy and aristocratic landlords in their fine homes and wretched, hard-worked peasants in their poverty-stricken villages, they fastened upon all the available public property and construction in the land as belonging to themselves and the large number of their progeny. The functions of government and full control over the life and death of their subjects were totally at the whim of the monarchs and their ministers, a despotism so chaotic, so inefficient, that the designation of a civilized nation in a largely civilized world had no meaning whatever under their rule. Above all, a venal system of exchanging bribes or so-called presents existed throughout the country, a system that controlled the lives of everyone from top to bottom and back again, an organized but unacknowledged method to insure that all official positions, all favors, authority and prestige, would fall upon those from whom the money came. The fiendish ingenuity of this cherished interchange, along with the savage cruelty and inhumanity of the prison system, its dire punishments and its willing executioners, constitutes, without a doubt, the lowest point in the spiritual and material life of the Persians.

The Qajar dynasty—with whom we shall be dealing in the dialogues—ruled in Iran from 1795 to 1925. Coming into Persia from converted areas in Central Asia they were well acquainted with Islam, and like other conquerors who had settled in Iran had been influenced by the dominant clergy to accept the current religious beliefs, in this case the orthodox doctrines of the Shias. The Shahs were persuaded, at least for public consumption, that they held the throne in fief for the Hidden or Twelfth Imam, a sacred trust that had fallen on their shoulders by the grace of Allah and would assure their final appearance in the highest paradise. This, the clergy insisted, would be brought to the proof when the Hidden Imam appeared in their midst to take over the rulership of Islam, a claim that was generally ridiculed outside of Persia and Iraq.

The Sunnis, as we have already indicated, possessed their own beliefs on the eventual Advent of one whom they too called the Mahdi or Mihdi, whose arrival would be announced by a prior or coinciding appearance in the Middle East of the prophet Jesus. Certain of the Shia sub-sects went along with Christ's return in this manner, and others departed from the belief in the Twelfth or lost Imam as the Promised One and held out for number seven—the Seveners— while some chose the Imam they most admired or who had left the most imposing legacy in his life and pronouncements. But the Twelvers were a large majority both in Persia and the holy cities in Iraq, and the doctrine of the Hidden Imam, Muhammad-ibn-i-Hasan-al Askari, who disappeared as a child in 874, was paramount when the Qajars came to the throne.

It was a matter, then, as to which of these various sects would give birth to the promised Apocalypse. That the claim of a new Revelation eventually came in 1844 from a group of humble scholars from the Shaykhi school in Iraq will be the subject of our final discussions in the present dialogues. Such a Revelation had been recorded in the Hadith or Traditions, the sayings and actions of Muhammad and his companions in his lifetime, as having been prophesied by the Prophet for approximately a thousand years from the end of the Imamate, at which time, the Tradition stated, nothing would be left of Islam but the name.

* * * * *

It will aid in understanding the background of the Persian personalities we shall meet in the dialogues if the meaning of certain male names, titles and designations are given here in the Prelude. The women, always secondary in Islam, and with no religious position, had a narrower choice, as I will point out below. Surnames in the Western style were not in use in Persia in the nineteenth century, and in order to identify one male person from another, all of whom might possess the same ubiquitous first name or combination of names gleaned from the roster of revered religious figures of the past, an ingenious system existed of titles, hyphens and hometowns or cities which pinpointed the individual in question. Thus, a member of the clergy from the town of Barfarush who was named after the Imam Hasan, a grandson of the Prophet, and who had been on a pilgrimage to Mecca (the Haj) was known as Haji Mulla Hasan-i-Barfarush, or if further identification was needed, his father, whose name was Jafar, would be brought into the sequence as follows: Haji Mulla Hasan-ibn-Jafar-i-Barfarush.

As for the combination and repetition of religious names, the practice was almost endless in Shia Persia: Ali-Muhammad, Muhammad-Ali, Abul-Hasan, Husayn-Ali, Ishmael-Rida, Karim-Mahmud and so on. As a rule, we shall present the names of our alien characters in the form in which they were used by those who personally addressed them or who knew them well, for example: Shaykh Ahmad, Siyyid Kazim, Mulla Husayn, and Mirza Aqasi. The particular titles in these names, along with a few others, have the following meanings:

A Shaykh is a man of learning, literate and often a leader in a mosque or in a religious school, a scholar of the Qoran and Traditions, and usually, but not always, fifty years of age or over. A Siyyid is a descendant of the House of the Prophet, entitled to wear a green turban and a distinguishing sash; his illustrious heritage was customarily venerated with a certain awe, especially if he attained at the same time the rank of a mujtahid, the epitome of expertise in both the customs and the legal aspects of Islam. The proliferation of Siyyids in Persia, however, like the spawning of excessive offspring by the monarchs and their harems, produced certain offshoots of Muhammad's bloodline whose characters were hardly compatible with their honorary title; they were either ignored or were fed and cared for by the populace as they wandered about the country.

A Mulla was a member of the clergy who was sometimes a learned scholar of Islam, sometimes a simple priest who rendered services to the people; most had sat at the feet of the Shaykhs in one or more of the many religious schools and colleges in Persia, or received their diplomas in the holy cities in Iraq. Mullas were often under twenty years of age, having begun their religious education in their boyhood. We shall meet later with a number of young Mullas in their twenties and thirties, who were both active and fearless in spreading the new religion. We would not be amiss in granting the young Mullas of Persia a primary place in the early proclaiming of a new Revelation.

The title of Mirza had no religious connotation as such, and as a prefix indicated a civilian status—generally a person in business or government—which corresponded to our

English Mister. If combined with the rank of Siyyid it signified that that person pursued a livelihood in some profession or occupation; if used as a suffix it denoted a princely heritage, either past or present. Such a title did not deter the recipient from involving himself in religious matters, according to his inclination and education; merchants, landlords, physicians and certain persons in government or at the court who were addressed in this manner were among the most ardent champions of the new faith, and suffered equally with the members of the clergy, the workers, the servants and the villagers, who dared to defy the state religion.

In addition, the title of Khan, used as a suffix, bestowed official authority and often the recognition of high birth on a person usually in government service, but was also used for the chieftains of the mountain tribes of the Kurds, the Lurs, the Bakhtiari and the Qashgai; the suffix Big is only slightly less complimentary. If all these various designations are kept in mind, including that of the Imam-Jumih, chief of the Mullas and leader of the Friday prayers in the main mosque of a town or city, as well as that of the Shaykhul-Islam, the leading divine appointed by the Shah in every city, there should be a minimum of confusion for the reader in making his way through the maze of alien names and titles.

It remains to deal briefly with the choice of names for the women in a closed society governed and directed in all its aspects by the male population. No religious titles were bestowed upon any woman at any time; her mind was considered incapable of understanding the nuances of religious teaching, and silence and invisibility were demanded except in the confines of the quarters for wives and daughters; there were those indeed who maintained that a woman lacked a soul. Nevertheless the selection open to the ladies was hardly plebeian. Khadija, the first and sole wife of

Muhammad from his twenty-fifth to his fortieth year, when she passed away, was a favored choice; the Prophet's diplomatic, political and humanitarian marriages during his Medina years provided others: Zaynab, Umm Salamih, Hafsa, Saffiya, Maymuna, Ayesha, Umm Habiba—there were eleven wives in all in the Prophet's household. Except for Ayesha, the young daughter of his close companion Abu Bakr, the other marriages of Muhammad were contracted with unprotected widows of dead heroes or friends, or divorced or unhappy wives of enemies or believers—a humane practice not unusual in the clans of the Qoraysh. By these women I have found no children reported, a rather strange circumstance for one whom the Christians have looked upon as a lecherous womanizer, going from one bed to another in his latter years. The women of Islam have worn these names with pride, and they have likewise carried on the names of revered ancestresses and romantic heroines in the works of the famous poets of Persia. Wives and daughters of the Imams and other religious figures were often chosen: Fatima, the daughter of Muhammad and the wife of the Imam Ali, was perhaps the most favored of all.

It was not until the eighteen-thirties that we meet with a definite departure in the recognition of a young woman in Persia as a prodigy of religious knowledge, and the consequent bestowal of a title upon her by Siyyid Kazim of the Shaykhi school in Iraq. Known by her household names of Umm Salamih and Fatima, and affectionately as Zarrin-Taj, the Crown of Gold, this young woman, as Doctor Varqa outlined to us in Tehran, was a poetess of renown, not only in her home city of Qazvin, but in aristocratic and sophisticated circles throughout the country, including the court. Not only because of the purity and religious passion of her poems and her acceptance of the teachings of the Shaykhi school in her correspondence with Siyyid Kazim, but also because of her reputation as a great beauty, the Siyyid conferred upon her the title of Qurratul-Ayn, the Solace of the Eyes. Later, as a declared and fearless believer in the new Revelation, she was endowed by the leader of the new faith in 1848 with the title of Tahirih, the Pure, the name by which she is known today throughout the world.

This charming young woman in her twenties, a miracle of erudition in such a male-dominated country, was a daughter in a family of religious jurists known for their strict orthodoxy and their wealth; her father and one of her uncles were considered the outstanding leaders among the ulama in northern Persia, and her husband, a cousin from whom she was separated—a fanatical young Mulla who would brook no departure from the norm of subservient women—was known in Qazvin for his cruel and neglectful treatment of his children and his wife. In spite of this orthodox background, Qurratul-Ayn became so famous for her unwelcome heretical views and such a thorn in the side of a disapproving clergy that her martyrdom was a foregone conclusion. Casting aside her veil in a male gathering of believers in 1848, she announced to the assembled company, as shocking as her deed would appear to them, that it constituted not only the initial bugle-call for the emancipation of women but primarily for the final separation of the new faith from the shackles of a dying Islam. In August of 1852 this phenomenal young heroine in the Cause of God was strangled without mercy in a dark garden in Tehran, and buried in a well. A firebrand of sacrifice in the path of the Herald Prophet of a new religion, we shall meet with her again in the dialogues.

* * * * *

Before I proceed with a list of our Western friends who joined us in our meetings, a word must be added on the spelling of alien names and places, a choice that we have made from many volumes on the Near and Middle East which depart time and again from one another in the matter of both vowels and consonants and the usage or non-usage of traditional marks. We have therefore chosen the spellings we felt most comfortable with and eliminated the marks which clutter up the pages. This does no harm to the places or persons depicted, and will, I believe, make for an easier intimacy with foreign names. Nor, I feel, does our use of the terms man and mankind denote any downgrading of the female sex; their use has covered for many centuries the full range of human beings—men, women and children—and it goes without saying that the equality of the sexes, as indicated by the sacrifice of Tahirih, is one of the outstanding principles of the new faith.

And finally, the personalities and appearance of four of our academic colleagues are presented here, as well as the wife of one of them and a Unitarian minister, who met with my husband and me in our home to discuss the matters we have dealt with in the Introduction and the Prelude. A blank and faceless group of eight people is not conducive to the interested attention we hope to generate in the dialogues, and the following details, though hardly biographical, will help the reader to image the speakers as they contribute to the tapes. They have read what I have written from my own point of view, and have graciously given me permission to describe them as follows:

Donald and Madilyn Heller—Assistant Professor of History and his wife, a poetess of distinction in the midwest, with no academic degree. Madilyn at thirty-six is a pretty natural blond with a sensitive patrician nose and dancing brown eyes, who seemed always to speak in our meetings in a happy voice. But Don, eleven years her senior, is quite different in appearance and temperament; a polarity in the latter threatened, according to campus gossip, to unravel the marriage. Black-haired and black-eyed, Don is a handsome man with a German-Semitic background, easily aroused to argument on a variety of historical subjects and especially on mankind's addiction to warfare and iniquity, which he perceived as ingrained and perpetual. Otherwise he appeared to be disinterested in the human condition—a habit that stemmed, I presumed, from his loss of cherished relatives in the Holocaust at the age of three, and his later assumption of atheism. Madilyn, on the other hand, is filled with constant optimism and a love of life, and pours out her exuberance in poems which reflect her intense interest in the Romantic movement in Europe which followed the rejection of the seventeenth century mechanical view of the universe portrayed by those two great giants of the mind, Descartes and Newton—a rejection which brought forth a corresponding flood of literature, poetry, philosophy, painting and music which looked toward a far better and more spiritual world.

It is interesting to recall in this context that the French Revolution from 1787 to 1794—coinciding with the Presidency of George Washington in America and a full-blown Industrial Revolution in England—was a turning point which seemed to augur the birth of a new age for mankind. But opposed to the many negative aspects of these revolutionary developments, the Romantic poets and philosophers, both in England and on the continent, presented to the Western world for almost half a century the vision and the hope of a universal brotherhood of man. Millenianism was a constant theme, and a rapid return to the beauty of natural creation and the simplicity of the natural man were everywhere touted as against the growing greed and inhumanity of mercantilism and the factory system, the displacement of religion by pure reason in the works of the new philosophers, and the increase of materialism on every hand. But the love of money and power had taken hold on both sides of the Atlantic, and by the late 1840s had succeeded in supplanting the short-lived idealism of some of our most celebrated Romantic writers, artists and poets. Madilyn had nevertheless clung to these universal themes in her own poems, and was therefore an avid listener to all that Ham and I had learned in the Middle East. In this connection it was gratifying to witness a gradual change in Don's attitude as the dialogues progressed.

Philip Simmons and Helen Rexford—Philip is our Professor of Atomic Physics, caught up in the view of many of the new physicists that the most recent discoveries in the sub-atomic world correlate with the mystic views of the East. Philip's keen blue eyes look out upon the world as if a new discovery could be made at any moment. Still a bachelor at thirty-eight, he has an eye for the ladies, and informed us that he would be happy to attend our gatherings if we also included the new Professor of Marxist and Soviet Studies, Helen Rexford, thirty-two, red hair, with milky skin and green eyes, by far the best-looking female professor, by consensus of both sexes, on the campus. Helen was aware of Philip's beguilement as well as his reputation, and although they were dating during the dialogues, Helen consistently showed her independence by teasing Philip whenever his erudition got out of hand. They seemed an ill-matched pair in spite of the brightness of their minds: he is six-feet-two, his appearance reminiscent of Danny Kaye, and Helen, with her slim figure and Botticelli face, reached in her full height only to his shoulder. What is more, Marxism and mysticism seemed hardly to go hand in hand, but we shall see in the dialogues that Professor Rexford had no personal interest in Communism, and possessed as searching a mind as her admirer.

Georgina Wentworth—Professor of Art and Architecture, fifty-four, pleasingly plump, unmarried, with a sweet round face and prematurely white hair. At times Georgina appeared naive in the midst of her colleagues, but she had authored four books on the art and architecture of many countries of the world, had traveled extensively in the East, and was considered a brilliant critic of both Eastern and Western art. Georgina had left the Catholic church in her late thirties, unable to confine her beliefs to a one-only theological view of religious truth; her studies and her travels had opened up a broad canvas of creativity engendered by religious convictions unacceptable to the church, and for a time it puzzled her that such beauty, such extraordinary accomplishments, should come out of such false and self-deluding beliefs. In New York she had been introduced to the Reverend Ardsley Ahearn at an art exhibition displaying a special showing of eastern sculpture; they had chatted at some length, and had met for tea the following day. A friendship ensued which transformed Georgina's religious views entirely, and in the end brought Reverend Ahearn to our campus town to establish a small Unitarian-Universalist church, to which Georgina belongs. Ham and I had gone there on two or three occasions, had found him extremely broad-minded, and were delighted when he agreed to attend the meetings.

The Reverend Ardsley Ahearn—Sixty-five, an aristocratic craggy face with deep blue eyes bright with empathy and wisdom, and a shock of iron-gray hair with matching beard and mustache. We could not have been more fortunate than to have this unexpected scholar of religion join us in the dialogues. Originally a member of the Church of England, he had found its hide-bound religious opinions restrictive and self-serving, had left London for New York, and discovered the Universalist church a year before it merged with the Unitarians in 1961. This combined church has continued the Universalist repudiation of the Trinity as taking away from the basic unity of God, and upholds the view that final salvation is possible for all mankind through a non-dogmatic approach to the faiths of the world, including one's own. They look upon the Founders of the higher religions as humanistic, charismatic figures in advance of their time, but Reverend Ahearn had concluded from his studies, and from the statements of the Founders themselves in the Scriptures of these world religions, that there was ample room to believe that they were guided and inspired by divine influence. As Ham and I had finally come to the same conclusion, his presence was a boon from start to finish. However, as no one in our gatherings had any knowledge whatever of the recent apocalyptic faith from the East, including the Reverend Ahearn, it came to all of them as a new and startling revelation.

Ham and Julia Adams—Self-description is a difficult procedure, and I will leave it to the reader to create whatever image he or she may glean from the Introduction and the Prelude, and this will hold as well for my husband. Physically, neither he nor I is distinguished for any unusual features; we are, in several ways, look-alikes: hazel eyes now in need of glasses and dark brown hair streaked with gray; in our middle fifties we fight the good fight to keep the weight down. Like Georgina we have written several books apiece, published by the University Press, and expect to write more if time in the future will allow us to do so.

My husband and I readily admit that this particular presentation is unusual, indeed unconventional, in its format, but the subject matter is far from ordinary, and we have dealt with it in a way that we felt could best lead the reader into the initial Revelation of the new faith which took place in Persia in 1844. All that we ask as we proceed with the tapes is that you stretch your minds and imaginations enough to examine without prejudice what millions in our world now perceive as one of the great turning points in religious history.

Ham's Preface to the Dialogues

A statement should be made here to explain the somewhat formal structure of the following conversations. In the several replayings of our tapes Julia and I realized that many of our collective thoughts and opinions, our questions and answers, expositions, diversions and interruptions, were scattered about in a rather haphazard manner as so often occurs in group discussions, and failed to give a fully consistent picture of the subject at hand.

As a consequence we decided to edit the tapes for a better continuity of the topic under discussion, and this we did by incorporating any scattered comments or opinions on the part of one individual into the larger statement of his or her thoughts or sentiments on the matter. Although this decision tends to stretch out the combined contributions of one individual into longer statements than were made at one time, we found nevertheless that it shortens the period of discussion in each chapter in what turned out to be on several occasions a rather prolonged evening of communication.

The reader should remember that six of the speakers are university professors accustomed to giving lectures in the classroom and to covering various points in a good deal of detail, as they have done in the dialogues. Reverend Ahearn is habituated as well to delivering analytic sermons from the pulpit, and Madilyn Heller, naturally exuberant in matters which pertain to her own interests, is equally expressive on the subjects of poetry and the brotherhood of man.

And finally, I must call attention to the fact that the following tapes have been stored away on a closet shelf for the past four years and more, from early in 1986 to the summer of 1990, while my wife and I were unavoidably occupied with other commitments. During these years tremendous changes have occurred throughout the world, some of them anticipated by the members of our group in Dialogues I. But a wide range of unresolved problems remains, and the primary purpose in a second series of dialogues will be to present and discuss the remarkable nature of the blueprint for political and religious peace as given to the world by the Revelators of the new faith in the Middle East.

I Feeling Our Way

JULIA: My dear friends, the tapes are on, and we are ready to proceed. You have long been apprised of our sabbatical itinerary and have viewed the required pictures along the route. Because of other commitments we have been a long time in relaying the information which came to us in the Middle East from the handsome gentleman you have seen in our snapshots, Doctor Ibrahim Varqa, who was brutally tortured and executed in Iran for his unorthodox beliefs. But tonight, with your participating help, we hope to launch an experiment with his memory in mind which we think might have a modifying effect on our usual patterns of thought, and will at least carry us away from the customary limitations of our own scholarship.

As you know, we shall deal here, among other things, with a new religion which arose in Islam in the nineteenth century and has subsequently spread around the world to establish itself as one of the most advanced and at the same time iconoclastic spiritual movements that have taken place on our planet. Whether or not you will agree with this assessment remains to be seen. But both Ham and I have found in this latter-day faith, as told to us by Doctor Varqa, some eye-opening changes from the usual model of our past prophetic religions. Although it incorporates a spiritual continuity with the faiths that have gone before it, there is an intellectual evolution involved that brings it quite firmly into the modern world.

I must also ease your minds, and perhaps your understandable prejudice, on its place of origin. Persia in the nineteenth century was the most corrupt and degenerate country it is possible to imagine. It was under the despotic, tyrannical rule of the Qajar regime, and its holy cities in the Turkish province of Iraq were governed from Constantinople by the autocratic Sultan of the Ottoman Empire. In spite of this unlikely area for the birth of a new and independent religion, we must remind ourselves that all of the living prophetic faiths of the world have arisen in the East and in regions weighed down with oppression, with hostile sects and cults, with no will for solving problems other than by warfare and contention, and with moral and behavioral qualifications way below par. Cruelty and inhumanity are almost always present, and a spiritual darkness that flouts not only the norms of civilized living but the very teachings in those areas that are upheld as the only truth for all mankind.

It seems logical, then, that the most downtrodden and spiritually bankrupt lands in the Eastern hemisphere—Persia and Turkey—should reach a point in the nineteenth century that required the intervention of a new Prophet of God—a title, by the way, that I shall employ in place of a Founder of a higher religion, for such a designation was used in their time for Moses, for Jesus, for Zoroaster, for Muhammad, for the Lord Krishna in Hinduism, and could equally well be used for the Lord Buddha, in my opinion, though that is contended by most religious historians. We will discuss later as to whether or not the systems of belief in the Far East, with their emphasis on reincarnation, can be said to correlate in any way with the great Semitic religions, Judaism, Christianity, and Islam.

Finally, I presume you will not be put off by the apparently supernatural manifestations which have appeared in the new faith. Again we must remind ourselves that the other-worldly aspects in all the higher religions exhibit these features in one way or another, even in Buddhism. Above all, it is well to remember that our own Christian commitment is based on Scriptures, both the Old and the New Testaments, which are filled with supernatural happenings, literally hundreds of references to both past and future events outside of one's usual or possible knowledge, a symphony of prophecies, visions and dreams, of unseen forces and divine beings, of communications from and through the world of the spirit. Where religion is concerned, dear friends, the rational mind must accommodate itself, if it can, to the observations of Shakespeare and other enlightened intellects that there is more to the universe than meets the eye or that the mind of man can possibly imagine.

But this is quite enough to start us off on a search for some meaning and purpose in man's existence, and for the possibility that the human race can attain at some future date a world of peace, harmony and brotherhood. Reverend Ahearn, do you take exception to anything I have said here as an introduction to our meetings? I defer to your understanding of the nature and course of the world's religions, which I am sure is equally as broadly based as my own.

THE REVEREND AHEARN: I shan't speak in these meetings, Julia, as a Unitarian. My small flock here knows that I depart in certain aspects from the purely humanistic view of the Founders of our major faiths, but not from the Unitarian stand that salvation is available for all mankind and that every religion has a right to be recognized, its teachings examined, and its Scriptures respected regardless of race, creed or color. Personally, however, these very Scriptures, as you have pointed out, cause me to believe that the Founders of religion—the Prophets of God as you have designated them—have not deceived the human race when they claim a supernatural connection with planes and powers beyond our comprehension, that they are more than advanced thinkers ahead of their time. In respect to the Christ this conviction is incorporated as well, of course, in those derivative beliefs stemming from Christianity, such as Mormonism and Christian Science, Jehovah's Witnesses, Seventh Day Adventists and the preaching of a large body of evangelists.

I believe we must come to some sort of understanding in these meetings as to whether a full-fledged religion is a necessary adjunct to man's evolution, or whether science has finally rendered traditional religion obsolete, at least in the West. But I cannot help but feel that man's propensity for creating, even in our materialist culture, an endless variety of cults and ersatz religious offshoots—deistic, secular or satanic—would indicate that an instinct for some sort of religious expression is implanted in the human species, however distorted it sometimes becomes. But where we can turn for the most advanced but always relative truths of the universe, is, as I understand it, what we shall try to decide upon here.

DON: A tall order, Reverend Ahearn. I know of no historical precedent that would give our small group the ability or the right to pass such a judgment along to the rest of the world. And I might say, Julia, that the rituals of our American Indians are hardly a derivative from any religion from the East, nor the beliefs of the Polynesians or the ancient cults of Central or South America. Since time immemorial the human mind has attempted to offset the pain and afflictions of the human condition by fantasizing gods and goddesses, messengers and revelations and commands from heaven, and building up whole systems on such unsound premises, only to have them collapse in the end due to their failure to improve the human lot. I don't mean to be combative, Julia —

JULIA: But of course, Donald, you always are—a valuable attribute for the range of opinions we have hoped for here. But you have just put forth a very narrow view of what religion has actually accomplished in the world—it's a one-sided opinion, Don, which is nevertheless understandable in the light of your concentration in your history courses on six thousand years of territorial hostility, of endless wars, and of man's inhumanity to man. Some of us deal with the other side of the coin, and I think the two aspects of the matter need to be put in balance before we give up on what man should eliminate in his life, his religion or his bad habits.

As for the systems of belief of the early races in the Western hemisphere, a number of respected scholars have claimed to have traced their roots back to India, to Asia, and even as far as Phoenicia, Greece and northern Africa, postulating that early wanderers brought the seeds of religious ideologies and rituals with them when they crossed the Bering Straits from East to West. Others have brought forward convincing sculptural and agricultural signs that early navigators from the East made several voyages to the shores and islands of the West, and could very well have brought with them the concepts and suppositions which developed eventually into the variety of religious beliefs of the Indians of North America and the Olmecs, Aztecs, Incas and Mayas to the south. The legends of the Polynesians and Melanesians are replete with echoes which hearken back to an undeniable source in Eastern lands.

But I don't intend to labor the matter—the main point is that the faith we shall soon discuss has followed in the footsteps of the major religions engendered by Moses, Jesus, Zoroaster in Persia, Krishna in India, Muhammad in Arabia, and the Buddha in both India and the Far East, all of which have arisen in the Eastern hemisphere. Is it quite out of order, dear friends, that a new religion should be born in the shambles of the dying faith of Islam, as the other faiths have likewise come into being in the wake of a former religion which no longer served its original purpose? This new religion, nevertheless, is more than just a regional replacement, as we shall see. Nor is it a synthesis, except in its spiritual pronouncements, of all the faiths that have gone before it, but a quite new presentation that combines science and religion, social laws and political behavior, in a Revelation meant for conditions as they exist for us today.

HELEN: You know, Julia, I am quite taken with the thought that these religions may be cyclical, as you are obviously saying. Cyclical behavior, which we accept for such things as the planets and the stars, the courses of the comets, the weather, the seasons—even, as some believe, the outbreak of wars and the death of Presidents in office, a dozen and one things actually, including the ups and downs of the stock market—is never applied to religions or civilizations except by a few philosophical historians such as Oswald Spengler and Arnold Toynbee. And no one seems willing to even imagine that what has happened before in the birth of a new religion or a new civilization can happen again. But whether any kind of organized religion can ever maintain itself indefinitely as one happy family I rather doubt—it has never succeeded in doing so in the past. I was brought up in Pennsylvania in the Quaker faith, and have always felt that religion should be a private matter with charity toward all, that its organization into great churches and ecclesiastical hierarchies only brings about internal divisions, eventual hostilities, and a final downfall.

In this connection, it might surprise you that I look upon communism as a form of religion. I am not a Marxist, as you well know, but my studies in the dialectical philosophy of Hegel and Engels, and of course Lenin whom they've made into a sort of god, have convinced me that almost all passionately held beliefs turn themselves in time into a form of organized religion, humanistic or atheistic as it may be. The rigid organization of the Soviet system, for example, is quite as exclusive and desirous of its own point of view as Christianity, Judaism, or Islam. It is interesting to take note of the fact that this atheistic faith, spawned in the West by Marx and Engels, traveled in the opposite direction to the East, and is the polar opposite of the theistic religions, which, as Julia has shown us, have traveled from East to West. Personally, I have no idea whatever why such an orientation exists.

I notice, by the way, that Philip is gazing at me with amusement, as if I were showing off for the benefit of my colleagues. Let us give him a chance to put out his own ideas, which may also surprise you. As a brilliant scientist and a closet student of mysticism, is there any scientific or mystical reason, Philip, why all the revelatory religions, so-called, should have their locus in the East? If you can answer me that we will all be grateful, I am sure.

PHILIP: I am quite in agreement with you, Helen—I haven't the slightest scientific or religious clue, or I would, heaven forbid, be God Himself. But I can suggest to you that it might be a matter of symbolism on the part of some overriding Intelligence—a First Cause, by the way, for which a good number of sub-atomic physicists have found an accommodation in their thinking processes. Einstein, as you no doubt know, my dear, was a prime example, and even Isaac Newton, who viewed the universe as a giant machine, was nevertheless a very religious man. I therefore make no excuse for my interest in mysticism, which engaged the attention of two scientific geniuses, Niels Bohr and Werner Heisenberg, and has stirred the imagination of many young devotees of the new physics.

But pertaining to the idea of symbolism in the orientation of East to West, let us consider, despite the fundamentalists and literalists, that symbolic language and expression is the very core of the Scriptures and writings of the higher religions, and this includes mysticism in both the East and the West. Material objects and human behavior which represent something on a spiritual level are quite properly accepted by all thinking people as basic forms of religious teaching—you have only to recall the parables of Jesus to understand what is meant here. If symbology is used in the instance of the rise of the great faiths in the East, I believe we might have a possible answer to a very unusual phenomenon.

From a scientific standpoint, of course, the sun rises in the East and sets in the West in relation to our planet. If one looks upon the higher religions as beacons of light for mankind—originally at least—it is not difficult to suppose that the Eastern hemisphere of our earth, in the mind of a Ruling Power, would be a symbolic area for the rise of the sun of a major Founder's spiritual and social teachings, which in time pass over to the West in a varied and sometimes quite different form. All the Eastern religions, in reverse, are now tainted with Western materialism, including Islam, regardless of its vaunted return to its medieval past. One can say, then, that these religions have finally "set in the West," and no longer have the ability to transform the hearts of their adherents or the culture in which they live. That is the best I can do for the moment, and it still leaves us with the burning question—can these cyclical and repetitious religions ever succeed in permanently changing the minds and hearts of men in both the East and the West?

HAM: We shall most certainly get to that in time. And may I say, Philip, that this bent of yours toward mysticism and symbolism has indeed taken me by surprise. But in feeling our way in these meetings I hope we will all continue to express our inner thoughts and convictions without the slightest embarrassment or guilt. It is only through such a free flow, and even through the clash of opinions, that we can come to some consensus on subjects that seem to Julia and me to be of paramount importance in an ever-increasingly dangerous and violent world.

If I may, I would like to comment on Helen's expression of distrust in organized religion. If the whole universe and the whole of nature here on earth is organized in the most staggering detail, as both the physicists and astronomers have clearly shown us, can religion be exempt from such a basic and universal phenomenon? Is it the organization that's at fault, or the use that people make of it? We hear a constant outcry against organized religion by those who maintain they are not "joiners," but Helen, there is nothing in the world that succeeds without organization, whether for good or evil, unless you wish to remain closed within yourself and to keep your heart and soul hidden from the world. Even lone artists, inventors, writers and solitary workers of all kinds need to organize their thoughts and what they are doing physically, or nothing whatever will result. Georgina should be able to contribute something here in relation to the art and architecture of the world. Are you in accord, Georgina, with what I am saying, or do you feel we should follow our own paths without reference to the group beliefs of an organized religion?

GEORGINA: But of course I'm in accord with you, Ham. The point is that one should join a group that is organized for good and for the peace of the world, and not for violence and destruction. As far as religion is concerned, if there were no organization you would not find on our planet the splendid temples, the magnificent mosques, the Gothic cathedrals, the masterpieces of sculpture and painting, and all the religious festivals and colorful scenes of pageantry that are half the delight of the human race—they simply would not have been produced. But on the other hand, whether the dichotomy of good and evil, which has emanated throughout history from the same source, is actually built into the universe and is grafted ineradicably onto the human species, I have no idea.

The fact remains that along with all the beauty it has given to the world, religion has been organized over and over again for reasons of hatred and warfare against one's fellow man, has toppled whole civilizations, and brought havoc and chaos everywhere, both to the innocent and otherwise. Today we are actually at war the world over, both religiously and politically—undeclared, to be sure—but as William James pointed out there is small difference today between peace and war. He stated, and I quote from memory, that "competitive preparation for war by the nations is a real war, and goes on permanently, unceasingly. The actual battles are only a public verification of the mastery gained during the so-called intervals of peace." Just how the deadlock can be broken in our time, no one seems to know.

PHILIP: A further word about organization from a physicist, before we leave the subject. If the universe were not organized, things would fall apart. But there is an uncertainty principle in the sub-atomic world, propounded by Heisenberg, which seems to leave room for a certain amount of disorder in an otherwise ordered universe, and for the possibility of accidents and catastrophes among the stars and on the earth. The same is true in our particular world for the illnesses of the human body and human mind, and includes, I presume, the often disastrous results of our religious beliefs. In other words, Georgina's dichotomy of good and evil, the possibility and even the probability that either good or evil can take place anywhere, seems indeed to be built into the universe.

But there is another discovery through quantum physics which brings mankind into the equation, and states that our very observation and measurement of the particles and waves of the sub-atomic world, of which all matter consists, changes the action of that world—in other words the human being, the human mind, is a participating element in the happenings not only of our own world but of the universe. There is a saying on that score that when a human being sneezes, nothing is ever quite the same as it was before. The idea is so staggering that when Einstein was told of this theory he indignantly declared that "God does not play dice with the universe." But he was able to say later, and I quote, that "the unleashed power of the atom has changed everything except our mode of thinking, and we thus drift toward unparalleled catastrophes." It seems to be the shattering truth, my friends—as Niels Bohr has written and the Eastern mystics have long maintained—that man is both a spectator and an actor in a universe that is interconnected in every last atom in existence.

HELEN: Well, Philip, you have taken us into realms of metaphysical conjecture that seem to have little to do with the down-to-earth subject of Julia's new religion. There are physicists, you know, who look upon all these mathematical theories as pure speculation. Do you actually believe that human behavior can bring about an earthquake, a tornado, a hurricane, or a downpour that produces a devastating flood—much less the happenings in outer space? I am not a scientist, of course, but conjectures carried to such extremes are a bit hard to believe.

REVEREND AHEARN: As a matter of fact, Helen, what Philip has had to say about the powers of the human mind to change the behavior of atoms and their constituents is one of the basic principles in faith healing and the transformations in one's life by positive thinking. It may also be a partial answer, and not only a sign from a Deity on High, to some of the apparently unscientific occurrences found in all the Scriptures of the world—the strange darkness, for example, that descended upon the area at the time of the Crucifixion of the Christ, the remarkable appearance of a new star before the Advent of a new Prophet, the conspicuous sweep of a comet coinciding with important events in world history and so on—not to mention the great epidemics when men's misuse of their minds and bodies reaches a morally unacceptable level. The synchronization of intense thoughts and of highly charged emotions and behavior with startling or devastating physical occurrences, especially in religious situations, seems to me to be a fairly sound deduction.

JULIA: I am glad to have you say so, Reverend Ahearn, as such occurrences are not lacking in the new faith, as Doctor Varqa was careful to point out. There are two of us here, by the way, without an academic doctorate, and something tells me that the contributions of Madilyn and Reverend Ahearn, who are not limited by the scholarship of the classroom, can take us into some unaccustomed realms in these discussions. Madilyn, you haven't offered a word as yet. Poets and prophets, they say, are able to reach out to non-physical dimensions denied to the rest of us, and bring us nearer to reality. Do you feel that this is so?

MADILYN: I hesitate to answer that, Julia, as pertaining to myself, though at times, when writing a poem in communion with nature, I feel for fleeting moments that I am one with what I am writing about—one with nature and the universe. It's definitely a religious feeling, a strange lifting of the consciousness, a momentary merging with the essence of being which the mystics talk about. There is a strong possibility, it seems to me, that poetry can be prophetic at such a time—the renowned poet Hafiz of Persia, for instance, appears to have foreseen the importance of certain locations in that country several hundred years in advance.

I think mainly, however, of the Romance poets of the late eighteenth and early nineteenth centuries in Europe, who expressed in their poems the great surge of religious feeling that swept over the West at that time, a wave of millennial expectation which included, through Scriptural searching by the Millerites in America and other groups in both East and West, the actual pinpointing of Christ's return for the years 1842 to 1844. From what Julia has said of the birth date of the new religion in the Middle East, this ferment of idealistic thought and expression, these paeans of praise in anticipation of a coming world of harmony and brotherhood coincided almost exactly with the lives of the early Forerunners and the Promised Qaim of Islam, the Herald Prophet of the new faith. I am grateful to Julia for answering some of my questions in advance, as I have always felt that something might have occurred in the wake of the French Revolution which caused not only the poets of that period but philosophers such as Kant with his "Critique of Pure Reason" and novelists, historians, composers—Beethoven, Schubert and Mendelssohn—as well as romantic painters, essayists like Carlyle, and even politicians, to join the jubilant expectation of a new and better world.

If I may, I would like to recall the fact that during the 1830s and early 1840s most of the ministers of the Gospels in England, and indeed on both sides of the Atlantic, thundered away in their pulpits, warning their congregations to be ready for the appearance of the Christ. The fundamentalists in America went so far as to sell their houses, to don white shrouds, and to stand on the rooftops prepared for the ascent to meet the Lord in the skies. It was an extraordinary period filled with impassioned individuals in both East and West whose names are even today quite unforgettable. And strangest of all, perhaps, was the settling down at the foot of Mount Carmel in Palestine of certain Christian orders and proselytizing travelers, to await there the Messiah's arrival on the slopes of that holy mountain.

It is the poets of that time, however, who fired my imagination and led me to attempt the same enthusiasm in my own poems for a new order in the world. Those of you who have an acquaintance with Tennyson know of his lyrical anticipation of a Parliament of Man, and perhaps will recall the visions of a different and more beautiful world in the poems of Shelley and Blake, of Byron and Wordsworth, Schiller and Goethe, Kingsley, Symonds, Matthew Arnold and Yeats—the list is formidable. Don does not agree that this sort of outburst of hope for a permanent Golden Age has any meaning or purpose whatever in the ongoing march of historical events, and he is, of course, quite entitled to his own point of view.

DON: I can only respond to that by praising Madilyn for her presentation. She obviously needs no degree for her knowledge of the periodic hopes in the past for the betterment of the human race. But let us be practical in these meetings. We have only to look about the world at present to perceive the exact opposite of what the Romantic era had looked forward to. From 1850 on, after the revolutions in Europe in 1848 failed in their purpose, we see the beginning of the search for wealth, the pursuit of property and power, an age of science and materialism, of agnostic and atheistic humanism and communism—quite the opposite of the hope for a spiritual renaissance.

Let us face the facts, friends. It all ended up with the fulminations of Nietsche against the assumptions of the idealists and utopians, with the iron-fisted diplomacy of Bismarck, the rationalism and agnosticism of the likes of Huxley and Renan, the atheism of Marx and Engels, the down-to-earth works of Ibsen and Freud, of George Orwell, Evelyn Waugh and Arthur Koestler, the wasteland poetry of T. S. Eliot which sums up the world as we see it today—and most tellingly, perhaps, the psychic pandemonium of Franz Kafka's inner man in the face of a world in which the demise of God is accepted even by members of the Western clergy.

If another religion is brewing around the world, mark my words, the backlash will call forth an opposite effect of resistance and persecution by both established religion and the humanists, and a vast indifference by the world at large.

PHILIP: This is the yin-and-yang effect, Don—the Chinese mystics centuries ago called attention to these periods of action and reaction, the swing from light to darkness and back again—it happens all the time. These cyclical components in man's history indicate that the low point on the totem pole where we are at the present time is not a permanent stopping place, that we shall start climbing up the pole again if we are patient enough not to annihilate ourselves before a polar opposite takes over. The recognition of this constant interplay in the life of mankind has been preserved down to our own day, in all its forms, in the three-thousand-year-old Chinese classic, the I Ching, the Book of Changes. The concept of yin and yang assures us that things must reach their extremes—their lowest or their highest point—before a true reversal will take place. Perhaps we can take heart from this that the darker the situation becomes in our present world, the sooner we can look for a transformation to something new. Who knows, my friends, Julia's up-to-date religion may very well be the catalyst that will change the face of the earth.

DON: All of this appears to me as so much nonsense, Philip. How any kind of religion can expect to unify the atheistic closed system of the Soviet regime and the democratic world of permissiveness and unlimited capitalism in America is beyond me. There is a basic schism here, and I cannot see that either side will give way without the type of warfare that will put us all under the sod. Unless one or the other collapses from internal problems, I see no possibility that any religion can overcome the spiritual inertia of the two most powerful nations in the world.

HELEN: Doctor Heller, I respect your point of view, but I believe you are overlooking some important points here. Marx's written philosophy, atheistic as it is, was nevertheless devoted to obtaining social and economic justice for the oppressed classes of the world, to eliminating a great gap between the rich and the poor. Surely that is a concept our prideful Western democracies could and should agree with, whether it is based on religion or not. Marx was totally disillusioned with the apathy of the church in these matters, and reflected the secularism of the nineteenth century when he denounced religion as the "opium of the people"—a fact that we might apply today to some of the traditional and evangelical beliefs in our own country which have no real power, obviously, to bring about the justice and true brotherhood, the universal human rights, which both our government and our churches are constantly preaching.

What I am saying is that both the Soviets and our own democratic and church systems make high-minded claims that parallel one another in any number of ways, but that both sides have failed to implement them in the real world. If the two systems ever break out of their hypnotic paranoia in regard to each other as permanent enemies, and agree to do away with endless confrontation and the deadly weapons of mutual destruction, they would find much in their common aspirations which coincide in a most remarkable way. Personally, I am weary of the everlasting criticism and backbiting, the lack of trust and respect, the continuous game-playing which goes on between the two governments, as well as the daily charade of political and individual accusations and denials, the lying and cheating and spying, that is part and parcel of our national lives. The potential of both systems to bring about the goal of true equality and a workable constitutional guarantee for the rights of all their citizens to live their lives to the fullest is therefore incapable of being realized without some sort of calamity. Philip may be right, of course—that we must go to a final extreme before the possibility of any change in attitude by the two nations can take place.

HAM: It's a grim situation, to be sure. In talking with us, Doctor Varqa pointed out, from the standpoint of his own religion, that nationalism in its present form is the greatest stumbling block to political peace. National pride, like the individual ego, prevents the governments of the world from acknowledging their own faults. They think nothing of quarreling within the confines of their own nation, but take offense when critics in other countries and the probing media, via television, the radio, the news magazines, the journalists, and a vast number of analytical articles and books show quite clearly and graphically that the large mote in the eye of one sovereign state is equally as blinding as the lack of perception in another. We have only to witness the behavior in the so-called United Nations to see the doggedness with which every country holds to its own point of view.

Actually, are we able any longer to define our Western world—if indeed one ever could—as composed of Christian nations? When we speak so arrogantly of atheism, does it ever occur to us that we ourselves behave as if the Christ had never lived or that the God we so glibly acknowledge is powerless to bring upon us either the punishments or rewards we deserve? No doubt the Christian psyche is imbued with the teaching in the church that we are forgiven for our behavior by the sacrifice of the Christ on the Cross for our collective sins. At any rate we see in our own country, year by year, an increase in violent and white-collar crime, in greed and corruption, in child and wife abuse, in obscenity, pornography and the worst kind of sexual deviation, in teenage pregnancies, abortions and suicides, the spreading problems of homelessness and hunger and mental illness, and the dangerous and deadly pollution of the land and atmosphere. I am sure you can dream up your own contributions—the economic uncertainties, the ever-increasing costs of education and medical care, the continuing inequality of the races, the still unbalanced status of women, and so on. Perhaps the most frightening of all is the flood of hard drugs and alcohol not only in the back alleys but in the schools, the workplace and in society at large, a fact that contributes to the overall problems that have grown in many cases into epidemic proportions. It is not an edifying picture for a great nation to present to the world.

Let us face it, friends, and not hide behind our books and our impartial lectures while the former values of our nation are plummeting day by day. If you feel that I am exaggerating, then all our sources of information are pure illusion, and nothing can be depended upon. Consider the obvious fact that we have replaced our reverence for the great religious figures, whose teachings aided us in building this great nation, by secular gods and goddesses of our own creation. The idols of a vast number of people today are the actors and actresses of the movies or TV, the very rich and the very famous from whatever walks of life and regardless of their behavior and their morals. Consider the general adulation of the highly paid figures in the world of sports, of the rock and roll artists, the entertainers on Broadway or in the gambling casinos, the sensational or controversial authors, painters, politicians and members of the press—those highly visible persons who are usually recognized with excitement as they pass through the airports, and are seen time and again in the National Enquirer. I repeat, it is not a culture that fits the dreams and visions, only two hundred years ago, of our founding fathers. Please be assured I am not a do-gooder or some sort of pious propagandist, but I simply cannot see any other way out of the impasse except a renewal of a dynamic, transforming faith or the unthinkable alternative of nuclear war, of environmental catastrophe or economic collapse.

DON: You should take to the road with this sad recital, Ham—you are very persuasive. But nothing in history will back up any hope for a permanent change from either religious or scientific sources. We will simply wear out our present customs and habits in time and replace them with new ones, equally good or bad. Even in the best of times the life of the human species has always been a mixed bag. If we are incapable of learning from our lessons, we will simply repeat them ad nauseum in varied and different ways. And allow me to say that your horrendous appraisal of the present does seem to me to be a magnified view of man's predicament. It has scarcely been otherwise in any civilization you can name.

JULIA: I'm afraid, Don, that I must disagree with you on the magnitude of the present problems. Humanity has never before possessed the nuclear bomb—you have seen its results at Hiroshima—or the consequent threat of possible annihilation. New techniques of terrorism increase every day, and we face a host of other dangerous and worldwide conditions which have no parallel in past civilizations. As for the frantic push for permissive personal freedom, for liberty at all costs, in both our own country and Europe—the two most civilized areas of the world before the World Wars and the Holocaust—we have seen nothing to equal its pervasiveness in any past era. Authority, if I may say so, is a dirty word, and this applies as well to the former authority of the Scriptures.

But we can easily develop an argument here with a formidable array of historical facts which will only prove, as we have all apparently agreed, that good and evil have gone hand in hand in the approximately twenty or so major civilizations which have preceded us on earth. At twenty-one this long line of our principal civilizations should by now have reached maturity. It is my opinion that Doctor Varqa's religion could very well lead us in that direction.

REVEREND AHEARN: As a fairly new citizen in this country, I feel I must call attention to the fact that America, even in recent years, has not been lacking in some of its finest hours. American generosity and humanitarian concern around the world and for its fellow-citizens in seriously troubled conditions is one of its characteristic attributes—it shows up in our abundance of charities, in our fund-raising for all sorts of good purposes, in the contribution of our celebrities, whatever their private lives, in alleviating world hunger and disease. And there is little doubt that liberal democracy and capitalism have raised the standard of living in the Western world, by and large, to its highest peak.

It is nevertheless sad that the general economic welfare in this country has burgeoned into the frantic pursuit of more and more income, bigger and better jobs and a superabundance of material possessions. To become a millionaire or better is a goal that appears to be paramount in American culture, whether by ill-gotten gains or not, and even among the very young. I have sometimes thought that the worst possible calamity for this nation would be an economic collapse or a drastic reduction in what we have all looked upon as the "American dream." I am not an economist, of course, but there are multiple signs in all sorts of places which herald a possible breakdown in our money culture as we have known it.

But Mammon is king today in both the East and the West—in the oil-producing countries, in the struggling states of the third world, and even in the deprived and discontented people under socialist or communist rule. It therefore seems to me that the loss of the world's money base, which is now a global affair, is a far more likely disaster than a nuclear war. As it is we are burdened in this country with a dangerous budget deficit impossible to balance with the world in its present shape, and the Soviets, according to our intelligence, are in ever-increasing trouble in the economic field. I am inclined to feel, then, that unless we cease spending the wealth of our nations on weapons to kill and maim our fellow men and instead proceed to clean up the ethics of our governments and the marketplaces everywhere, we shall finally see a world that is bankrupt both morally and economically.

All this, of course, is what one might call a "worst scenario." Disasters could very well arrive in any number of other ways or creep up upon us unexpectedly on "dove's feet"—we have already experienced an unending series of dire happenings which unfortunately have engulfed far more innocent people than those who were guilty. But I would like to take note here that in spite of the detrimental elements in our society one can read daily in our papers and magazines of the kindly and even heroic acts performed by any number of good and caring people—there are families and individuals, devout and otherwise, who automatically observe the Golden Rule and follow the injunctions of the Ten Commandments, even though they may not recall them in their written form. People still crowd the concert and symphony halls, give standing ovations at ballets and operas, and show a genuine appreciation for good art, good theatre, good politics, and good principles and ethics. So all is not lost by any means. I have traveled the world over, dear friends, and I venture to say that if some transformational occurrence takes place on our planet the potentialities of this nation will blossom in the end above all the others.

JULIA: This is a positive view of our country, Reverend Ahearn, which is not only generous but factual. It is my contention, however, that a very serious imbalance exists between the outward achievements and the moral integrity of an overwhelming number of our citizens. I give you the brief example of a brilliant Nobel Award scientist who is later accused of continuous wife abuse. And we all know of a well-respected church organist in our college town, a fine composer devoted to his music and his parish, who suddenly disappeared with the church funds, along with a young lady in town whose reputation was very bad indeed. I am simply saying that our general acceptance of the dichotomy between a display of mental or artistic achievements and the unbridled exhibit of one's emotions, sexual or otherwise, contributes to the increasing moral decline, and until this imbalance is corrected there is little hope for any kind of transformation in our society.

Let me say as well at this point that I am not looking for perfection on earth. This world is not a place of perfection, but a school for learning lessons. We apparently cannot do it alone but need our religions to help us. In rejecting that aid we witness everywhere that no matter how assiduously governments and individuals attempt to deal with the troubling issues that confront everyone on this planet, we seem impotent to find any lasting solutions to the great majority of our difficulties. We do, however, seem to be increasingly aware of our deficiencies. In spite of our failures in so many directions, our own government, slowly and inadequately as yet, to be sure, is making sincere efforts to deal with the basic problems of our time—drug and alcohol addiction, pornography and sex abuse, catastrophic illness and medical care, poverty, crime, corruption, pollution, international terrorism and the continuing encroachment of the Soviets on whatever countries they are able to control or seduce. I believe, friends, that we cannot stress enough in these meetings the outstanding wrongs in every portion of the globe, for without the recognition and disapproval of their existence, we are quite unable to attend to them.

Since our sojourn in Tehran, however, and in listening to the cosmological and sub-atomic explanations of the physicists in our midst, I am convinced that creation is evolving toward some distant goal, some unknown spiritual state in which a mature humanity may constitute here on earth—if I may use the orthodox Christian terminology in this regard—one of the kingdoms of God, wherein, as the Scriptures assert, His Will will be done as it is in heaven. If one believes in the prophetic powers of the Christ, as all Christians aver that they do, would he have taught us to pray for such a condition if it were not possible of attainment? Would the Founders of the world's religions have looked forward to a time of fulfillment on earth when the human species would reach a stage where the fatherhood of God and the brotherhood of man would be universally recognized, if such an eventuality were impossible for mankind? Such a transformation may seem quite unlikely at our present stage of evolution, but in spite of the dark nights that from time to time have descended upon the world, the vision of a day on earth when the spirit of good in the human heart will prevail over evil has never departed from the human race.

GEORGINA: Transformation—a wonderful word—so beautifully symbolized by the marvelous change from an immature larva to a butterfly. I believe this may be the whole purpose of our life here—a change in our nature and character. Actually, this kind of transformation has occurred in millions of individuals whose lives, following a religious conversion, have been completely turned around from their former conduct to a far higher level of thought and behavior. Anyone who has read and absorbed William James's "Varieties of Religious Experience" will be struck with the fact that a new consciousness entirely seems to result. And this eminently intellectual psychologist records that in all the genuine cases he has known and studied the change has been a permanent one.

I have also been impressed in the past by the works of Professor Frederick Myers of England, of Doctor R. M. Bucke of Canada and Carl Jung of Switzerland, who totally agree with James—as do Philip's Eastern mystics and a long line of poets, as Madilyn well knows—that our present consciousness, our rational consciousness, so-called, is only one of many levels of consciousness which exist all around us, below us, above us, and deep within us—that though they are ordinarily sealed off from one another, when a breakthrough occurs from time to time enormous energies can flow through and change the lives of individuals, of groups, and of whole regions of our planet. In the case of the Founders of the major religions this outpouring of spiritual energy appears to be so great that it can change the face of the earth. New arts appear, new sciences, new creations of all sorts, new institutions and modes of thought—what Philip would call, I suppose, a fundamental swing from yin to yang.

I can assure my colleagues that I have seen quite clearly in my studies of art and architecture what a remarkable transformation occurs in this field when a new religion is established. And indeed almost everything undergoes a change—past misconceptions are forgotten, and in the building of another civilization on the base of the new beliefs a form of resurrection takes place which has its day, passes through its allotted cycle, eventually loses its impetus and gradually descends into the darkness of what we see today on every hand. In my own field this can be illustrated quite well, I believe, by comparing the glorious art of Raphael, Michelangelo and Leonardo da Vinci with Picasso's broken faces and bodies, Dali's neurotic distortions, and Andy Warhol's soup cans. Such a vast difference in the quality of one's perception of mankind's primary place in the world surely reflects, as Professor Toynbee has noted, a serious schism in the soul.

I understand from Julia that the new religion is not regional but planetary, that it claims to be the beginning of a universal cycle, a culmination of all the religious cycles that have gone before it in recorded history. At the same time, she has told me, it makes no claims to be final and states that the system of the Prophets of God is eternal, has existed from time immemorial, beyond any record known to our present race. If such outpourings from the Prophets of God are eternal, then perfection is forever a relative term for mankind, and we never cease to evolve. In that case it is quite possible to conjecture that the universe itself is evolving, that it has its own days and nights in the periods of cosmic expansion and contraction, and that cycles within cycles within cycles have no beginning and no end. This is truly a stupendous thought, and undoubtedly far too transcendental for the human mind to encompass.

HAM: We are delighted, Georgina, to have such thoughts expressed in these meetings. In fact, we have managed to plow some new ground here this evening, and certain seeds have been sown that should produce the results Julia and I are looking forward to in our further discussions. I must stress once again that we are not in the business of proselytizing our friends in behalf of any particular religion, but due to our enthusiasm for what we learned from Doctor Varqa in the Middle East we have wished for some time to present a remarkable movement that appears to us to carry with it the solution to a great many of the world's ills.

So much that is scandalous and false has been attributed to this new religion in the land of its birth, and still is, that we feel it a boon beyond our wildest hopes to have had access through Doctor Varqa to actual records and eyewitness reports, including contemporary manuscripts of events in both Persia and Iraq. I was able to take voluminous notes from both the Arabic and Persian writings in the doctor's possession, and was thankful for my decision to study these languages while working on my doctorate. In time we intend to send for the large amount of literature available in this country in English, but meanwhile there is so much of mystery and suspense in the story of this faith that Julia and I have decided to present it to you in a chronological order that will take us from its earliest beginnings to the open drama of the execution of the Qaim by firing squad in the barracks square in Tabriz.

Meanwhile we urge you to inject any thoughts or opinions as we go along, no matter what they might be, contrary or otherwise. This is a group project, and we are humbly respectful of all individual input. We will not unduly prolong these evening meetings as the subject matter calls for a good deal of concentration, and most of us in academia are in need of our periods of mental relaxation. When the tapes are shut off let us forget our solemn search after truth, always relative as it is, and engage only in small talk. In two weeks we shall meet again and begin our review of the early inception, the spiritual genesis, of the new faith.

One last observation before we go to the sideboard for coffee and cake. In one of his letters to a friend, William James wrote of his final conviction that religion as a whole, in spite of the often extravagant dogmas and the theological superstitions to be found in man's manipulation of a Founder's Revelation, has nevertheless been the most important, the most productive enterprise in the life of mankind. And just recently a well-known anthropologist in a leading university in an eastern state has shared his opinion with me, in a statement uncharacteristic of a scientist, that if science and religion could be combined in the highest and most creative forms to be found on earth, there is no reason why a Golden Age could not be brought about at some future date for every man, woman and child.

With this possible goal in mind we hope that you will stay with us, and we shall do our best to enlighten you and ourselves on what may very well be the first religion in the history of mankind to conquer the planet.

II The Forerunners. 1753-1844

JULIA: Welcome to our second meeting, friends. It's most gratifying to see that you have all returned. Ham has given you the basic differences between the Shias and the Sunnis before the tapes were on, and if necessary we will enlarge upon them as we go along. He and I, of necessity, will take over the general direction of our discussions from now on, but do not forget that a dialogue is expected on any statement or point of view that is brought forth here. We will be presenting our findings to you as given to us by Doctor Varqa, not only because of our conviction of his great integrity and spiritual stature, but due to the fact also that he, his family, and his ancestors in the nineteenth century were deeply involved in the actual events, the factual realities of the new religion, now of global proportions.

We were able to take many notes in Doctor Varqa's presence, as well as in his library, and we shall refer to these as we go along. Our first business is to lay the foundation of how these events came about in the Middle East, and this will take us back as far as the birth of a boy in the town of Ahsa in northeast Arabia in 1753. His father was a minor though literate official whose ancestors on the island of Bahrayn in the Persian Gulf had converted from the Sunni to the Shia sect. The family was poor, humble, and certainly without any danger at that time from the Sunni authorities then in control of Arabia. However, a puritanical spirit was rising in the Sunni strongholds of Mecca and Medina, and the Shias were increasingly criticized as idolatrous worshippers of the Shia saints, of the shrines and relics of the Imams in Persia and Iraq, and the Hidden Imam as the future ruler of Islam. At the same time the Arabian Sunnis disapproved of the lax practices of the Ottoman Caliphate—a circumstance which led eventually to the Wahhabi uprising in Arabia, caused the overthrow of the Turkish rule in that country, and in time brought the strictly traditional Saudi family to power.

The household name of our young boy has not been recorded, but he is known to the new faith as Ahmad, a favored name among the Shias. Even as a child the boy was so spiritually sensitive that he was given to strange dreams and visions which seemed to be preparing him for knowledge beyond his years. Ahmad's father, recognizing the signs in his son of a future vocation in the clerical ranks of Islam, made the decision to return his family to Bahrayn, the island of his ancestors off the eastern coast of Arabia. There a Shia majority had established an ecclesiastical school renowned for its deep study of the Qoran, of the sayings and traditions of Muhammad in his lifetime, and the prophecies and pronouncements of the Imams of the House of the Prophet. Before long Ahmad's reputation as a brilliant pupil had guaranteed his rapid rise to the rank of teacher in the school.

Ahmad remained on Bahrayn for almost forty years. Examining minutely every detail in Islamic literature, he delved as well into the teachings and prophecies in the various Scriptures of the world. His spiritual and intellectual sensibilities were profoundly disturbed by the lack of unity in Islam, the perversions and spiritual degradation of both sects, and the literal interpretation of a multitude of passages which were obviously filled with symbolic meaning. Now a venerable Shaykh surrounded by a large number of students from various areas in the region of the Persian Gulf, Ahmad determined to leave Bahrayn and share his knowledge and convictions with the Shias in Persia and Iraq.

DON: Was this man, Julia, an Arab or a Persian? I am sorry, but I must admit to you that the world of Islam is not a part of my scholarship. I am learning things here of which even my graduate studies failed to enlighten me. You are no doubt aware of the fact that during my days in college, and except for special studies on the Eastern hemisphere, the history departments of the West were generally involved in teaching historical events from the standpoint of the Western world, beginning with ancient Greece and going on from there to Rome and Europe and the American continent. As to what happened elsewhere it was judged more or less as to how it had affected the West. I would like to say that after our first meeting I checked out from the library a few recent books on the history of Islam and hope to be more knowledgeable when we meet again. However, I will need a good deal of persuasion to concede that any religion of lasting value could possibly arise in such a superstitious part of the world.

HAM: Nevertheless, Don, Islam itself arose in a spiritually decadent milieu of outright idolatry, and both Christianity and Buddhism, the two greatest influences on the West and the Far East, came into being when the former religions in their respective areas were in serious decline. Just stay with us, Don, we can use that bright mind of yours. We'll look forward to sharing your response to the books on Islam. It seems that Madilyn's interest in the marvelous poetry that has come out of Persia has given her a less critical view of the Middle East.

As for Shaykh Ahmad, we gathered that he was an Arab whose ancestors stemmed from an ancient tribe of Arabia, the Bani-Sakhr. Because of his later history in Persia and in the holy cities in Iraq he has been looked upon by the more recent believers in foreign lands as a Persian. But as Doctor Varqa pointed out, his mission was hardly dependent on his genealogy—he was destined to arouse the Shias of Persia and Iraq to the imminent Advent of the one whom they called the Hidden Imam, the Promised One of Islam, the Qaim. We informed you before the tapes were on of this Shia doctrine of an Apocalypse through the return of the last Imam, an event which in time would reform and renew the declining powers of the Muslim faith and establish Islam as the primary religion for mankind. But we shall see that Shaykh Ahmad departed in several ways from this thousand-year view of the Shias, and we will explain this to you as we go along.

JULIA: Actually, the idea of an Apocalypse, the return in glory of a spiritual luminary known in the past, or the Advent of a different individual with new and advanced teachings for mankind, is inherent in all the religions, including certain schools of Buddhism, and we will quote later from the various Scriptures involved to establish this fact. Christianity and Islam have designated this future event, this messianic Apocalypse, as occurring through a former figure of their own faith—in Christianity by the Christ, in Shia Islam by the Twelfth or Hidden Imam, and in the ranks of the Sunnis by the Mahdi, a rather difficult figure to pinpoint due to the differences of opinion in the various sects of the Sunni persuasion. Surprisingly there are Sunnis who echo the belief of various Shia sects who look forward to the return in glory of the Imam Husayn—the youngest grandson of the Prophet who was martyred with all his family on the plain of Karbila—or of some other Imam of their own choice. Some have gone as far afield as to opt for certain non-Imamate sons of the Prophet's House in Medina, while others hold out for a latter-day descendant of Muhammad who will carry the name of the Prophet combined with that of the Imam Ali. However, the lack of a formal and united doctrine on the exact personality of the Mahdi of the Sunnis, unlike the majority choice of the Twelfth or Hidden Imam of the Shias, has left the matter open to any number of ambitious claimants, usually politically motivated. We have seen an historical example of this when a native of Sudan, claiming to be the Mahdi and bent on ridding the country of the British and Egyptians, was responsible for the death of General Charles Gordon in Khartoum in 1885, and shortly afterward passed away without attaining the recognition he looked for. As a consequence, the Advent of the Mahdi, like the long wait for the World Messiah in Judaism, remains perpetually, and often indifferently, in the future.

HELEN: It appears to me, Julia, that all this looking forward to some sort of future delivery from the mishmash the Muslims have made of their religion is identical to the Christian belief that the Christ will descend again and save us from the stagnation of our own former traditions. It is all so irrational, so based on hidebound literal interpretations of mostly non-comprehensible religious texts that indifference would seem to me the proper approach to the whole subject.

JULIA: I am able to agree with you, Helen, where these two religions are concerned, but fortunately this is not the entire picture. Contrary to such an exclusive view we shall quote later from certain passages in the Scriptures of Hinduism, Judaism, Buddhism and Zoroastrianism which leave the idea open for a World Teacher with a new personality, a new name, and new truths never before revealed to the world. Even in Christianity we find in the Apocalypse, the Book of Revelation—almost entirely symbolic, by the way—the intimation that another heavenly figure, "like unto the Son of Man," will appear in the latter days with a new name—a prophecy implied likewise in the Christ's statement that "When he the Spirit of Truth cometh, he will lead you into all truth." Surely the modern mind can no longer believe that "all truth," either in connection with the Christ or in any other way, descended upon his early followers at the time of Pentecost, nor that the pronoun he is applicable to such an occasion. The fact remains that the final truth of all the higher religions and of our very existence in the universe is still far beyond our grasp—it was Edison, I believe, who declared that we know less than one percent about anything. But this should not prevent us from using our increasing religious scholarship to continually investigate what many of our most searching minds have looked upon, in conjunction with the illuminating findings of science, as the greatest transforming force in the life of the human species.

Before we return to the teachings of Shaykh Ahmad, we should take note that certain Muslim sects, both Sunni and Shia, include the appearance of the Prophet Jesus in the Middle East concurrently with the Mahdi or the Hidden Imam—in other words a double Advent combining these two sister religions into one powerful Revelation that will sweep the world and establish the truth of Muhammad's mission. At the same time we encounter in the Qoran a similar declaration of which the Western world is unaware. It states that at the time foreordained for the spiritual resurrection of mankind the blast of "Two Trumpets," one following closely upon the other, would find the world in a condition of material consternation and spiritual torpor, its plight beyond retrieval by the people of that future age. In the sayings of the Imams the Prophet is purported to have asserted that the Advent in those latter days would bring a new Cause and a new Book, and this would occur when Islam had run its destined course for a full thousand years. The time of the sudden and unexpected sound of the Trumpets was designated as The Hour, The Great Announcement, The Resurrection and The Day of Judgment.

Ham and I brought back with us many notes on the prophecies of Muhammad and the Imams, and when the proper moment arrives we will share with you the remarkable concordance of these declarations with what is actually the moral condition today in both the East and the West. I will quote just one of them from the Hadith, the Traditions of Islam, which foretells quite accurately, it seems to me, the degraded state of affairs in which the Middle East finds itself at this particular period:

"The Prophet of God said: There will come a time for my people when there will remain nothing of the Qoran except an outward form and nothing of Islam except its name, and they will call themselves by this name even though they are the people furthest from it. Their mosques will be full of people but they will be empty of right guidance. The religious leaders of that day will be the most evil religious leaders under the heavens; sedition and dissension will go out from them and to them will it return."

It is natural that the orthodox Sunnis of Islam have maintained that Hadith prophecies of this sort are forgeries, concocted by the Shia Imams or by later adherents of various sects to forward ambitions or opinions of their own. But Shaykh Ahmad vigorously disagreed. He emphatically discarded the orthodox beliefs of both the Sunnis and the Shias, and claimed that their doctrines of the Mahdi and the Hidden Imam, including the actual appearance of the Christ in the Middle East, were only partially correct, that no personal return of such past figures would take place, but on the contrary, two new Prophets of God, born anew of woman as all the Prophets have been, would soon be manifested on Persian soil. These Twin Prophets were designated by the Shaykh as the Promised One of Islam, the Qaim, and a Universal Teacher, the Qayyúm, whose mission would encompass the entire planet. I think you can agree with me that with these statements he automatically pointed out the cyclical nature of religion and the principle of progressive revelation by successive Manifestations sent to mankind for that very purpose.

REVEREND AHEARN: These are extraordinary observations, Julia. I have never investigated the future expectations of the world's religions, aside from the Second Coming of the Christ, except in a most perfunctory way. With seventy or more schools of thought in the Muslim world, with many thousands of denominations within the fold of the Christian religion, and numerous divisions within Judaism, Buddhism and Hinduism, it's a major struggle to obtain a clear perspective on the basic beliefs. That a Shaykh of the Shia persuasion should come to the conclusions you have outlined is quite remarkable. Surely we can admit to something unusual here, a breakthrough that seems to have led to an independent religion different in its underlying theology from most of the Scriptural sources from which he received so much of his knowledge.

HAM: As far as we could gather from Doctor Varqa, the Shaykh appeared to possess an endowment of intuition far beyond that of the average man—a direct perception of certain truths not necessarily based on the powers of reason. One of his main contentions was that the truth behind the sacred writings could not be discovered through literalism alone, but primarily through an understanding of symbolism, the spiritual language of the Prophets. At the same time there were many esoteric developments in his teaching which stemmed directly from Shiism and Sufism, and which, as far as the end results are concerned, would be superfluous to outline in these meetings. Most of the orthodox ulama were hard put to follow the intricate weavings of his intellect, and there were many who disapproved of his teachings as heretical. But he never swerved from his convictions, aware that he had been chosen, as others have been chosen in the past, to open the way to a radical reform in religious thinking.

JULIA: One of the Shaykh's most pronounced teachings was at variance with the Muslim and Christian belief in the resurrection of the physical body. He maintained that there was a duplicate body in man, subtle and ethereal, which escaped destruction at death and passed into other realms of being, eventually drawn to the place where its spiritual attainments, or lack of them, had attracted it. But when the Shaykh went so far as to maintain that Muhammad's Night Journey to Heaven from the Rock in Jerusalem was not accomplished in his material body but by the spiritual body of the Prophet, this was unacceptable to the orthodox ulama and caused a great many rival scholars to accuse him not only of blasphemy against the powers of the Prophet, but in certain extremist cities, such as Qazvin and Qum, of being an agent of the Devil. Nevertheless the Shaykh's intellectual brilliance, the eloquence of his lectures and the fluency of his writings—reminiscent, many said, of the famed Islamic scholars and philosophers of the past—were to give him an entree into all but the most fanatical circles. Many of the more liberal clergy would later declare themselves as Shaykhis, both in Persia and Iraq, and his influence spread from one city and town to another as he traveled and taught constantly to reform the thinking of Shia Islam.

REVEREND AHEARN: The doctrine of some sort of unearthly body is certainly in keeping with that of the Jewish Pharisees, and this included a former Pharisee, St. Paul, who declared that there was both a natural body and a spiritual body. And surely this can be inferred from the sayings of the Christ in the Gospels—recall his promise of Paradise to the thief on the cross—as well as the afterlife scenes described by Muhammad in the Qoran, symbolic though they may be. The same is true in the teachings of the Zend-Avesta, which records the statements of Zoroaster. In fact I have found no Scriptural religions anywhere, including Buddhism and Hinduism, where the concept of other worlds of being is totally absent. Unfortunately the two latter religions depart from Judaism, Christianity and Islam in accepting the reality of reincarnation, the return to earth again and again to achieve perfection. Personally I have never given the subject much consideration, and admit my ignorance as to just how the idea of rebirth came into being.

JULIA: Beginnings are always difficult to pinpoint, especially in religion. But you have brought up an important dichotomy between two sets of religion which needs some discussion. This division in what is presented as the universal system for man's development has come up on many occasions in the classroom and if we find the time this evening I will attempt to point out where and when the idea of rebirth seems to have taken hold of men's minds. For the present, however, I must follow through on the Forerunners, and introduce you to that other remarkable figure, Siyyid Kazim, who became the assistant and then the partner of his mentor, Shaykh Ahmad. How these two came together is a story that I will pass on to you as we come to it.

Doctor Varqa informed us that when the Shaykh departed from Bahrayn he had gone first to the holy city of Najaf in Iraq, and then to nearby Karbila, and was soon recognized by the resident ulama as an outstanding scholar of Islamic theology and law, as well as of many thousands of recorded traditions of the days of the Prophet and the Imams, which he declared, in contradistinction to others of spurious value, to be authentic. In spite of their understandable prejudice against certain of his novel statements and interpretations, the ecclesiastics came in droves to sit at his feet, and when he applied for the title of mujtahid—a renowned exponent of Shia jurisprudence able to make independent judgments in his own name—it was bestowed upon him with only minor dissensions.

When the Shaykh departed from Iraq for the city of Yazd he stopped off at the port town of Bushihr on the Persian Gulf and in the city of Shiraz in the province of Fars. The doctor pointed out that both of these sites were a part of the territory of ancient Elam in the days of the Zoroastrian Achaemenian monarchs Cyrus, Darius and Xerxes of the first Persian Empire, from the sixth to the fourth centuries B.C. The conquest of this famous line of rulers by Alexander the Great took place in this region, and it was not until the third century A.D. that the local dynasty of Sassanian kings in this same area rejuvenated the Persian Empire and the Zoroastrian religion. Over this vast second Empire they ruled for four hundred years from such cities as Ishtakr, Ctesiphon and Firuzabad, metropolises which had replaced the former Empire cities of Pasargadae, Persepolis, Susa, Ecbatana and Babylon.

I have mentioned this prolific region of southern Persia for several reasons. It was in ancient Elam, in the city of Susa, near the lower banks of the Tigris, that Daniel, still in captivity in the East, experienced in the reign of Cyrus the Great his prophetic visions of the time of the end, and was told that the meaning of what he had seen and heard would be kept secret and sealed until those final days had arrived. Jeremiah had prophesied in this same region that the Lord would take away the might of the kings in Elam, that their power and kingdoms would be no more. The prophecy then goes on to say that after the fall of the kings in Persia the Lord would "set his throne in Elam," and in days to come would restore the fortunes of that sad and corrupted land.

Whether or not such prophecies impress us in these secular times, we should recall that the Christ, in speaking of the day of his return, warned that mankind would need spiritual understanding in order to know him. "When ye shall see the abomination of desolation spoken of by Daniel the prophet," he said, "stand ye in the holy place (whoso readeth, let him understand)." This hardly appears to be a terrifying descent from the clouds, when all the inhabitants of the earth, their free will a thing of the past, will be forced to recognize the sovereignty of the Christ. If, however, he should come as a thief in the night with a new name, there can be no foregone conclusion that the Holy Spirit will not appear once more in an area little known to the West—an event that would indeed test the spiritual understanding of those who await a world Apocalypse in the latter days. Ham, you have the notes with you on the Shaykh's journey through the ancient province of Elam. What he had to say in two particular locations on this journey was not only surprising to his hearers, but will prove to be important to our story at a later time.

HAM: It seems that one of Doctor Varqa's ancestors, Haji Mirza Jamal, a merchant of Kashan and the grandfather of Mustafa—who was then a mere child, and whose later journal in part we now have in our possession—happened to be in the port town of Bushihr on business when Shaykh Ahmad arrived there on his way to the city of Shiraz in the uplands of the present province of Fars. Bushihr was a hot and dusty town and hardly a locality for enthusiastic acclaim. But according to Mustafa's later writings, Mirza Jamal was astounded to hear the Shaykh extol the virtues of Bushihr in such extravagant terms that he wondered if the heat had somehow affected his mind. The Shaykh continued to lavish such praise upon the town in his public talks that the clergy, aware of his remarkable erudition in all other matters, were completely nonplussed.

Mirza Jamal was apparently a sensitive and literate man who had formed the habit of writing down unusual events during his business trips, and had also encouraged his three sons, the father and two young uncles of Mustafa, to take notes of any interesting happenings in Kashan which came to their attention. Intrigued with Ahmad's acclaim of a site that was not in the category for such praise, he decided to follow the Shaykh to Shiraz in the hope of further enlightenment. Once again, such verbal homage was paid to the city of Shiraz that Mirza Jamal wondered if the Shaykh's intuitive powers had sensed in these places the coming of some future event. He jotted down these two locations in his notebook with a question mark. Later in Kashan, in relating these unusual accolades to his son Mirza Jani, one of the uncles of Mustafa, he gave him a full account of what he considered a very strange circumstance. Shiraz, to be sure, had always been lauded by the poets and the rank and file alike for the beauty of its plains, its blossoming orchards, the roses, cypresses and nightingales for which it was famous, but Bushihr was a different matter altogether. Without any further clue the merchant and Mirza Jani, occupied with the family business in Kashan, soon put the unprecedented incidents out of their minds.

Upon his arrival in Yazd, the Shaykh settled down to write the greater part of his scores of essays, commentaries and prophetic interpretations of Islamic writ. His lectures were not only well-attended in Yazd, but his fame soon spread throughout Persia, attracting the attention of the monarch Fath-Ali-Shah, of the Crown Prince Muhammad-Ali Mirza and other members of the court, as well as a number of the leading clergy in Tehran, Kirmanshah, Hamadan and Isfahan who found it fashionable at that time to declare themselves as Shaykhis. But others ridiculed his assertion that the Advent of the Promised One was not far off, and they looked upon his symbolic reading of Islamic Scriptures and Traditions as not only unorthodox but in most cases pure imagination. As for his ability to quote from Scriptures which preceded the Qoran, they declared it a waste of time, as the Qoran was not only the final Revelation for mankind but superseded and nullified all other teachings and customs before it. There were certain fanatics indeed, especially in Qazvin and Qum, who were biding their time, awaiting an opportunity to bring about the downfall of the Shaykh as a dangerous heretic. All of this will no doubt sound familiar to anyone who has been a scholar of religious behavior, both in our modern day and in the past. A consensus of opinion is rarely found when new theological interpretations are presented to the world.

REVEREND AHEARN: Heresy has been the key word for persecution in every religion on earth. Do the Christians not remember that the Christ himself was looked upon as heretical, a false prophet, from his earliest teachings to his death on the cross? The Bible tells us that many turned aside from what he had to say, and came to hear him no more. But rejection of this sort is no proof of ultimate failure. In time these great teachers and their early followers become the kings and princes of the earth, their names known and their words quoted the world over. I presume that Shaykh Ahmad, as the earliest pioneer of the new faith, is now revered within this fold in the same manner.

JULIA: He is indeed—and not only the Shaykh but his spiritual companion as well, Siyyid Kazim. Their intellects and their intuition, according to what Doctor Varqa had to say, are equally revered by the members of the new faith, who maintain that their very existence was foreordained to prepare the way for the coming Advent of the Twin Prophets. Their story is therefore as important to the members of the new religion as that of John the Baptist to the mission of the Christ. Both Ham and I feel very strongly that a résumé of their lives together should be given here for a full understanding of their dedication to an imminent Apocalypse. Through thick and thin, through successful recognition and heartbreaking rejection, they held to their firm convictions without a moment's hesitation.

HAM: How these two unorthodox members of the Muslim clergy came together in the city of Yazd is ample proof, in my estimation, that they were destined to do so from the very start of their lives, even though they were born in separate areas of the Middle East. The family of Siyyid Kazim were merchants in the town of Rasht near the Caspian Sea, and even in his early youth the young Siyyid was known and admired for his scholarship and religious devotion, his character and humble deportment. Ever since his childhood days he had spent many hours committing the Qoran and a vast number of Traditions to memory, and by the age of twenty-two, aware for some time of the teachings of Shaykh Ahmad, he recognized that his own conclusions in relation to a coming Advent and to other pronouncements of the Shaykh were surprisingly in accord. The Siyyid continued his profound studies and his written commentaries until he found himself able, at twenty-six, in the wake of a vivid dream urging him to do so, to leave his home in the province of Gilan and travel to Yazd to become a disciple of the Shaykh.

I might say in passing that the northwestern area of Persia near the Caspian Sea has been alleged by some historians to be the birthplace of Zoroaster. Doctor Varqa stated that a number of well-known ecclesiastics in that area have proudly put forth the claim to be direct descendants of that Prophet, and others have done likewise in the provinces of Mazindaran and Khurasan, where this first monotheistic teacher in Persian history had taught his dualistic doctrine of the One God Ahura-Mazda versus the satanic forces of the Big Lie, and had passed away in old age—or as some say was murdered while praying at a fire-altar—in the region known as Bactria. The family of Siyyid Kazim, however, made no such claim, content to be authentic descendants of the Prophet Muhammad.

When the young Kazim reached his destination in Yazd he found that the Shaykh was making arrangements to depart for the city of Mashad in eastern Khurasan, where he intended to declare the coming Advent at the Shrine of the Imam Rida. It was soon apparent, from the overwhelmingly warm reception of Kazim by the Shaykh, that the latter's departure had been predicated upon the arrival of his new disciple from the north. In short order Kazim was groomed to take over the pupils in place of the Shaykh and to teach them the conclusions that he himself had deduced from the Scriptures. It was not long before he had won over the hearts and minds of his audiences and dispelled any jealousy of the older disciples by his dignity, his knowledge, and his unpretentious demeanor.

Upon the Shaykh's return from Mashad the two teachers began their travels together, and eventually, at the invitation of Fath-Ali-Shah, received a royal welcome at the court in Tehran. The Shaykh had expressed to the Shah a desire to visit a famous village in the district of Nur in Mazindaran, the country home of a wealthy landowner, Mirza Buzurg, one of the more liberal ministers at court. But the Crown Prince, the most religiously tolerant of the large brood of the monarch's sons, and now governor of Kirmanshah, requested the Shah to send his visitors to that city, where he might provide them with his patronage and protection. There in Kirmanshah the two theologians remained, surrounded by crowds of listeners, until the untimely death of the Prince in 1821, when Shaykh Ahmad made the decision to return to Iraq and to open a school in Karbila.

In telling us the history of the Forerunners, Doctor Varqa conjectured that had the Crown Prince lived on and come to the throne later in Tehran the fortunes of the new faith might very well have taken a different turn, for a time at least. This could possibly have been the case as well, he said, if the deceased's brother, Abbas Mirza, the new heir to the throne—considered the most reform-minded and the least corrupt of the Qajar princes—had not been obliged to conduct a series of humiliating wars with Russia in the north, in which Persia lost her provinces in the Caucasus, including much of Adjerbaijan, and most of her former rights in and around the Caspian Sea. The heavy indemnities against Persia came close to bankrupting the nation, and Abbas Mirza, in a state of deep depression and shame, lost his will to live, and passed away in 1833. A year later Fath-Ali-Shah followed him to the grave, and in 1834 Muhammad Shah, a very different character from his father Abbas, ascended the throne, with disastrous results in the 1840s, as we shall see, for the spreading faith.

Once established in Karbila the Shaykh and Siyyid Kazim began to feel the loss of their former court patronage. The orthodox ulama of the holy cities now found the opportunity to begin their verbal assaults on the heterodox teachings of the school. The attacks were spearheaded by Siyyid Ibrahim-i-Qazvini, a fanatical and pretentious mujtahid who had no intention of giving up his leading role in Karbila for the founders of the new school. In his earlier years in Qazvin, Ibrahim was a friend and admirer of the city's two principal ecclesiastics, the father and uncle of the poetess Qurratul-Ayn. The mutual animosity of these three influential clerics toward Shaykh Ahmad's unorthodox approach to the teachings of Shia Islam was so vitriolic that the day the Shaykh and Siyyid Kazim arrived in Qazvin during their early lecture tours in Persia they were treated with such public discourtesy and disdain that they were forced to withdraw from the city.

There seems to be little doubt that the ambitious Ibrahim, during his later prominence in the holy city of Karbila, was jealous in particular of the charismatic Kazim, whom he came to look upon as a threat to his own authority in the town. In time, after Shaykh Ahmad had returned to Arabia, to die there in 1834, and Siyyid Kazim had himself attained the illustrious title of mujtahid, the acid-tongued Ibrahim spent most of his time denouncing the school, its leaders and its pupils, and attempting to arouse the populace on every public occasion to expel them from the town. Although these tirades against the respected Kazim were unsuccessful, Siyyid Ibrahim remained an active enemy of the school for the next twenty years, contributing his malicious share in 1844 and 1845 in denying the legitimacy of the Advent of a new Messenger from God, and lending his venomous influence in the persecution of the first believers in Iraq. In all fairness we must say that this portrayal of Siyyid Ibrahim, produced in later accounts by followers of the tenets of the Shaykhi school, is counterbalanced by those orthodox ulama who expressed an admiration for his dignity and reticence. Such portrayals, from opposite sides of the fence, are found in every religion, and until we can judge in a more scholarly manner of the true character of this mujtahid we are obliged of necessity to accept the reports of his actions as they have come down to us through the accounts of young Mulla Mustafa and other writers of the time.

I believe that this is as good a place as any to take a break from our Forerunners and to deal with a subject brought forward by Reverend Ahearn— the controversial theory of reincarnation. Because the new faith has denied that this is the system that God has ordained for man's perfecting, Julia has made an attempt in her more recent studies to discover where and when this Hindu and Far Eastern doctrine, so appealing to its advocates in the West, first appeared in the long history of religion. In our next meeting we will return to the school in Karbila and go behind the scenes, with the help of Mustafa's contemporary journal, to become more intimately acquainted with the teachings and some of the pupils there and to bring us closer to the crucial years of the 1830s and 1840s. I shall now hand things over to Julia who has delved into the past on the matter of the soul's rebirth on earth, and we shall look for as many comments as you care to make on a most contentious and touchy subject.

JULIA: I will state immediately and forthrightly that, try as I might, I have found no foundation for the doctrine of the reincarnation of a human soul into the body of a new-born child in any of the Scriptural religions preceding Hinduism and Buddhism—not in the ancient Sabeanism of the flourishing civilization of Arabia Felix on the southern shores of that sub-continent, not in the early untainted Vedism of the conquering Aryans, that "noble race" from the area around the Black Sea, or in the sacred writings of Sumeria, Babylonia, Egypt, Palestine or the Far East. But if you will bear with me we must go further back to the religions of early man whose primitive beliefs—animism, totemism and fetishism—may very well have planted the seeds for the idea of transmigration through the four kingdoms of nature, or from one kingdom to another—forms of reincarnation still accepted as truth by various indigenous peoples who have clung to their primitive ways. Transmigration beliefs are still to be found among the Hindus and in certain schools of Buddhism, but not until the establishment of the caste system in India in the fifteenth century B.C. am I able to find anything to resemble the present mode of an almost endless return of the self-same human soul, life after life, to pick up one's fated karma in another human body on earth. We will make time in another meeting to quote the words of the Buddha himself from the early Pali Canon—a surprising denial of a hard-core personal soul or self that reincarnates after death. This statement appears to be little known, and if known is generally ignored.

Meanwhile we should be aware that many of the ideas of early man are still existent in our modern culture, and whether they are strongly implanted or only a lingering trace they prove the continuity of man's development throughout long periods of time. The primitive mind was far from stupid, nor did it drift about in a sort of unbroken "dream time," quite disconnected from the real world. On the contrary, the closeness of early man to all four kingdoms of nature—minerals, plants, animals and man himself—was far beyond anything we experience in our own lives, and this produced a feeling of empathy towards his surroundings and his fellow man akin to brotherhood. There were certain humans and certain things that were harmful, to be sure, but he invented fetishes to protect himself, as we today carry a good luck charm in a pocket, place a St. Christopher's medal on a windshield, rub a rabbit's foot or knock wood to avoid unpleasant results.

We should note here that in animistic beliefs all things in nature possessed a soul and a consciousness—forces that worked for either good or evil and needed to be placated or pacified and when necessary confronted by an equally powerful soul-force in man's own being—the "mana" of the Polynesians and the Melanesians, for example—which kept life bearable and on a fairly even keel. Because of the pervasive presence of these forces everywhere and in everything, animism seems to be in early agreement with our scientists today that all existent things are not only interconnected, but in certain of their aspects interchangeable. At any rate a balance was maintained that brought early man through a time of physical danger and apprehension until a new era of gods and goddesses dawned upon the scene.

This early interconnectedness between man and nature is important to the idea of transmigration between the four earthly kingdoms, mineral, plant, animal and man. The relationship with animals in totemism is a case in point—the belief that certain birds, animals or creatures of the sea were ancestors of a group or tribe and that these progenitors must be protected, must not be killed or eaten, and must be cared for as brothers. Thus such groups were known as the "buffalo clan," the "bear clan," the "shark clan," the "eagle clan" and so on, depending on their locations and means of contact. The reverence for the cat and other animals in ancient Egypt may very well be an example; and the sacredness of cows in India, still a case of massive animal protection, stems, in my opinion, from the same source. Is it too much, perhaps, to see an echo here in the Russian bear and the American eagle, the choice of a plant or flower, an animal or a species of bird to represent a country or a state, or our preoccupation with certain animals, birds or fish as our special pets?

I do not mean to be flippant here, friends. I am only suggesting to you once again that a continuity of thought, welling up from the subconscious underlying every man's existence, can be found today in all sorts of activities and in all sorts of places. My feeling is that an inclination toward the transmigration beliefs of early man is still alive in the present devotees of reincarnation, and without any scientific proof, then or now. As for Hinduism and Buddhism, we have an additional factor—the caste system—that brought this belief to fruition in its present form, and I will ask Ham to clarify the extremely complex political development on the Indian subcontinent which brought about the merging of Aryan Vedism and primitive indigenous beliefs in India to produce the Hinduism we know today.

HELEN: My dear Julia, the strange and sometimes baffling subjects you and Ham are bringing up in these meetings are taxing every ounce of my mental capacity. I frankly admit nevertheless that I am fascinated with all this offbeat material—it would carry no meaning whatever in a Marxist classroom, and I welcome the change. I'm obliged to say, however, that the idea of reincarnation has always seemed ridiculous to me, weighed down as it is, at least in this country, with returned Cleopatras, Joan of Arcs, Alexander the Greats, Napoleons, Mary Magdalenes and so on, and seldom, it seems, with ordinary, simple individuals unproclaimed in the history books.

I am speaking, I assure you, from first-hand knowledge on this score. A young cousin of mine in California, who writes to me often with an intent to convert, is an addict of certain New Age beliefs which include mediumistic teachings delivered from other dimensions by those who no longer need to return to earth, and whose wise directives, if adhered to, will save our souls and our benighted planet. She and her friends of all ages are well into the practice of Eastern rituals, of recalling past lives, of automatic writing, of unraveling the meaning of flying saucers, and attending an endless round of meetings and classes on what they maintain is a New Age outpouring of the spirit for these troubled times. I am not a fundamentally cynical person, but I cannot see that all this activity, superior as it no doubt is to a purely self-centered life, is the definitive way to perfect ourselves nor our sadly deficient society. If a system of rebirth is required for perfecting mankind, why do we see so few results in our grossly imperfect world—a Mother Teresa perhaps or a few recorded saints from the past. As far as I can see there seems to be little intellectual examination applied to such beliefs.

PHILIP: My dear Helen, you are fastening upon one of the pseudo-religious expressions that have spread so rapidly in our modern day, especially in the open atmosphere of our Golden State. In my estimation they do little harm, except to divert their devotees from scientific reality and the ever-increasing necessity, as Julia has brought to our attention, of examining the great religions at the base of our world civilizations. I am told that twenty percent of our American citizens believe that reincarnation best explains the good and evil in the world and the apparent injustices suffered by those who have led hurtful and unproductive lives in a past incarnation. This is one fifth of the population, and a formidable challenge to four of the world's Scriptural religions—Judaism, Zoroastrianism, Christianity and Islam—whose Prophet-Founders and their followers made no mention whatever of such a doctrine.

As for Hinduism and Buddhism, they are very much in vogue in the West these days, an interesting departure for those who maintain that the four faiths I have just mentioned are now old and outworn, that they no longer have any relevance to the present day, while completely ignoring the fact that Hinduism, and much that we find in Buddhism, is more ancient still. But all this New Age thinking seems to be fairly innocuous compared to the crippling drug cults and satanic rituals which appear to be increasing, especially among the young. Here is where the real danger lies—a true descent into hell for those who have had no education in our society as to what constitutes a valid religion.

REVEREND AHEARN: To be quite fair, there are New Age philosophies, humanistic and secular as most of them are, which appear to be psychologically and scientifically sound. They look to an evolutionary rise in man's consciousness to bring about the establishment of global unity and brotherhood and a sane and holistic approach to politics, technology, medicine, education, and the methods of communication—in other words to the dawn of the "global brain" first posited by a Catholic scientist, Pierre Tailhard de Chardin, whose remarkable works center on the belief in God's evolutionary purpose for mankind. The claims of most of the modern expressions of hope for the world, however, seem to be lacking in the one element that has the power, as witnessed over and over again in every part of our planet, to unify large segments of humanity. The missing component is the recognition that our Creator, a First Cause or First Intelligence if you wish, not only lies at the base of all existence but that no dynamic or lasting spiritual results can be achieved without a profound feeling of relationship with that unknowable Essence behind all manifestation. And this includes our recognition of those great Educators, the Founders of the world's faiths, whose exalted and unifying teachings confirm their mutual connection to that unseen Essence.

I have recently read somewhere that a poll was taken to discover the number of our citizens who believe in God. More than ninety percent proclaimed this belief, and many included the conviction that nearness and remoteness from God after death constituted their idea of heaven and hell. This is all very well, very impressive, but where are the practical results of this declared belief in transforming our society and our personal behavior? Another recent poll tells us that fifty percent of our citizens believe in unidentified flying objects, a poll arousing far more interest than one's belief in God. Our peripheral beliefs have taken the place of our Scriptural religions, and surely no one can deny the flagrant consequences in every segment of our society. And so I say again that the new faith presented here by Ham and Julia may very well be the catalyst for turning our minds to the true purpose of religion in these latter days—a God-oriented movement embodying both the practical and the superphysical, a strict morality in all worldly endeavors, and a unity in diversity of all men, women and children in a world without war, without confrontation, and without the many personal and political evils endured for thousands of years in the past.

DON: If I might say so, Reverend Ahearn, any practical man will tell us that, given the ingrained characteristics of our species to be both personally contentious and prone to warfare, no religion, judging from the failures of the past, can be counted on to overcome these tendencies. He would also maintain, and to my mind quite correctly, that as long as communism continues its control over huge areas of the world's population, as I have pointed out before, it is quite unlikely that any religious solution will bring about world peace without a drastic change in both the Soviet Union and China, including their satellites.

HAM: In that you are quite correct, Don. But I predict that the system of communism—if you will pardon my presumption, Helen—will collapse early in the twenty-first century, if not before, from economic stalemate and the discontent of its people. The eventual recognition that man cannot live by bread alone—especially when the bread itself is unsatisfactory—will, I believe, bring about a counter-revolution calling for genuine democracy and an open society. Once this takes place the bonds will be loosened for a spiritual revival that is already simmering below the surface, a circumstance that will pave the way for an international global community—a final transformation, as Philip might put it, from the present darkness of yin to the brightness of both yin and yang, and to the long-awaited maturity of mankind.

I would like to add here that the new faith has prophesied the downfall of the communist system, as it had also warned of the disappearance of the arrogant and militaristic kingdoms of the continent of Europe and Asia from 1870 to 1945, and the loss of ecclesiastical authority in one country after another. But these subjects are for a later day, and for the time that is left this evening let us take a backward look at what we believe to be the initial cause of the present doctrine of reincarnation in India.

Now that the issue has arisen in this meeting we are more than ready to give this doctrine, denied by the new faith, some special attention. Julia and I believe, as did Doctor Varqa, that several widely held convictions in both the East and the

West need to be eliminated through reason and scholarly analysis before the world as a whole will accept the new Revelation. One of these centuries-old beliefs, the return of the human soul to earth again and again, has already given way to an astonishing acceptance of the new faith by numerous Hindus—indeed India today has the largest number of believers in any country anywhere on the globe. This will give you some idea of the power of a major Prophet of God to change the mode of thinking of large masses of people in preparation for a universal cycle of transformation throughout the world—a cycle, in my opinion, Philip, that will not only diminish the present preponderance of the scientific, technological and masculine elements in our Western culture, but will combine them in harmony with the intuitive, spiritual and artistic principles of the feminine yin—a balanced combination of the left and the right hemispheres of the brain. Doctor Varqa quoted for us a metaphor from his own religion—a bird cannot fly, it says, with one wing. Likewise a mature civilization cannot be established without the two wings of science and religion in the proper balance, as well as the equality of the two sexes to engage in the running of the world. Balance is all-important, and without it there can be no coordination of the many and diverse peoples of our planet.

Additional obstacles to any new theological revelations are the three Semitic religions which cling to the exclusive view that their own Prophet, as well as a latter-day rejuvenation of their own faith through a final Apocalypse, is the last best hope for mankind. Other formidable stumbling blocks, as we have already noted, are humanism and the New Age philosophies, the existence of communism and atheism, and the overall materialism and corruption that has spread throughout both East and West. I am gratified that all these subjects, including the habitual ostracism of any religious belief aside from one's own, have arisen in such short order in these meetings. We shall see later, in a portion of Mustafa's journal, how certain members of the Shaykhi school, in their scholarly exegesis of various Scriptures, dealt with the Christian doctrine of the one and only Son of God, the sole Redeemer for all mankind, and the adamant conviction of the Christians that without this recognition a man cannot be saved. At least the Hindu religion—or, I should say, the many religions that seem to have coalesced in India to create what we now designate as Hinduism—is far more open to other faiths than the three Semitic religions I have just mentioned, and for that, along with the depth of its thoughts on the workings of the universe, we must give it some very high marks.

GEORGINA: Before you analyze the Hindu belief in the theory of rebirth, Ham, I would like to make some observations, if I may, on my former image of India. Before I came to this campus in my thirties I made my first visit to that totally distinctive, wholly paradoxical land. I had little knowledge of its true nature, and at the time, because of my Catholic affiliation, I was filled with self-righteous prejudice against any departure from the dictates of my own church. I considered the Hindus a pagan people, mired in polytheism, reincarnation, and a rigorous caste system to control a swarming population. However, I knew from my studies that the art expression of a people can be outstanding in its merit no matter what its beliefs, and this has been true since prehistoric times. Consequently I went to India in the interests of a book I had in mind, and to my amazement discovered a wealth of art and architecture, including magnificent temples, exquisitely wrought artifacts, and sculptures in bronze and stone, on a par with much that I had hitherto admired in the West. The Taj Mahal, the fairylike palaces, and their garden settings, were brought into being, of course, by the Muslims of the Mughal Empire in India in the sixteenth and seventeenth centuries, which brought to my attention once again that the artistic expression of mankind, in this case within the faith of Islam, was no respecter of my personal intolerance, for the fine arts function where religion is in full force and decline as man's faith declines. I learned a great deal in India in spite of its appalling backwardness in so many ways. When I returned on sabbatical two years ago—

DON: Pardon the interruption, Georgina, but I have been in India myself, before I married Madilyn. It reinforced my opinion that religion is not only superstition, but the more God-intoxicated the people the less civilization is evident in the culture. I was horrified at the pitiful hunger and wasting diseases on every hand and the deaths taking place daily in the streets of Calcutta and Bombay. It was a shock to see the masses of people bathing for special merit in the highly polluted waters of the Ganges, the wasteful worship, in a hungry nation, of thousands upon thousands of wandering cows, and the utterly futile practice, by followers of certain forms of yoga, of seeking perfection and indifference to the material world by lying on painful beds of nails. The attempt to escape reincarnation and the caste system seemed to me to be paramount in India, and the consequent apathy on living a reasonably happy and healthy life simply prolongs the misery. It may all be very colorful, of course, but surely this type of religion has no place whatever in the twentieth century.

GEORGINA: Well, Don, I have no argument with you on these observations, as I witnessed such activities myself. But negative or backward aspects, though they may differ in character, can be found in every religion on earth. As a Unitarian I've become aware of the long list of unhealthy as well as barbaric acts on the part of Christians, Muslims,

Buddhists, Hindus, agnostics and atheists alike, and they are still taking place in the supposed enlightenment of the twentieth century. Even the Jews, who returned as the chosen people of God to their homeland in Palestine, hoping in time to produce the Messiah for the world, are by and large today a secularized nation of defensive militarists, obliged to ignore the demand of Moses' commandment "Thou shalt not kill," and making no distinction between those who are armed against them and innocent women and children. Man is still in his adolescence, Don, as Julia has pointed out, and emotions are largely in control. What we are looking forward to in these meetings is the possibility—and in my mind the probability—of a transformation to a higher level of consciousness—a leap to maturity which often occurs in an unbridled youth in a surprisingly short time. At any rate, our species will get nowhere if we keep our minds preoccupied solely with the negative facets of our planetary history.

Let me say in this respect that on my return to India as a Unitarian two years ago my attitude toward Hinduism had undergone a great change. For prior to this second visit I made a great effort—though political matters are not as a rule my cup of tea—to understand what had happened to that land since the Aryan conquest in the second millennium B.C. And I learned that India had been wracked with both political and religious division for almost three thousand years and how the people had managed to cope with overpowering odds against the unification of the subcontinent and the rise of a more enlightened civilization. With Reverend Ahearn's aid I discovered that religious speculation was the way the Indian mind, especially in the more recent centuries of the post-Vedic era, has held its soul together through thick and thin, that behind the backward rituals which still meet the eye there exists another system of belief so profound, so all-embracing, that no other cosmological or metaphysical conjecture can exceed it.

During my stay in India I read the Rig-Veda, the Upanishads, the Manu-Smrti, the various forms of Vedanta, and the two great historical records which sustain the imagination of the people, the Ramayana and the Mahabharata—the latter contains the most beloved of Indian Scriptures, the Bhagavad-Gita. The concept of rebirth, so ingrained in the psyche of the people, and fed by reports of young children who claim to recognize the members of their former families, as well as by numerous persuasive accounts in occult publications in both East and West, is still a basic belief in popular Hinduism, but appears to be stressed less and less in the most recent writings of the modern Hindus. Considering all its aspects I would say that the Indian religion consists of the Many within the One, and as a consequence there are no religious paths to that One Universal Source which are unacceptable to the Hindu mind.

HAM: Your observations are right to the point, Georgina. And it has always been obvious, of course, that unstable politics, due to the mixture of religious beliefs, has for generations been a drawback to progress in India. It was hoped for a time that the separation of the majority of Muslims in the country into the two states of Pakistan adjoining India to the east and west, and the independence of both India and Pakistan in 1947 after eighty-odd years of British control, would bring about a more substantial democracy to that turbulent land. But this is not possible, I feel, while religious division keeps the nation disunified, no matter how democratic the government may be—to wit, the rebellion of the Sikhs who combine Muslim and Hindu beliefs, and their recent assassination of the Prime Minister, Madame Gandhi. Nevertheless there are basic changes taking place, however regional they may be. The lower castes and the outcastes— the untouchables—are decreasingly looked upon by modern Hindus as animals eternally reborn to do the menial work for those above them, though poverty, unfortunately, keeps them enslaved in their former condition. Residual practices, though disapproved of by the government, still occur behind the scenes—widow-burning, for example, and divorcing or doing away with a wife in order to obtain another with a better dowry. With an increase in education, however, and the further spread of the new religion, these aberrations should give way by the twenty-first century to more rational and humanitarian views.

PHILIP: Georgina, you have mentioned your reading of the Rig-Veda. I don't mean to hold up Ham's explanation of the Hindu belief in reincarnation any further, but if I may I would like to quote a passage from those ancient Scriptures that for any imaginative physicist contains an astounding resemblance to the theoretical description of a potential universe before and after its latent energies burst into sub-atomic life—in other words, the bursting of the Cosmic Egg—the Big Bang. I recall it very well, as do a number of my colleagues:

> "Then was not non-existent nor existent; there was no realm of air, no sky beyond it...
> Death was not there, nor was there aught immortal; no sign was there of the day's and night's divider.
> That one thing, breathless, breathed of its own nature; apart from it was nothing whatsoever.
> Darkness there was; at first, concealed in darkness, this All was indiscriminate chaos.
> All that existed then was void and formless; by the great power of warmth was born that unit.
> Thereafter arose Desire in the beginning, the primal seed and germ of spirit...
> And there were begetters, there were mighty forces, free action here and energy up yonder.

Who verily knows, and who can here declare it, whence
it was born and whence came this creation?
The gods are later than this world's production. Who
knows then, whence it all came into being?"

I can only conclude from such remarkable insight that the
pre-Hindu religion of the Aryans was closer to monotheism
and scientific wisdom than we give it credit for. The polytheism of the vast array of gods and goddesses in the Vedas
might very well have been a symbolic means to express the
many aspects and attributes of the Eternal Being, the One
who is lauded in the Vedic hymns as "the god of gods" and
"none beside him," "the lord of all created beings," "sole
ruler of all that breathes and slumbers," and from whom
"sprang the gods into being." I am inclined to believe that
monotheism has been an inherent tendency at the base of
man's many and diverse beliefs, that his division of the One
into the Many, his endless inventions and rituals and theories, have been a necessity for lesser or developing minds
unable to conceive of an unknown God as the sole ruler of a
vast and, to them, an unimaginable universe.

MADILYN: And now we have scientific minds like yours,
Philip, probing into the farthest reaches of the cosmos,
delving for the unifying essence behind all existence, and
flirting with the idea of advanced civilizations in the vast
reaches of space. But I am bound to remark as a poetess that
without the wide variety of beliefs that have created what
Georgina has called the colorful pageantry of our global life
there would be a great lack of inspirational themes on which
a poet might concentrate his or her imagery in this world. We
deal with the Many, and leave the One as a rule to religion,
and therein lies the appeal of a poet to all peoples everywhere,
no matter what their beliefs. I might have no personal interest
in the doctrine of reincarnation, for instance, but neverthe-

less I can read and enjoy the many fine poets who have clung to this idea and expressed it in the highest of spiritual terms.

Who of us, for example, has not read the poetry of Kahlil Gibran, and kept a copy of "The Prophet" among our cherished books? And surely no one would toss aside the lyrical poems of Rabindranath Tagore because of his affiliation with the Hindu religion. Indeed we cannot overlook the fact that in recent times there have been Hindus such as Ramakrishna, Vivekananda, Mahatma Gandhi, Nehru, Aurobindo Ghose and the former President of India, Sir Sarvepali Radhakrishnan, to name only a few, who have raised the level of Hinduism, in their various ways, to as high a degree of religious, political and scientific thought as one can find today in the East. I do not believe that time is being wasted here on dissecting the beliefs of a nation which still holds fast to its spiritual heritage, whatever its forms, in a world of nations increasingly indifferent to the spiritual issues of their own religious backgrounds.

Before we come to a close this evening I would like to say that I deeply appreciate my inclusion in these discussions. I have listened intently to everything that was said here, and have been as captivated as the poet Keats upon discovering the wonders of Homer—he felt, he wrote, "like some watcher of the skies when a new planet swims into his ken." And I am looking forward to Ham's analysis of the doctrine of reincarnation—I am ignorant of any other attempt to explain its inception. All these matters are grist for the mill of a poet, and I do not turn aside from anything that will appeal to the mind or emotions of a human being, whatever his or her faith might be.

DON: It is evident, I think, that Madilyn and I do not see eye to eye on a number of things. But if an explanation is possible for the widespread belief in the theory of rebirth, I would like to hear it. I am learning a good many things here—

and realize that in this company I am decidedly a misfit. Madilyn and I will be visiting relatives at the University of Chicago for the next ten days, and perhaps we should decide then as to whether or not to return to these meetings. We have personal decisions to make as well, and in such uncertain circumstances I feel it might be best to discontinue our affiliation with my colleagues here. I can only thank you for putting up with me, and later perhaps I might obtain one of the tapes to ascertain your final decision on whether this decadent world can be salvaged or not.

HAM: Don, my good friend, you consistently underestimate yourself. If you can remove the blinkers of your pessimism there is no doubt that your life and your outlook will vastly improve. All of us here are behind you and Madilyn, and sincerely hope that your visit to Chicago will prove to be of great benefit to both of you. We will happily welcome you back here, and meanwhile our good wishes are with you all the way.

I will now sum up as concisely as possible what not only Julia and I but a number of political and religious analysts believe may have brought about the theory we are pursuing here. When the light-skinned Vedic Aryans invaded northern India around 1500 B.C. they had already overrun much of the then known world to the south and southwest of the Caucasus including the plateau of Iran, spreading in the process their pantheon of gods and goddesses and the Aryan language, later known to the world as the Indo-European tongue. This fair-skinned people were known everywhere as the "noble race," and their imprint on the peoples of northern Europe would call forth the obsessive admiration of Adolph Hitler and those who followed his racial idealogy.

At any rate, the conquering Aryans who poured into the Indus Valley in the second millennium B.C. discovered to their amazement the still-flourishing remains of a civilization extending for a thousand miles along the Indus River and its tributaries and into what is now known as Pakistan to the west and Bangladesh to the east. Archaeologists have verified that this civilization existed from as far back as 3000 B.C. to the time when the Aryans overran its main cities, Harappa and Mohenjo-Daro, and brought their political and religious life to a standstill. The culture of its cities was equal to that of the centralized states then existing in Mesopotamia and Egypt, but with certain advanced material developments, such as elaborate baths and a drainage system unseen until the days of Rome. To maintain, then, that the subcontinent of India consisted totally of aborigines and animists before the advent of the Aryans is incorrect, and one has only to read of the temple structures, the pillared halls, the expansive streets and the skill shown in the artifacts to realize that this civilization in the Indus Valley was a culture in the final stages of a Golden Age, its religion of gods and goddesses, sacred animals and divine kings in keeping with the archaic cultures then flourishing within the great arc of the Fertile Crescent— that green and river-fed stretch of land that some look upon as the Biblical Garden of Eden.

I mention this Indian civilization for several reasons, but primarily because of the strong echoes that still exist in India of a dark-skinned Prophet known as the Lord Krishna whose teachings spread throughout the northern region of the subcontinent sometime between 3000 and 1500 B.C. If this was indeed the case we can only surmise that he was born into the civilization along the Indus River and taught the monotheistic and cosmic doctrines that are later found in his name in the Bhavagad-Gita—a portion, as Georgina has said, of one of the great epic histories of the Indian people. As none of the archaic civilizations nor any Prophet of God known to us has taught that a person's soul returns to earth again and again to attain perfection—nor, as we shall see later in these meetings if time permits, did the Buddha—we can assume that Krishna's monotheistic teachings were later mingled with the Vedism of the Aryans, the superstitions of the Tamils and Dravidians, and the later results of the caste system, to take root throughout India as a new conglomeration of complex beliefs, rich in the rituals and pageantry still to be found there, and with levels of doctrinal choice for all segments of society.

The main point here, however, has to do with the caste system. The Aryan people who came into northern India were already divided into three male classes which embraced the priests of the Vedic religion, the warriors and ruling nobles, and the scribes, artisans, builders and cultivators. A fourth division, which included the women, carried on the menial tasks for the three privileged groups above them—an oppressive legacy to India that has burdened its people for centuries. As time went on, and the Aryans spread throughout the subcontinent, they encountered more and more of the dark-skinned and smaller inhabitants far beneath them in development, and in order to maintain the racial purity of the conquerors and prevent intermarriage between the two peoples a system came into being based on the color of one's skin—indeed the word 'caste' in Sanskrit implies this very concept. Between 1200 and 800 B.C. the number of castes had increased to three thousand or more, an incredible separation of peoples, one from the other, as opposed to the declared purpose of the Aryans to rule the land with justice and tolerance. As one would expect, this system of separation, instituted as part of the Vedic religion, and obviously imposed in the interests of racial protection, failed to obtain its objective, for assimilation took place nevertheless, as it has everywhere, and a large number of Hindus today are a mixture of their Aryan forefathers and the ethnic attributes of the early indigenous inhabitants.

With such a repressive system it should not be difficult to note the possibility of a final belief in a universal and inescapable law—that one was fated to return again and again into one's appointed caste. As for the lower castes and the untouchables, the long, hot and weary days of performing the same repetitive actions with no hope of upward mobility must have long ago caused a revolt of some sort if the system itself was not considered a religious requirement that came directly from Brahma and his vast horde of ruling gods and goddesses. Eventually a loop-hole was discerned in this system whereby the few who earnestly sought and attained a spiritual detachment from the earth-world could arrive at a state of emancipation from this ever-recurring round of rebirths and reach a plane of enlightenment free from the karma of the past. There are many ramifications to be noted of this continuing theory, but time is of the essence and this summing up, as incomplete as it may be, must suffice for the present status of reincarnation in both the East and the West. As we have pointed out, a good many changes are taking place in the country where this doctrine was conceived, but the powerful hold of this basic conception on its people will continue, in my opinion, for an indeterminate period of time.

JULIA: A final word on the gradual replacement of original Vedism in India, mainly ritualistic as time went on, by what Ham has outlined for us as popular Hinduism. Both are intertwined, but between the sixth and fourth centuries B.C. a great eruption of Indian thought took place in the outpouring we have hitherto mentioned of new and profound writings which began the process of Hinduizing the Vedic religion. This was the period as well that saw the early reformist teachings of the Buddha on Indian soil, an influence that, though it failed to displace the tenacious beliefs of the Indian mind on the subcontinent, spread to the Far East and has flourished there ever since. The Buddha was a Hindu, a fact to remember when we contemplate the far-reaching impact of these two Indian religions on the rest of the world.

We shall return to Karbila in our next meeting, and meanwhile there's a cherry pie to be shared, and a well-deserved rest from our mutual efforts to understand a complex and often bewildering planet. Whether or not we are able to arrive jointly at some final conclusion on the remedies needed for a very sick world remains to be seen.

III   Genesis in Iraq

HAM: Before we go forward to our most important objective—the search for the Qaim and the Declaration in Shiraz in 1844—we should first of all describe the changes taking place in the 1830s at the court in Tehran, and the ensuing effect upon the Shaykhi school in Karbila. With the aid of our notes and Mustafa's journal we shall present these facts to you as they were given to us in Tehran, and will also recapitulate certain important points that are pertinent to the ongoing developments of the Shaykhi expectations.

In 1832, at the age of seventy-nine, Shaykh Ahmad, considering his mission to be accomplished and his teachings ensured in the hands of Siyyid Kazim, had departed for Mecca and Medina, had died in the latter city two years later, and was buried there in the cemetery of Baqui near the tomb of the Prophet. We have told you of the death of the Crown Prince Muhammad-Ali, the Governor of Kirmanshah, in 1821, of his brother Abbas Mirza in 1833 and their father Fath-Ali-Shah in 1834, all of whom, along with their Sufi leanings, were sympathetic to the Shaykhi teachings.

We should make mention also of another of the many sons of Fath-Ali-Shah, known as the Zillus-Sultán. He attempted to take the throne at the death of his father, but after four months was put aside with the help of the British in favor of the son of Abbas Mirza, a nephew of the Zillus. The able Viziers of the two deceased Crown Princes and the Grand Vizier of Fath-Ali-Shah were all disregarded for court office by the new ruler, Muhammad Shah, at the instigation of his chosen Prime Minister, Haji Mirza Aqasi, who persuaded the Shah in his own interests to dismiss two of them and behead the other, wholly ungrateful for the aid they had given the new monarch in attaining the throne.

There can be little doubt that the British, the French and the Russian envoys then accredited to the court in Tehran came to regret the choice of the grandson of Fath-Ali-Shah, who would prove to be as weak, as vacillating, and as ineffectual as they supposed would be the case with the Zillus-Sultán. They had not counted on the new Shah's appointment of his former tutor, Mirza Aqasi, as Grand Vizier, nor the fact that this crafty and deceitful new minister, bigoted, intolerant, prejudiced against Christians and Jews in particular and foreigners in general, would shortly become the power behind the throne. One has only to read contemporary accounts of this period to agree that this disagreeable individual succeeded in bringing the country to its lowest point, morally and spiritually, in its already decadent history.

I should say here in all fairness that as far as we can discover from our many pages of notes, Muhammad Shah, though constantly wavering from one point of view to another, was nevertheless—relatively speaking—a fairly temperate fellow if left to his own devices. This seems to be borne out when he dispatched a personal envoy—the eminent theologian Siyyid Yahya, now known to the faith as Vahid— to investigate in Shiraz the truth of the new Revelation and report his findings to the court. The total capitulation of this trusted envoy to the claims of a young descendant of Muhammad in Shiraz caused the Shah to express his wish that both the claimant and Siyyid Yahya be brought to the court in Tehran for interrogation, a wish that was unfulfilled due to the intervention of Mirza Aqasi.

And once again, at a later date, the Shah, astonished at the wholehearted acceptance of the claims of the Herald Prophet by the powerful Governor of Isfahan, a trusted friend of the monarch, took matters into his own hands and sent a personal letter to the Governor that the claimant, then visiting in that great city, should be transported secretly to meet with him at the court. History has recorded how the Prime Minister dealt with these two overtures by the monarch, and how his prevention of any meeting at the court may have forestalled a more tolerant treatment of the new faith by the Qajars. Because of Aqasi's implacable hatred of any departure from the orthodox, his manipulation of the monarch, and his crafty machinations to obstruct any possible capitulation by Muhammad Shah, this calculating and cunning man has become known in communities the world over as the Antichrist of the new Revelation.

Perhaps we can sympathize further with Muhammad Shah when we know that he suffered from severe attacks of gout and was subject to other painful ailments as well. As a consequence, except for riding with his ill-trained troops in the field when his health allowed, he preferred the company of his wife and children in the women's quarters to the business of governing the nation. He appears to have looked upon Aqasi as a father figure, depending upon him, as a former tutor and spiritual guide, to supply the answers to the problems of the court. That he seemed to be oblivious to the man's insidious ways, his insolent manners, his indolent approach to the niceties of his dress and his crude choice of words, is almost inexplicable in a nation's ruler. Other members of the court, on the other hand, were well aware of Aqasi's character, though unable to express their hatred of his arrogance and power. It remained for foreign writers of that period to categorize him as a man of such insatiable greed that he amassed a large and illicit fortune by appropriating the possessions and property of others, both rich and poor alike. One foreign envoy wrote of him as a consummate hypocrite of miserly habits who would not have given up his avaricious ways had the Hidden Imam confronted him in person on the matter.

Regardless of the character of the Prime Minister, the orthodox clergy were quick to take advantage of his disapproval of the Shaykhi school. Whenever the government sided with the interests of the dominant clergy the combination could be lethal for any departure from the norm. Consequently, many of those outside of the school who had formerly declared themselves as Shaykhis when Ahmad was still alive began to withdraw from any affiliation with the sect in Karbila, and muted their own belief in an imminent appearance of the Promised One. In spite of a thousand years of lip-service to the Hidden Imam's return in glory, neither the Shia ulama nor the court were prepared to forego in his favor their own authority and power.

During this same period there were certain disciples within the school itself, in particular Haji Mirza Karim Khan and his uncle Mirza Muhit, both with close connections to the Qajar family, who showed unmistakable signs of independence from Siyyid Kazim after sitting for many years at his feet and receiving from him the highest accolades for their loyalty and devotion to the teachings. One of these disciples, the eminent scholar Hasan-i-Gawthar, would later succeed, at Siyyid Kazim's demise, in taking over as Master of the school, and Karim Khan, then established in new headquarters in Kirman, would declare himself the head of the Shaykhi sect, with the backing in Karbila of the influential Mirza Muhit. These names will arise again in the struggle between the believers and the non-believers which followed the Declaration in Shiraz in 1844. We can add them to the names of Siyyid Ibrahim in Karbila, of Najib Pasha, the Sunni Governor of Baghdad, of Husayn Khan, the ruthless Governor of Shiraz, and of Mirza Aqasi in Tehran, as initial factors in the trials and persecutions, as time went on, of thousands of innocent victims.

A further word in respect to the Zillus-Sultán. He seems to have been an amiable and pious man and hardly a person to threaten the life of his nephew, the new Shah. He was nevertheless banished to Karbila, where he became a friend and admirer of Siyyid Kazim, who saw to it that the exiled and impecunious expatriate did not want for the proper sustenance when the money ran out. Such were the twists and turns in the order of things which decided the negative fate or the good fortune of large numbers of helpless subjects of the Qajars, including members of the royal family itself. As T. S. Eliot has so well expressed it, "The world turns and the world changes, but one thing does not change . . . However you disguise it, this thing does not change: the perpetual struggle of good and evil."

PHILIP: Forgive me for interrupting, Ham, but curiosity has overcome me on a rather strange phenomenon in relation to the Qajars. Julia has said that this family—and I presume that one may as well include the Shah's so-called spiritual guide, Mirza Aqasi—was interested in Sufism, or at least had leanings in that direction. I have never put my teeth into the subject of Islamic mysticism, but the overall tenets of the mystic view are pretty much the same the world over—a personal one-on-one approach to the Ground of All Being, an attempt to merge with its essence and achieve an escape, at least psychologically, from all forms of material manifestation and from all human desires. This One Thing, this Basic Essence, is called by different names in different parts of the world—Brahman, the Tao, the Absolute, the Cosmic Intelligence, Nirvana, the Universal Soul—or, if you prefer, the Ultimate Unknown Deity or Godhead, the primary source from which all creation emanates. Certain advocates of the new physics have seen in this final essence the closest approach to what they hope to come upon eventually through the science of advanced mathematics—a unified field theory.

But how can this mystic path in Islam possibly square away with the orthodox Muslim devotion to the Prophet Muhammad as the mediator between this First Cause and the world of man? In addition, how do the Shia Sufis manage to bypass the Imams of the Prophet's House, whom the majority of Shia believers consider, in conjunction with Muhammad, to be the mediating channels of God's Will? A confusing dichotomy here, which needs some explanation. I find the incorporation of Sufism into Shiism a baffling combination of contradictory beliefs.

JULIA: You've brought up an interesting subject, Philip. Sufism is little understood in the Western world, and like most religions-within-a-religion, it has caused a good deal of disunity among the Muslims. Sufism is as old as Islam itself—its development and complexities over a period of a thousand years or more could easily engage us for the rest of the evening. As Philip has raised the question, and as it constitutes a subsidiary element in the background of the new faith, it should be discussed at this point. Doctor Varqa had a strong predilection for reading the great Sufi poets, Rumi and Jami, and certain of the writings of the Qayyúm himself are composed in the Sufi mold. Even in the nineteenth century most boys of the upper classes in Persia, although they received scant education outside of the Qoran, were made familiar with the Sufi poets along with the art of calligraphy, proper horsemanship and manners acceptable to the court.

The inception of Sufism can be traced back to the days of the Prophet and the Imams, when certain believers, drawn to the life of simplicity and self-denial, displayed their leanings toward asceticism by wearing garments of coarse wool, or suf, in imitation of the rough clothing of the Prophet's companions, including his son-in-law Ali. This detachment from worldly affairs gradually attracted more and more of those believers who looked with dismay on the change from the unpretentious life of the first four Caliphs to the luxurious living and secular pleasures of the Umayyad and Abbasid Caliphates and their courts. This puritan movement did not coalesce into a sect, but by the second Islamic century it had penetrated into all the Muslim divisions of belief, Sunni and Shia alike. During this period both the orthodox and the unorthodox found a common ground in Sufism to express their reaction against the sterile intellectual argumentations taking place under the Umayyads and the strict application of the legalistic laws of the Qoran at the expense of the spiritual development of the inner man. It was a movement that was open at that time to the influence of Greek, Christian and Indo-Aryan mysticism, and by the fourth Islamic century a full-blown devotion to the mystic way had replaced among the Sufis the traditional forms of worship and the orthodox approach to God.

I must add that the history of Sufism is far from consistent, varying in its influence from century to century depending on the approval or disapproval of the current clergy or the dynasty in power. In general it remained among the Sunnis as a strong force within the faith, while in Persia and among the Shias elsewhere its prestige waxed and waned, even to the point of persecution, according to the attitude of the Shia mujtahids and the reigning Shahs. It stands to reason that the basic Shia doctrines would tend to keep the extreme forms of the mystic approach—the belief in a merging with God and a partnership with God—a matter of minority interest.

There were periods nevertheless when conquering families such as the Qajars had imposed their Sufi leanings on the people, and during the eighteenth century Persia had been obliged to follow the powerful forebears of the Qajars in Tabriz and allow the Sufis to flourish and multiply. By the nineteenth century a reversal took place in Persia which brought the orthodox ulama once more into prominence—a change brought about by Fath-Ali-Shah, who needed the backing of the clergy to strengthen his hold on the country from the new capital in Tehran. But a lingering attraction to Sufism remained at the court, and was inextricably entwined with certain aspects of Shiism itself, even in the Shaykhi school.

HAM: Shaykh Ahmad and Siyyid Kazim did not discourage the practice of personal meditation or contemplation or direct prayers to or conversations with God, nor did Islam itself. Muhammad's primary doctrine of submission to the Will of Allah—the same One God, he asserted, as the Jews and the Christians declared—needed no dictatorial rule by churches or synagogues, no intervening clerical institutions, no sacramental rituals or any central authority beside the Will of God in the Qoran, but only the sacred mosques for prayers of submission and the free exchange of religious views and expressions within the boundaries of the Book, the Traditions, the Sunna and the Sharia.

This original pattern—intended to include not only the Muslim religion itself but the very basis of Islamic civilization and culture—was later breached by new ideas, either from within or imported, like everything else in a changing and evolving world. We have seen this not only in the escape through Sufism from increasingly impersonal, legalistic rules and customs in Islam, but since the oil boom in the Middle East we have witnessed the exact opposite effect brought about by enforced modernization and Western technology—a process that has so materialized and politicized the ways of the believers and broken down their inner spiritual aspirations that vast riches and abundance of expensive possessions, unknown even in the Western world, have replaced the yearning for a closeness to God and a better life in the realms beyond. This seems to be the case as well in puritan Arabia, the original heart of Islam, a land where strict and xenophobic Wahhabism under the Saudis is in constant conflict with such declared aberrations on the one hand as Sufi mysticism, and on the other hand with the material and political demands of building and maintaining a twentieth-century oil-producing nation of enormous wealth.

I bring these things to your attention to illustrate that there is nothing more certain in this world than change, and that changes in religion are no exception, either in the East or the West. Shaykh Ahmad was well aware of this, but his own mission, as he saw it, was to cleave to his appointed place within the boundaries of Shia Islam, to remain adamant in his loyalty to the infallibility of the Prophet and the Imams, and to stand fast in the intuitive knowledge that, according to his reading of the Qoran and the Hadith, two new Prophets of God would arise in Persia from the ranks of the Shia sect.

With this expectation as the basis of the teachings of Ahmad and Kazim in the Shaykhi school, the disciples were free to express their worship of God in private as their souls directed them. This is as close to the freedom of the Sufi approach to the Deity as we have been able to discover from our notes and Mustafa's journal, and it is evident from these sources that any affiliation with the Sufi brotherhoods, orders, fraternities and institutions, later established in almost all Islamic countries in a widespread network, was not at any time a part of the consecrated concerns of the school. The near-worship tendered to the heads of these Sufi orders by their initiates, the representation of their ruling Shaykhs as intercessory saints for the Sunnis and Shias alike, and the consequent glorification of the shrines and tombs of these "perfect men," was incompatible with the basic Shia belief in the primary authority of the Prophet and the Imams.

REVEREND AHEARN: Most people in the West, I suppose, if they have any idea at all in relation to Sufism, have connected it by and large with whirling or pirouetting dervishes, with hypnotic chanting, singing, dancing and other pantheistic rituals employed as a means to achieve the ultimate spiritual enlightenment, an ecstatic merging of the human soul with the Godhead. It is unfortunate that these developments, these extreme examples of getting in touch with the Infinite—often carried to the most absurd lengths and thoroughly frowned upon by the orthodox clergy and the moderate Sufis alike—have obscured the very real love and reverence for God that we find in the metaphysical poems and philosophical writings of many of the great Sufi intellects of Islam. Ever since the blessing bestowed upon the spiritual claims of this movement by the most prominent theologian and philosopher of the twelfth century, Al-Ghazali, the divines of Islam in general, except for the ultra-orthodox, have willy-nilly accepted in one degree or another its fundamental tenet of a personal and intimate approach to the Source of All Being.

I have only in recent months discovered the extent and the metaphorical beauty of the literature of Sufism, especially of the brilliant use in its poetry of worldly similes or allegories to veil its spiritual meaning from profane or disapproving eyes. Through opening my mind to a new and fascinating study I have come to understand at last the psychological results of the so-called mystic path, not only in Islam, but in India and the Far East and within the Christian fold as well— the exalted feeling of being free from the material universe and the consequent certainty that one has escaped into the Basic Source behind all manifestation. At the same time we should realize that this psychological experience by itself has had little effect in bringing about the needed social changes, the civilizing processes so necessary for an evolving world. It is effective and satisfying only for the small number of individuals attempting to escape from that world.

JULIA: Reverend Ahearn, I am always delightfully surprised at that ever-inquiring mind of yours, and am grateful for your well-balanced comments in these meetings. Nothing in the life of mankind is entirely black or completely white, as we know, and it is necessary to dig as deeply as possible in our searchings in order to unravel what seems to be both right and workable for the common good, as relative as that may be. There is no doubt in my mind that ignorance of the long historical processes of other religions and other cultures, as well as one's own, is the basic cause for the hostilities still endemic in every nation on earth. There is only one remedy for this, as I see it—a worldwide education in world history. A great number of our students today are woefully lacking in and indeed indifferent to all but their own self-centered concerns, and I am quite aware, as are many other professors attempting to impart a liberal education in their courses, that the attendance of these students in our classrooms is not primarily to educate themselves in the ways and the thoughts of other peoples, but to sit through four necessary years of waiting for the best jobs available in the marketplace. As Reverend Ahearn has commented in one of our former meetings, it may take a catastrophic downfall in the world economy before such students awaken to the fact—engendered to be sure by the culture we live in—that their narrow view of life, defined on one side by their vaunted sexual freedom and on the other by the drive for monetary success, is not the liberated utopia they had bargained for.

HAM: In connection with the proper kind of education, Doctor Varqa informed us that neither Ahmad nor Kazim nor their close disciples were unaware of the psychological and scientific studies then taking place in Europe or the burgeoning Western studies in the field of comparative religion through a critical examination of the world's Scriptures. We shall see later, from Mustafa's journal, that the private library of Siyyid Kazim was not solely Islamic, but a cross-section of the philosophical and religious thought of many regions and many ages. Only a few trusted scholars and older companions of the Master of the school were admitted to this inner sanctum—a protection not only against the prying eyes of Siyyid Ibrahim and his band of fanatical rowdies and spies, but to minimize the possibility that certain disciples in the school itself, not yet open to the literature of non-Muslim intellects, or still antagonistic to alien religions, would eventually turn their backs on the teachings or complain to the leading divines in Najaf. The library, Doctor Varqa said, also included, along with the works of Shaykh Ahmad, three hundred or more commentaries and unpublished manuscripts written by Siyyid Kazim.

In the fall of 1839, Mirza Jamal and his grandson Mustafa accompanied the latter's uncle, Mirza Jani, on a business trip from Kashan to Karbila, crossing the Zagros range via Hamadan and stopping off for some time in Kirmanshah. There they encountered a number of Shaykhi merchants who had sat at the feet of Ahmad and Kazim during the latters' stay in that city as guests of the Crown Prince, and learned from them of the claim of the Shaykhi school that the Advent of the Promised One of Islam was not far off. Recalling his past experience of listening to Ahmad's extraordinary public extolment of Bushihr and Shiraz, Mirza Jamal determined that he would visit the school in Karbila and ask for a meeting with Siyyid Kazim. As a leading merchant in Kashan, and well known for his generous contributions to the shrines of the Imams in the holy cities, he felt that this request would not be refused.

Julia and I have agreed that the most personal and intimate way in which we can carry on an exposition of what can rightly be called the cradle of the new faith in Karbila, is to see things through the eyes and mind of our young journalist, Mustafa. In response to his orthodox father's desire, Mustafa had spent some time in one of the seminaries in Qum, enabling him to assume the title of Mulla. But after two years of routine studies from which he received no intellectual impetus whatever toward answering the many questions that burned in his eager mind, he persuaded his reluctant father to take him into the family business. This fateful decision was responsible later, as we shall see, for a large number of staunch believers in Kashan, of whom Mirza Jani and Mirza Sabeh, the young uncles of Mustafa, stand out prominently in the history books of the faith as eminent writers on the Shaykhi history and beliefs.

I would like to inject a few words here to express our gratitude for your respectful silence while we lay the foundation for what Julia and I have come to believe is a very real breakthrough from higher planes of consciousness. We realize that this is hardly a popular view in our day when the ruling philosophies in American and European culture are based, by and large, as Julia has remarked, on the accumulation of property and an unrestrained freedom to do as one pleases. Such philosophies, though carried to extremes in our own culture, are due in part to European thinkers such as Hobbes, Locke, Rousseau, Heidegger, Weber and the later Nietzsche, and include the various schools of psychology and psychiatry following in the footsteps of Freud. The excessive liberty resulting from the materialistic application of these philosophies, while at the same time metaphysical and paranormal interests are put aside as sheer superstition by most scientists, has denuded man of his soul and his higher nature, allowing him the right, within the laws of his government, to do anything he wishes to do, and making self-interest his highest priority. Such philosophies and permissive psychology have displaced the moral demands of Scriptural religion as the guiding influence for our modern lifestyles—for doing freely, in the vernacular, "what comes naturally." Unfortunately, what man chooses to do naturally has not only brought us to the brink of nuclear war, but can be heard and seen every day of the week on television, in our schools and universities, in the newspapers and, in fact, all around us. Personally I see no chance whatever that the groping of men's imperfect, culture-conditioned minds can bring about the "ultimate solution" for man's behavior, while the universal God-directed approach of the higher religions, in their original intent at least, is thrown to one side.

At any rate, this is the conviction of both Julia and myself, and we hope we can persuade you that the teachings of the Karbila school are not just another disorder within the Islamic mind, but a logical basis for a renewed outpouring of progressive revelation. If there are no questions or comments, Julia will read a revealing portion of Mustafa's earliest observations of the school, and you can make your own judgments as to whether or not this iconoclastic group of scholars deserves the opprobrium heaped upon them in the 1840s by the people and the clergy of Persia.

JULIA: The text of the journal was translated for us by Doctor Varqa, and the part that I will read to you this evening will take us directly into the center of things. Remember, friends, that we are dealing here with a backward nineteenth-century culture. I think that you will therefore agree with me that what Mustafa has to tell us of the openmindedness, tolerance and depth of religious analysis fostered by Siyyid Kazim—a Muslim scholar within a Muslim clergy considered by the West the most superstitious and bigoted clerical order imaginable—is not only extraordinary, but is something, I believe, that is quite out of the order of natural events.

Again, whether or not you are able to concur in such a view, I am sure you will find the documentation in Mustafa's journal an enlightening experience.

"We arrived in Karbila from Kirmanshah in the late fall of 1255, or 1839 in the Christian calendar," Mustafa informs us. "With the usual bargaining and a number of expensive presents we obtained a small house not far from the Shaykhi school and prepared our goods for business. Pilgrims were at a minimum, the town was quiet, and the time seemed right for an approach to the Master in his residence, adjoining the classrooms of the school. On the third day Mirza Jamal and Mirza Jani left me in charge of our business affairs and went off to pay their respects to Siyyid Kazim.

"Imagine my delight when they returned with the news that all three of us were welcome to attend the lectures in the main classroom of the school. The Siyyid, they reported, was a most impressive man, fine-appearing, warm in his manner, and obviously extremely perceptive, his penetrating eyes seeming to reach into one's very heart and soul. He had suggested that one or two of us could come to the school at a time, in order not to leave our business unattended. His courtesy and consideration had won them over completely, and Mirza Jamal had made arrangements for Mirza Jani and me to be present in the classroom the next morning at nine o'clock.

"As strangers to the school my uncle and I took our seats humbly, and somewhat apprehensively, on a carpet at the rear of the room, where we faced a large number of backs in black or brown robes topped by the turbans of various divisions of Islamic life, all attentively concentrated on the dais in the front of the classroom. Within a short time the Siyyid appeared from one of the side doors and took his seat on the platform carpet, facing his audience with raised hands and a welcoming smile. Picking up some books at his side, he glanced through some of the pages, leaving one of the books open in his lap. I had brought my notebook, my pen and an ink-box to the lecture with the Siyyid's permission, obtained through Mirza Jamal, and am able to recount in detail the things that were said and done on my first day in the school.

" 'Today,' the Siyyid said, 'I intend to give you a few of the statements and prophecies which look forward to an apocalyptic occurrence in what has come to be known in various Scriptures as the Last Days, the Day of Judgment, The Hour of Resurrection, the Time of the End and so on—the days when the Jews will return to the Holy Land, when the Biblical Scriptures will circle the globe, and the names and basic teachings of the Prophet-Founders of at least five of the still-living religions will be known to the world. This is the time characterized by the prophet Daniel as the "abomination of desolation," a time of planetary troubles and widespread immorality when men's fears would turn their minds at last to a vision of a new and different life for mankind.

" 'We have already acquainted you with the veiled prophecies in the Qoran and the open statements in the Hadith which place this period at approximately a thousand to twelve hundred years from the death of the Prophet Muhammad. And let me remind you that, although most of the orthodox believers today will stop up their ears when other Scriptures are brought forward to back up the apocalyptic statements of Muhammad and the Hadith, we should all remember that large portions of the Qoran are devoted to retelling the teachings and events of our Jewish and Christian brethren, that the Prophet looked upon them as People of the Book, the Holy Bible, and commanded respect and tolerance for their beliefs. There must be no persecution, he affirmed, of other faiths. Islam has turned its back on these teachings, and today we are faced in Persia and the holy cities with the most virulent prejudice to be found anywhere.

" 'Before we quote from still-existing prophetic religions on the Advent of a world Apocalypse, let me refresh your memories with prophecies from the Hadith purporting to come from Ali and from subsequent Imams in Medina, undoubtedly stemming from the words of the Prophet himself. I shan't dwell on the statements which foresee the proliferation of scientific developments in a highly secular world, nor the influence of women in religious and national affairs, nor political conditions which foster tyranny, corruption and war. But I will list some of the signs of moral decadence in the nations of the world that will run parallel to the Advent of the Qaim and the subsequent World Messiah, the Qayyúm—that latter-day Prophet anticipated in the books of the Parsees of the Zoroastrian faith, of Judaism, Buddhism and Christianity, in the Bhagavad-Gita of the Hindus, and most recently in the teachings and expectations of the Shaykhi school in Islam.

" 'Now I have mentioned these six living religions many times, but there is a seventh whose Founder, before the time of Abraham and Moses, is unknown, and we have no record of its prophecies for the future. This ancient religion, Sabeanism, is mentioned by Muhammad in the Qoran as a faith with a Holy Book, and its surviving signs can still be found in unenlightened areas of Arabia Felix, such as the kingdoms of Saba and Yemen. Judging from the conversation between the Queen of Sheba and King Solomon during her visit to Israel, as recorded in the Old Testament, this faith was still practised by her subjects in semi-idolatrous form, its early spiritual teachings having lost their potency after many centuries. Some say its Founder may have been Enoch or the Prophet Noah, or even a predecessor of that mystery figure in the Old Testament, Melchisedek, to whom Abraham paid his humble respects in the land of Canaan, and to whom the mission of the Christ was later compared as "in the order of

Melchisedek." But such far afield conjectures cannot be proved, and we should not waste our time in the classroom on totally obscure and unprofitable matters.

" 'On the other hand, it is quite possible that Abraham, the most widely traveled of the post-diluvian Prophets, was responsible for spreading the principles of this early mono-theistic religion, not only in Mesopotamia and Canaan, but even as far south as Arabia Felix. For we must remember that Abraham was not only the forefather of the Hebrew tradition in the Near East through his second son Isaac, born to his formerly barren wife Sarah, but he also received the promise of God that his constancy under a most severe series of tests had guaranteed that his descendants through his later wife Katurah and Sarah's maid-servant Hagar would cover the earth as teachers and Revelators of His Will for mankind. We should not be surprised, then, that through Abraham's eldest son Ismael by the Egyptian maid-servant Hagar and his visits to that son in the settlement of Mecca, where Hagar had taken refuge from the jealousy of Sarah, that this great Prophet of the Hebrews is also claimed by the clergy of Islam as the forefather of Muhammad, a descendant of Ismael. The Muslims likewise declare that Abraham was responsible for embellishing and consecrating to the One God the ancient idolatrous cube in Mecca which today is the major point of pilgrimage, the Kaaba, for the vast numbers who perform the Haj. I shall return to this subject later, for the ramifications of God's promise to our Father Abraham, especially in regard to Ismael and his posterity, should later extend as well to the Qaim and the Qayyúm and to those Manifestations who succeed them in the future.'

"The Siyyid paused and looked out over his audience. How handsome he is, I thought, with his pale Persian skin, his black brows winging above those large black eyes, and the neatly clipped moustache and beard. The turban of a Siyyid ballooned about his head, and his dress, though largely unadorned, was of excellent quality and in the best of taste. His noble appearance was enough to engage one's interested attention, but the words that came forth from that platform were so different from the repetitious discourses I had had to endure in Qum that I soon became aware, as ignorant as I was in that scholarly company, that here was a man whose erudition and spiritual wisdom were far beyond anything I had yet been privileged to encounter. I could see that Mirza Jani at my side was equally affected—he had not moved an inch since the lecture began.

" 'The prophecies of our Islamic Traditions,' the Siyyid continued, 'are more specific in relation to that future Day of God—the Day of the Promised One of all religions, when renewal must come upon the earth and a new order must be established in a world of corruption and tyranny—than in any other records available. It remains for the people of that Day and its aftermath to judge as to whether or not these prophesied conditions are indeed true to the facts in that time of the world's afflictions, when religious faith will have no further influence over man's behavior and godlessness is rampant in many nations of the globe. These conditions will intensify both before and after the Qaim and the Qayyúm depart from the earth, and will grow in strength and power year by year as mankind, including the greater part of Islam, ignores the new Revelation from God. Calamities and catastrophes will erupt everywhere with unprecedented severity, and the terror of devastating and prolonged wars, civil, religious and otherwise, will hang over men's heads like the sword of Damocles.

" 'The prophecies state likewise that truth among men and nations will die out, and lying will be looked upon as permissible. Love, brotherhood and the former bonds of family life will be hard to find, and people will grow cold toward their neighbors and mistreat the members of their own households. Moral depravity will openly manifest itself, and men will be increasingly content with men and women with women. People will live together like animals, adultery will be accepted and praised, and the breaking of religious and social laws will be done flagrantly in public, while the doers will not be prevented, nor will they excuse themselves. The drinking of alcohol and the use of mind-destroying substances—forbidden by Muhammad—will overwhelm the nations, and the places and other means of entertainment will cater to the lusts and appetites of men, while the wombs of the women will be cut open to prevent childbirth and bring to an end the unwanted results of their careless sexual desires.

" 'In addition, the Hadith affirms that injustice will prevail everywhere, that most of the leaders of men will be corrupt and will further their own aims instead of that of the people, forbidding things that are beneficial and making legal that which is harmful. The women of that day will leave their homes unsupervised to assist their husbands in trade to obtain more of the things of this world, and will no longer raise their children to obey the commands of the Books of God. A number of religious leaders of that end time, caught in the toils of materialism, will devote themselves to affairs other than religion, and when away from the pulpits from which they enjoin the fear of God they will seek the wealth and prestige of this world in common with the secular culture in which they live. Contributing to these adverse conditions, the undisciplined productions of science, bedazzling the world with miraculous accomplishments unheard of in bygone ages, will have unloosed upon the earth such lethal weapons and substances so dangerous to the human body and to nature itself that civilization and the life of the human species will appear to be at stake.

" 'But Shaykh Ahmad has assured us that the God-ordained system of the Prophets precludes the annihilation or complete degeneration of life on this planet, a system that guarantees that the end of one era or civilization will see the rising of another, that the evolution of our planetary life is far from over. Added to this assurance are the prophecies in our world Scriptures of a future Manifestation whose mission is far beyond our imagination—a turning point for mankind that every former Prophet of God has looked forward to, a time that will bring about a major transition in the life of our planet and a world order without parallel in the past. An eternal succession of Prophets, appropriate to the evolutionary periods and birthplaces of their appearance, is a reality upheld by the Hindu Prophet, the Lord Krishna. In explaining his own rank and assigned task to his young warrior disciple Arjuna, he revealed this age-old system of the Lord of Lords, the Creator and Ruler of the universe.'

"The Siyyid picked up the book in his lap, and in a deep-toned melodious voice he read from that portion of the epic Mahabharata, the Bhagavad-Gita, which contains the revelation of Krishna that the Hand and the Mind of God periodically and eternally overshadow the affairs of men.

" 'As the years have passed by,' the Siyyid read, 'the noble teaching of the past has decayed and its light has grown dim. Almost lost has become its inner spirit and men know naught but its letter. Such is the fate of truth among the race of men.

" 'But once more I declare that truth, and the great mystery of creation. Know that whenever the world declineth in virtue and righteousness, and vice and injustice mount the throne, then cometh I, the Lord, and revisit my world in visible form, and mingle as a man with men, and by my influence and teaching do destroy the evil and injustice and reestablish virtue and righteousness. Many times have I thus appeared; many times hereafter shall I come again. He who is able to pierce my disguise on earth, and who knoweth me in essence, when he quitteth his mortal frame is granted the joy of dwelling with me in the spiritual world.'

"The Siyyid put the book aside, and reached for another. 'Now when a Prophet is spoken of as the Lord—Lord Krishna, Lord Buddha, Lord Jesus—you are not to suppose that the Creator behind all manifestation, the First Cause Itself, descends to earth and takes on the semblance of a man. There are some who believe this—in particular the post-Vedic Hindus who were many centuries away from the Prophet Krishna, and incorporated such a belief, in respect to Krishna himself, in the stories and teaching in the Gita. In Christianity this occurred as well with the Prophet Jesus, declared by church councils in the fourth century to be a third part of the Supreme Being, and indeed is thought by many Christians to be God Himself. As for the Lord Buddha, the Indian Founder of one of the great religions of the world, no such claim can be found in the Buddhist Scriptures, but nevertheless we have discovered in the Pali Canon that the Buddha made the following statement to his early disciples which parallels the declaration of the Lord Krishna.

" 'I am not the first Buddha who has come upon the earth,' the Siyyid read, 'nor shall I be the last. In due course another Buddha will arise in the world, a Holy One, fully awakened, abounding in wisdom and goodness, unsurpassed as a guide to mortals willing to be led, a teacher for both men and angels, an Exalted One, even as I am now. He will thoroughly know and see face to face the universe and its world of spirits, and reveal to you eternal truths, as I do now.'

" 'We have all heard,' the Siyyid went on, 'that the Buddha taught an atheistic philosophy, with no mention of God or the afterlife as taught by the Christians and Muhammad. But let us remember that Siddhartha Gautama, the heir to a throne in the region of Nepal and living in the luxury of the ruling caste in India, was born into a culture of illiterate masses so God-obsessed and at the same time so disoriented within the material world in which the human species is ordained to begin its journey toward the apex of the spiritual world, that development of the body and the mind had come to a virtual standstill, and misery, suffering and disease prevailed throughout the land. Prince Gautama, awakened by his observations of these conditions, departed from his palace and his family, searching for the answers that would alleviate the bodily and mental illnesses not only of his own people but of all mankind.

" 'The teachings of the Buddha are remarkably conducive to a state of tranquility in the midst of the world's afflictions, but whether or not they are philosophical, scientific, psychological or religious—and they have been looked upon as one or the other or as all four in the schools of Buddhism itself— he taught his followers the relativity of life, that everything in the universe is of a transitory nature, and that by the proper use of the mind and the body, by higher thought and right conduct, and by meditating deeply on the doctrine of samsara, which declares it an illusion that all things are static and forever set as they appear to the eyes of men, one may reach a state of emancipation which nullifies the mental and physical suffering of the human condition.

" 'Likewise, in connection with the impermanence, the evanescence of all created matter and life in the universe, he declares that the soul of man itself is in flux, that there is no compact, solid, hard and fast entity or self that can pass intact from one body or world to another, that the soul changes from day to day, indeed from moment to moment. The state of the soul—attached to the body through the mind but not within it—depends upon one's mental, emotional or spiritual development at any given point, and this includes one's current desires, ideas, judgments, decisions and motivations.

The spiritual energies and forces of the soul, he tells us, respond constantly to the use of our God-given free will, that without this flexibility, this opening to change and transformation, there would be no possibility of our spiritual progress or the opposite movement into retrogression. These energies or forces, in whatever state they exist on one's deathbed, are reborn in a spiritual body at the moment of death, and in that ethereal form, in which our personalities are still recognizable to those who knew us on earth, we either progress or retrogress according to our final beliefs and desires, and gravitate to that plane of existence to which the use of our free will has brought us.

" 'There is more to be said on these matters, complex and difficult to express as they are, but one simple fact must be noted—that the souls of the Manifestations, unaffected by the world's cultures and the learning of mankind, reflect as in a clear mirror the justice, the love and the universal knowledge of the Creator, and represent in the material world the purity, the beauty, and the creative power of God's attributes. In common with man these great Prophets retain their individual personalities in their spiritual bodies and exist with great power and glory in the supreme and unimaginable world of the Will of God, the goal of all those souls who become aware, either slowly or rapidly here on earth or in the spiritual world, of the true meaning and celestial purpose of universal life.

" 'As for the teaching of the Buddha, perhaps we may call this particular system of enlightenment a scientific or psychological religion which applied—as all religions apply to various aspects of man's existence at certain periods of our evolutionary history—to the people of a retrogressive and scientifically ignorant age who neglected their earthly development in favor of an obsession with Hindu superstitions and rituals, a vast pantheon of gods, and the circumscribed bonds of the caste system. Contrary to the belief of some people that the Buddha advocated a denial of material pleasures, he himself lived a joyful, healthy and long life, maintaining that by the proper use of the mind and the body all men could do likewise. In fact the Founders of the world's religions have invariably proffered solutions to the men and women of each age which would bring them, as the Christ expressed it, a more abundant life on earth, while they prepared themselves at the same time for what might await them in the world beyond.

" 'And now, my friends, what did Zoroaster—our own revered Prophet more than a thousand years before Muhammad—have to say about a World Teacher whom he called the Shah Bahram? Just as the Buddhists look for a World Buddha whom they have designated by the name of Maitreya, Zoroastrians refer their fellow believers to that portion of their Scriptures known as the Dinkird, wherein the Prophet declares that a great Teacher will appear in Persia two thousand and two hundred years from the final waning of his own faith and the beginning of the end-time of the Arabian religion. In that day a descendant of the ancient kings of the Persian Empire would be raised up as a Universal Educator for mankind.

" 'As some of you are aware, the Semitic religions— Judaism, Christianity and Islam—have many names for this latter-day Prophet of God. Judaism is still expecting the Messiah, the Lord of Hosts, the Everlasting Father, the Glory of the Lord and so on. Unlike Christianity, which holds all such titles as belonging to the personal return of the Christ, the Jews do not anticipate the return of their own Prophet Moses to lead the world to his own faith, nor have they recognized the Christ as other than a minor prophet among the Jews. The Messiah they look for will raise the posterity of Israel and Judah once more to their appointed rank as the chosen people of God and bring them back to rule once again in Palestine.

" 'Of all the religious blocks to the recognition of a future Prophet in a different guise from the past, the established doctrines of the Christian religion and those of Islam are the most difficult to overcome. We all understand the orthodox doctrine of the Shia faith in connection with the return of the last Imam or, as some believe, the Imam Husayn, the grandson of the Prophet, or some other choice from the House of Muhammad. These beliefs, and those of the Sunnis, with certain deviations, have been a part of the Muslim religion for over a thousand years and it is not likely that any change of heart will result from a new Revelation. Quite the contrary, as Shaykh Ahmad has warned us, and you must be prepared for the most severe forms of persecution. The tenacious adherence to a material return of some revered being from the past, rather than the appearance of the same Holy Spirit in a succession of Chosen Souls, does not coincide with the prophecies of Muhammad in the Hadith, and I exhort you to cleave to the symbolic statements of the Prophet and the Imams about that future Day of God.

" 'That Day, my dear friends, will be the prophesied Day of Reckoning, the Day of Mutual Deceit, of Sighing and Severing, the Day when the First Trumpet will be sounded and the latter-day Muslims will stand before the judgment seat of the Promised One of Islam, the Qaim. And this is but a small part of the prophecies of the End Time when both the First and the Second Trumpets, following one upon the other, will announce the beginning of a new era for mankind. Shaykh Ahmad discovered in his long years of study that the laying of the foundation of this Apocalypse, the day of the First Trumpet, would begin in our Muslim calendar in the year 1260. This is known to all of you who are pupils and disciples here—the pivotal teaching around which the rest of our instruction revolves in the Shaykhi school.

" 'When we come to the Christian religion, a good deal of deep study of both the Old and the New Testaments has been essential, and we shall take this up at a later time. For the rest of our class today I wish to emphasize once again, as I have on many occasions, that the primary obligation of the members of this school is to set out at the expected time to search for that Promised One, the Forerunner of the Qayyúm. Once more I lay upon you the duty of leaving your homes and families at my demise, for I shall pass into other realms no later than the year 1259 or the early part of 1260. As Shaykh Ahmad informed me before his departure for Medina, neither he nor I would live to see the Advent of the Promised Ones on earth. It remains for those who are dedicated to our mission to arise at all costs and to declare themselves as disciples of that Holy Soul, the Qaim. Do not feel that any one of you is exempt from this duty unless great physical weakness interferes. There will be many, regardless, whose bodies are frail and whose purses are low in substance who will lead the way to that blessed being, the Dawnbreaker of a New Age.'

"At this point a figure appeared at the rear doorway to the courtyard, close to where we sat. Hesitating there he put a finger to his lips as one of the pupils in the back row recognized the youth standing in the entrance and half-rose from his seat. The movement engaged the attention of the Siyyid, who called out from the platform with apparent pleasure.

" 'Muhammad-Ali! Come in! Come in! How splendid—you have come all the way again from Barfarush. Your friends will be delighted to greet you. This time you will be with us for a longer stay, I hope.'

"The Siyyid rose and stepped down from the platform, waving a hand in dismissal of the class. A group of smiling young pupils surged toward the visitor, a handsome youth who appeared to be still in his adolescent years. I could only presume that he was a former member of the school, and I whispered to Mirza Jani that we had best depart, and return at a less intimate time.

"We slipped away through the door to the courtyard, but not before we had heard the Siyyid address certain members of the group surrounding the new arrival. I was already aware of the names of certain disciples whom he now called upon to meet with him, and have since ascertained the names of the others.

" 'Mulla Husayn,' he said, 'please join with me in the library with Mulla Ali, Mulla Jalil, and Mulla Yusuf. I will ask Shaykh Hasan-i-Zunuzi and Siyyid Husayn-i-Yazdi to be present also. There are many increasingly difficult problems arising here in Karbila, and Muhammad-Ali can give us word as well of the recent demonstrations against the Shaykhi believers in northern Persia. We hope to alleviate what has come upon us from many directions, and I fear will soon intensify.'

"Mirza Jani and I hastened back to our quarters, anxious to relay to Mirza Jamal all that we had seen and heard at the school. There was no doubt in the minds of my uncle and myself that we were now wholeheartedly enlisted in the Cause of the Promised Qaim. And we declared to Mirza Jamal that we were ready to undergo the trials and vicissitudes that we now knew would be heaped upon us in the days to come."

JULIA: This is as far as we planned to go in the journal this evening, friends, and it seems as good a place as any to discontinue this particular chain of events until the next meeting. As a teacher of religious history I am highly gratified at your attention to a subject so far removed from the scientific and secular matters that engage the majority of our Western professors. I have no doubt that there are questions and comments on the tips of your tongues, and even serious disagreement on the time spent on details which most of our colleagues in academia now look upon as a tiresome repetition of ancient themes no longer applicable to more enlightened times.

I can only say of this present-day put-down of religion by many intellectuals of our Western world that it is time we possessed a modern documentation of how the never-ending renewal of faith takes place when a new Prophet declares his mission to the world. This documentation is available today in hundreds of eyewitness accounts by Muslims and Western diplomats alike, by writers and artists in both the East and the West, and from a stunning array of those who caught fire from the Teachings which came to their hands or ears in the nineteenth and early twentieth centuries.

I will list here a number of their names, which are surely familiar to all of you—Leo Tolstoy, Queen Marie of Rumania, the eminent Swiss scientist and psychiatrist Doctor August Forel, George Townshend, Archdeacon of Clonfert and formerly Canon of St. Patrick's Cathedral in Dublin, Professor Pitrim Sorokin of Harvard, Edward Benes, President of Czechoslovakia, Y. T. Tsao, President of the University of Shanghai, the Western historians Herbert Adams Gibbons in America and A. L. M. Nicholas in France, the distinguished English clergyman and author the Reverend T. K. Cheyne, and Doctor Benjamin Jowett, Master of Balliol at Oxford, who wrote of the new faith as "the greatest light that has come into the world since the time of Jesus Christ." The full list, given to us by Doctor Varqa, is compelling, and includes two well-known writers in the nineteenth century, Le Comte de Gobineau and Sir Francis Younghusband.

But perhaps the best known of all the enthusiasts of the new faith was the renowned orientalist, Professor George Edward Browne of Cambridge, who spent a good part of his academic life, both in England and in Persia, in calling attention to and writing extensively on the dramatic events in the Middle East, which seemed to him of paramount importance. Although he was mistaken in a number of views pertaining to what he called the apostolic successorship which followed the martyrdom of the Promised Qaim, he extolled the movement as unparalleled since the days of the Christ and Muhammad.

I have brought these particular persons to your attention, for none of them can be labelled by any stretch of the imagination as nonentities with an ax to grind or fanatical religious figures in search of an alien Messiah. I hope these names will help to keep your interest alive as we continue in our next gathering with the dangers of extinction to the Shaykhi school and describe the devastating attack on Karbila by the Ottoman governor of Baghdad. Although Mustafa's grandfather and uncle returned to Kashan after a week or so in Karbila, Mustafa remained in charge of the shop in the holy city, and from this new young disciple's journal we shall learn of several important events which took place there from the fall of 1839 to the death of Siyyid Kazim in January of 1844—the year 1260 in the Muslim calendar.

We have a surprise for you tonight. It is Philip's birthday and Helen has brought for the occasion a delicious-looking pineapple dessert and a bottle of champagne. We salute you, Philip, and one and all we thank you for your ever-ready and pertinent contributions to our explorations here. There will come a day, I predict, when none of you who have listened so attentively and given of your opinions and your scholarship in these meetings will regret the mutual exchanges we have so far experienced, and which Ham and I look forward to in the future. Although we have spoken of the absence of Don and Madilyn this evening before the tapes were on, we hope that their longer stay in Chicago will be conducive to our seeing them back here together again by our next meeting.

Helen, will you preside over your birthday offering, my dear? And Ham will happily, I am sure, assist you in pouring the champagne.

IV Critical Days in Karbila

HAM: Welcome once again, friends. It is splendid to have Madilyn and Don in our midst once more, and to hear the extraordinary news before the tapes were on that Don's cousins, professors at the University of Chicago, are members, along with their families, of the faith we have been discussing here. I cannot help but look upon this discovery as a remarkable case of synchronization, an occurrence that appears to take place frequently where this faith is concerned. Something quite contrary to the expected course of events occurred on that visit, and we would appreciate it greatly if Don and Madilyn will reveal for us on the tapes just how they have achieved the new relationship so obvious to all of us. The choice, of course, is theirs, but they can add immeasurably to Doctor Varqa's contention that the new faith is capable of healing disharmonies and attitudes that sometimes seem insurmountable.

MADILYN: I feel that there is no need for secrecy in these meetings, Ham, and if you will bear with us I believe that our recent experience will prove what you and Julia have been telling us in these meetings and what we have learned in Chicago—that the new faith is indeed a healing mechanism delivered to the world by an All-Knowing Physician. At the same time we want to assure you that our promise to Julia on our return here will be strictly kept—we will not divulge any knowledge we received in Chicago that goes beyond the chronological boundaries you have set for the dialogues. However, the results of what we discovered there and what happened to ourselves have been so remarkable that both of us are more than willing to share with you the amazing transformations promised by the new faith.

The immediate and most surprising thing to both of us was the obvious happiness and outgoing warmth we encountered in Don's two cousins and their families, whom we had not seen for several years. On our last visit as guests in their homes the atmosphere had been filled with negations and arguments between the professors and their wives, and their grown children were in constant conflict with their parents. I knew, of course, that Don's relatives as young boys had gone through the same losses as he too had sustained in the Holocaust, had experienced the same disillusionments, and had turned away in their twenties from the former consolations of their Jewish faith.

When we received a letter a month or so ago inviting us to visit them again, I naturally pictured the gloomy and depressing environment of these households and attempted to persuade Don to go there on his own. He had been talking for some time of giving up his position here at the end of the college year and applying for a possible associate professorship at the University of Chicago. After several days of back-and-forthing I felt that this might very well be the end of our relationship, and I finally capitulated and agreed to accompany him on the trip. I can only suppose now that our marriage was fated to undergo a final test, and one that could very well have failed if it had not been for the unexpected metamorphosis we came upon within a few moments of our arrival at the airport.

The astonishing changes that were immediately evident in Don's relatives were so overwhelming to both of us—and indeed a matter of some confusion—that nothing was said on the matter until we had joined the two families at dinner. Within a short time Don had begun complaining about the lack of opportunity in the midwest for getting ahead in the history department and the various situations that kept him from achieving the success he desired. He was, of course, looking for support, but the conversation suddenly took a turn in another direction, and we found ourselves listening to a recitation of how the two families had discovered a new worldwide religion which had transformed entirely their outlook on life.

You can well imagine that when names and places began to emerge we both realized with amazement, incredible as it seemed, that these relatives of Don's, their wives and the rest of their families had become staunch and active members of the new faith we had been introduced to by Julia and Ham. I was so astonished, so excited by this discovery that I was seized by the thought that a marriage so close to disintegration as my own could possibly be recovered if Don's chronic despondency about the world could be lifted. As we talked and listened day by day to these happy people, perceptible changes occurred in Don's attitude, and when he suggested that we remain for another week I was quick to concur. But I feel it is up to Don to give his own version of how he slowly awakened to the self-centered opinions and points of view on life he had fostered for so long a time, and how he was struck with a sudden determination to see the possibilities of his work and marriage in a different light.

DON: To begin with, these two cousins of mine—now successful professors of biology and chemistry respectively—are older than I, and since my childhood have always been very much admired by me. While visiting our Jewish grandparents here in America as children we experienced at a distance the dreadful trauma of the Holocaust that wiped out every last one of our mutual families and other relatives in Germany. It was a blow that the three of us were unable to adjust to, and we fed upon one another's grief and depression and the abject feelings of racial rejection to such an extent that it is proof to me now how infectious and life-destroying such negative interchanges can be. As these older cousins had eventually repudiated our former faith and had persuaded me that the human species was incurably hostile and untrustworthy, I followed in their footsteps, becoming more and more maladjusted to the world as time went on.

The sudden discovery in Chicago that I was now alone in my self-pity and my soured perspective on almost every aspect of man's existence produced at first a painful feeling of alienation from the two families I had counted on for emotional support. In desperation I turned to Madilyn, asking what she thought of attending a meeting of believers with our hosts, as they had suggested we do while the opportunity was open to us. She unhesitatingly agreed, and I think I can say that from that first meeting onward I felt a cloud lifting from my mind and an unaccustomed urge to reach out for the same kind of happiness, the same knowledgeable approach to the world so evident in the members of the new faith. I learned that realism and chronic pessimism are two different things, that in keeping with our meetings here with Julia and Ham the members of this faith do not shy away from the recognition of the evils and imperfections of a slowly evolving world, but on the contrary are engaged in spreading the means to alleviate them.

After a second meeting—a large gathering of obviously successful people—it came to me forcefully that I must return to this campus and try for a book that would increase my chances for promotion and tenure. At the same time I began to realize very clearly that the optimistic viewpoint that Madilyn had been advocating for the twelve difficult years we had tried to adjust to one another's mental perceptions was not only correct but that I could not possibly face any future life of accomplishment without her support and the love that we shared together in the first part of our marriage. I can only say that results have been unbelievable, that I feel myself renewed, and I am anxious to take up a creative relationship with my colleagues. Above all, I must express my gratitude for the patience you have shown here as I attempted to undercut a religious movement that has the obvious power to raise the consciousness of millions of people around the globe. We are counting on hearing the tapes we have missed, and I am looking forward to adding a positive note to our discussions here.

JULIA: Our smiling faces, Don, will tell you and Madilyn the pleasure we all feel in this marvelous transformation in your lives. As for Ham and myself, we account it a partial victory for Doctor Varqa, who constantly assured us that miracles of change can occur when one is introduced to the faith and finally recognizes the power of a Prophet of God. And about that book, Don—we are ready to aid you in any way we can. In my estimation you should choose an educational approach in relation to the intellectual apathy in our schools and colleges—something to galvanize the thinking of those in control of our educational programs. It is a project that needs the courage of a crusader—a positive act of service to the young minds of today.

PHILIP: A book is the thing, old man, and I'll be glad to assist. I'm on the board of the University Press, and can steer you on the proper way to handle the matter. I've read some of your papers and you write well, but give it a lift, Don, accentuate the actual facts with the requisite research and eliminate the personal criticisms indulged in by so many cultural writers today. Nothing religious, at least to begin with, or you won't sell. And above all take your time—this sort of project is not accomplished overnight.

HAM: We are all in back of you, Don, and are ready to help if you need us. I presume you and Madilyn will now be considerably more cognizant of certain aspects of the faith than we are yet prepared to introduce in these initial meetings. We deeply appreciate your agreement to hold in reserve your additional knowledge while we present the faith in as chronological a manner as possible to the rest of our friends here. Nevertheless we welcome any correction if you find us seriously off the mark in our presentation.

Meanwhile we must go forward with certain events in the Shaykhi school and the holy city itself during a very crucial period. It was a harrowing time in many ways, not only from the growing independence within the school of Haji Karim Khan, his uncle and his friends, in relation to Siyyid Kazim, but due as well to the increasing hostility between the holy city and the Ottoman authorities in Baghdad. At the same time Siyyid Ibrahim continued to insert his disruptive spies into the classrooms of the school, and to incite his small army of rowdies to add their strident voices to the demand of the populace of Karbila, as a holy city of the Shiites, for autonomy to govern themselves. There were nevertheless rays of light persisting amidst the gloom—a steadfast and continuing search after knowledge by the pupils of the Siyyid and an unremitting application of this knowledge to the Advent of the Qaim. To all those scholars who had come from places near or far to await the apocalyptic year of 1260, Siyyid Kazim had repeatedly reminded them of Muhammad's statement that "Whoever leaves his home in the search for knowledge walks in the path of God," and that this search should never end but continue from his early years to the day of his death.

The growing rebellion of Karbila against the government of the Sultan during this period is difficult to envision without postulating what one might term an outbreak of contagious insanity, a reckless disregard of the consequences which seems to take hold of the collective religious mind when frustrations reach a certain breaking point. The inept response to this situation by the Turkish authorities then in control of Baghdad and the holy cities in Iraq served only to increase the animosity of the Persian Shias toward the Ottoman Sunnis. The anger of the Sultan's government in Constantinople finally erupted in the sudden recall in the summer of 1842 of the Sunni governor in Baghdad and his replacement by Najib Pasha, who features prominently in the ongoing affairs of the Shaykhi school.

The new governor was under orders to refrain from attack unless the unruliness became unmanageable, and he seems to have done his best in a calm and patient manner to hold off a final reckoning. He consulted on a number of occasions with Siyyid Kazim, Siyyid Ibrahim, the Zillus-Sultán and the Persian consul in Karbila, but in spite of the prodigious efforts of Siyyid Kazim to bring things under control and the governor's attempt at a peaceful solution of the matter, the madness continued, infecting the pilgrims and threatening to precipitate a march on the city of Baghdad. We learn of what follows through the sixty-six page report of the British Special Commissioner then in Tehran, an almost incredible account which reveals the disastrous results of the stubborn mind-set of religious and political fanaticism.

I realize that I am ahead of myself here, friends, but I will inform you nevertheless that all this led to a siege of the town which had no salutary effect on the populace and resulted in daily insults and rock-throwing from the top of the walls and the emptying of garbage on the soldiers below. His patience exhausted, the governor ordered an attack in force in January of 1843, a military explosion in which the school itself, though put off-limits to the rampaging and marauding troops by Najib Pasha, was unavoidably engulfed by scores of wounded and terrified Persians fleeing from other areas of the town, resulting in scenes of misery and horror beyond belief in the classrooms and in the residence of Siyyid Kazim. I think I can say without exaggeration that this Ottoman attack on Karbila—the cruel massacres in the streets and in the houses, on the walkways at the top of the walls and in the courtyards of the Shrines—is a glaring example of the abominable pit into which members of the same religion can fall when worldly power and politics are at stake. We will leave this appalling event in abeyance, however, and return to certain occurrences within the school with the help of Mustafa's journal and the notes we gathered in Doctor Varqa's home.

JULIA: We learned in our last meeting that Mustafa, his grandfather and his uncle Mirza Jani established in Karbila, in the fall of 1839, a branch of their family business in Kashan. Mustafa would remain in the holy city in charge of this enterprise until the spring of 1260, or 1844, when news from the southern river port of Basra caused him to leave the shop in the care of his bookkeeper, and to make his way to Bushihr. Meanwhile he had written of certain events affecting his business and the Shaykhi school, and a quite extraordinary account of a gathering in the Siyyid's library which should be of interest to us all—an analysis in depth of the claim of the Christians that only through the Christ, the one and only Savior for all time, could men everywhere be accepted into the Kingdom of God. I have not run across a more perceptive exegesis of the Christian Scriptures, and it has aided me in clarifying my own thoughts on the strange discrepancies not only between the four Gospels, but also between the Gospels and the writings and teachings of St. Paul. The expressed theologies in these two sections of the New Testament can only appear to the eye of a Biblical scholar as two quite separate religions.

This sort of analysis of other Scriptural faiths within the school had no affiliation whatever with the attempt at disparagement of the type engaged in by rival religions. Such bigotry, according to Mustafa, was strictly forbidden by Siyyid Kazim in keeping with the command of Muhammad for tolerance of other faiths. Where Christianity in particular was concerned the primary purpose of such an examination was to uphold the teachings of Shaykh Ahmad that many Prophets of God had appeared in the past and would continue to do so in the future, that St. Paul's missionary zeal in proclaiming the Prophet Jesus as the only Word of God for all eternity—the very Son of God on a par with God Himself—did not square away with the statements of the Christ in the Gospels or the declarations to be found in the Apocalypse of St. John, which we will come to at a later time. Such delving into other Scriptures, anathema to the orthodox in the holy cities, had finally been forbidden in the classrooms by Siyyid Kazim to avoid the resulting disruptions. Undaunted by such hostile episodes, the brightest young scholars in the school and the closest companions of the Master now collected for Scriptural discussions in the Siyyid's private library, where even the disturbing lutis, the rowdies in the town, did not dare to penetrate. Ham, will you read from the journal, please? It will carry us forward in a number of ways—and do not hesitate to comment on the contents, friends, when the reading comes to an end.

HAM: "Until the first month of 1256, or 1840 in the Christian calendar," Mustafa writes, "I was kept busy at the shop in Karbila attempting to handle the rush of business, which spoke well for the quality of our textiles and accessories and promised our continued success. As a consequence I was not able to attend the school classes more than twice a week, but this enabled me to establish a personal friendship with a number of the younger scholars and to be accepted as a member of their inner circle. This was not a group who intentionally stood apart from the other members of the school, but by a natural endowment of mental ability and a greater capacity for the Cause they had chosen, they stood above the others, in my opinion, in their readiness to give their lives for the coming Revelation.

"I soon learned from these friends that the Master had lost so much support among the ulama that he was planning to send an emissary on a mission to Isfahan and Mashad, hoping that he could obtain anew the good graces of one of the most influential ecclesiastics in Persia, Haji Muhammad-Baquir of Isfahan, and of certain prominent clergy in the holy city of Mashad in the province of Khurasan. When finally he called for volunteers for this service he found that both the rigors and dangers of the long and difficult journey and the pressing necessity to provide a livelihood for their relatives in Karbila were holding back the ready acceptance of this honor. At last it was Mulla Husayn who stepped forward, much to the Master's delight. The knowledge and eloquence of this outstanding member of the school, his moral stature and his spiritual humility could not be matched among the young scholars except perhaps by Mulla Ali. Indeed, these two disciples were so revered that there had been conjectures among the pupils at one time that either one or the other might be the Promised One of Islam. How the Master succeeded in putting down such speculations, which at various times had included himself as well, I shall reveal on another occasion.

"It will clarify later events if I insert here in the summer of 1260 that Mulla Husayn, unavoidably occupied at that earlier period with the care of his mother and other members of his family in the holy city, was unable to depart from Karbila until the early spring of 1257, or 1841 in the Christian calendar, and that he spent almost three years on the journey, much of it in grueling travel by foot, by mule and by horseback. Though only twenty-seven at his departure and frail in appearance, his loyalty, his endurance and his humble eloquence in addressing large groups of the clergy gained the respect and the renewed allegiance of Muhammad-Baquir of Isfahan and laid the foundation in Mashad for his later and productive sojourn in that city with Muhammad-Ali of Barfarush. Unfortunately it is necessary to report that the death of Muhammad-Baquir a few months before the beginning of this prophesied year of 1260 nullified Husayn's initial success in Isfahan. Upon the untimely demise of this leading mujtahid, and in spite of the claim of the city's clergy to stand above all others in the country in their espousal of the doctrine of the Hidden Imam, the Shaykhi believers among them rapidly fell away from their apparent pretensions and withdrew their support of the school, a state of affairs largely brought about by the now hostile disciples of Muhammad-Baquir and the enmity of the orthodox ulama.

"I was told by Mulla Ali that when the Master was informed of these developments he shook his head sadly and predicted that the city of Isfahan would prove to be one of the most active areas of persecution against the believers. But there were two faithful souls in that city, he said, who would not be budged from their loyalty to the teachings of the school—the steadfast Mulla Sadiq of Khurasan, advanced in years, who had sat at the feet of Shaykh Ahmad in Yazd, and was sent to Isfahan by Siyyid Kazim to teach whom he could and to proclaim the Advent of the Qaim when it occurred, and a young wheat sifter, Mulla Jafar, who had listened carefully to Mulla Husayn on the latter's visit in 1257 and was filled with the certainty of what he had heard. Never deviating from spreading the word to all who would listen, and exposed to the ridicule and abuse of their neighbors and the clergy, these two staunch believers, the Master declared, were destined to appear in the history books as outstanding martyrs for the Cause.

"As for Mulla Husayn, he returned to Karbila in January of 1260 to a scene of mourning and indecision which followed upon the Master's death a short time before. The disciples had been overwhelmed by this event on the very brink of the prophesied year of the Qaim's appearance, and lacking direction as to how to proceed with the Siyyid's instructions they were not yet prepared to start off on a journey whose final destination was still unknown. In spite of his own grief Mulla Husayn attempted to rally his companions to set out in search of the Promised One, but his urgent appeals for departure in various directions were to no avail—they would go later, they said, that for the present they were needed at the school, that the Master's bereaved family must be cared for, that their own families were in need of their presence and so on. Convinced that this phase of indecision would soon pass for those who were deeply devoted to the teachings, Mulla Husayn ceased his exhortations and persuaded his brother and his cousin to accompany him to the ancient mosque in Kufa to pray there for guidance. Just how this succeeded in arousing his friends and companions to follow in his footsteps will have to be left until a later time."

DON: I would like to make a comment, Julia, on the youth of so many of the followers of Siyyid Kazim. The Muslim books on Islam from the college library have treated this circumstance in a most off-hand and cursory manner, stating that the Shaykhi school was in the nature of a revolutionary youth movement engendered by visionaries among the unorthodox clergy who looked to the young clerics to bring about a change in the customs of Islam—that the school was in favor of religious syncretism and democratic permissiveness. The books declare that this radical movement, which included the downfall of the Qajar monarchy, was not a lasting success, that most of its agitators were put to death, and that its advocates today, still deluded by religious pretensions, are properly deprived of the rights of Muslim citizens, are imprisoned as morally dangerous, and in many cases executed by firing squad or hanged. We found in Chicago that this appraisal of the new faith, as you have shown us, is not in keeping with the facts, but one thing at least is correct—the incredible persecutions continue in spite of the protests of the United Nations, the various Parliaments of Europe, and by the members of our own Congress. Personally, I believe that these books should be withdrawn from the library as subversive of the truth of this faith.

JULIA: In my estimation, Don, this is not the way to handle the enmity of rival religions. A few books by either Muslims or Christians who have no understanding of the new faith cannot hold back its steady spread around the world. Such biased writers have no intention of impartially investigating the actual history and tenets of any Revelation subsequent to their own, nor the slightest desire to give up their long-held beliefs. Surely this reactionary response can be understood by those who are seeking the truth on such matters, and the way to approach these unyielding minds is to leave them to the evolutionary process. But the question of youth is something I would like to address when we finish the next segment of our journal. Mustafa will acquaint us in short order with some of these so-called revolutionaries in the Shaykhi school. It hardly appears that they were plotting the downfall of anybody or anything other than the misconceived interpretations of certain passages in the Christian Scriptures, as you will see.

HAM: The journal reads that "During my second month in Karbila, Mulla Jalil dropped by the shop to invite me to join some of the young scholars in the Master's library to examine certain doctrines of the Christian religion. Shaykh

Hasan-i-Zunuzi would be in charge, as the Siyyid was away in Najaf to discuss the agitation in Karbila with the leading ulama in that holy city. The Master had suggested that I be included to take notes on what was discussed. He had been corresponding with Mirza Jani, who had mentioned the rapidity with which I was able to write down the detailed contents of a meeting or the words of a lecture or of any other discourse. Naturally I accepted the invitation with alacrity, thrilled with the thought that a wholly new area of knowledge would now be opened to me.

"On the appointed morning we gathered discreetly in the library, and I found myself seated in a circle among nine of the brightest scholars in the school, our legs folded in the Persian style, and all pleasantly aware, I am sure, that we were outwitting the enemies and spies who surrounded us in Karbila. Present were Mulla Husayn of Bushrui, Mulla Ali of Bastam, Mulla Ahmad of Maraghi, Mulla Muhammad-Ali of Barfarush, the Mullas Yusuf, Jalil and Mahmud from Ardabil, Urumi and Khuy respectively, and Siyyid Husayn from Yazd, a close friend of Shaykh Hasan. It was only I who knew nothing of the Jewish or Christian Testaments, and I was soon amazed at the telling details from various sections of the Holy Bible which were brought forth around that circle of scholars.

"Shaykh Hasan lost no time in opening the Bible to the New Testament. 'Without an understanding of the history of this Book,' he said, 'we can have no true knowledge of the actual station of the Prophet Jesus. You need no reminder that the Christian churches are immovable on the unique rank of the Christ as the one and only religious figure through whom all mankind can obtain salvation and forgiveness and begin the spiritual journey to the throne of heaven. Certain Christian sects believe that upon his reappearance on our planet only a small number will be gathered together as the proper spiritual material to inherit the earth, that all the rest of mankind will be shut out from sharing the glories and rewards prepared for them by God the Father and His only Son.

" 'Now what distinguishes us here in this school is our assertion that such rigid dogmas are mainly due to the extraordinary difference between the statements of the Christ in the Gospels and the doctrines of St. Paul in his Epistles and in the Acts of the Apostles. We are not here to criticize the Apostle to the Gentiles, who above all men in the time of the earliest Christians, before the Gospels had been written, contributed to the upbuilding of the first churches in pagan lands and their unification in an often confused and disorganized community of believers. But the fact remains that in the Gospels and in the teachings of St. Paul we are faced with conflicting expositions of the position and rank of the Prophet Jesus in relation to God and to the people of the world.'

"Mulla Ali raised his hand, requesting permission to speak. 'We must not forget that Paul was born in Asia Minor, in Tarsus, an area of the world which combined in its beliefs the Hellenistic philosophies of the Greeks and the pagan ideas of the lands that surrounded Palestine. As Saul of Tarsus he was well aware of the Greek doctrine of the Logos—the preexistent creative principle behind all things material and immaterial—as well as the rituals and suppositions of the mystery religions of Greece and other pagan cults. When, as a Jewish Pharisee, he left Asia Minor to make his home in Israel, he became an ardent and active member of that sect, looking forward with all his fellow Israelites to the Advent of the Jewish Messiah, that World Redeemer who was also known in those days as the "Son of God." Saul had never encountered the Christ, had little idea of his life and teachings, and was unsympathetic to the beliefs expressed by

Jesus' followers after the Crucifixion, who regarded their Lord, according to the latter's own statements, as the Prophet foretold by Moses—the one "like unto me," as Moses declared, who would succeed him as an Educator for the Jews. At the time this belief was an abomination to the zealous Saul, a strict adherent of the everlasting Laws of Moses, who proceeded to persecute by word of mouth and physical abuse the early Christians in Palestine.

" 'All of this underwent a great change, as we know, subsequent to Saul's conversion on the road to Damascus. And what developed thereafter is well documented by the history of the early churches presided over by the new convert—now known as Paul—in the Gentile lands of Asia Minor, Greece and Rome. Paul was filled, ever since his vision of the Christ, with a burning devotion to the One whom he now looked upon as the World Messiah, the Son of God, the Logos or controlling Word behind all creation, the One by whom "all things were made." And Paul gave to these early churches a new religion, high-minded and spiritually effective, and adaptable to the former pagan beliefs—a religion that, since the Gospels were not compiled until approximately 65 to 120 A.D., subsequently caused a wide disparity of doctrines in a multitude of denominations.

" 'Now we can find, of course, the same disunity in Islam and the other great religions of the past. They constitute a "house divided" both between and within themselves and as a consequence possess no remaining spiritual force for unifying the peoples of the future. It is understandable, then, that religion as we know it at the present time no longer carries the authority to guide the thinking and behavior of mankind, and has left our past religions impotent to deal with the pressing problems of today and tomorrow.

" 'It is well to remember, in any attempt to reconstruct the true Christian religion, that Jesus spoke of himself in general as the Son of Man, merely acknowledging the title Son of God when mockingly confronted by his persecutors, and he likewise declared in this connection that if his teachings were adhered to they would make "sons of God" of all those who obeyed him. The use of such titles among the Jews has led to misinterpretations that, combined with the set doctrines of the Councils of the Church, have caused many centuries of division and hostility, of persecution and warfare, among the Christians themselves. Mulla Mahmud and Mulla Yusuf have studied the Gospels with great care, and we should listen to what they have to say. They will leave no doubt in our minds that the statements of the Christ himself as reported therein are a total refutation of his deification and his role in the world as the sole Redeemer of all mankind.'

"Mulla Mahmud leaned forward to oblige. 'First of all,' he said, 'the Prophet Jesus makes no claim anywhere in the Gospels to be the final Word for the world. If so, what can we make of the declaration that "I have many things to say unto you, but ye cannot bear them now. But when he, the Spirit of Truth cometh, he will guide you into all truth." And as Moses declared of the Prophet who would follow him among the Jews, Jesus in turn states of this Spirit of Truth that "He shall not speak of himself, but whatever he shall hear, that shall he speak, and he will show you things to come." The mental capacity of his hearers in his own time, then, was the criterion for the amount of truth to be delivered, and further revelation would follow at a time, as he informed them, "known only to God."

" 'When Mulla Yusuf and I began our examination of the Holy Bible we were utterly confused to find two separate religions contained in that Book, and we understood then why the Prophet Muhammad made no mention of the doctrines of St. Paul or the later Councils of the Church, but spoke of the Christ as a Prophet like himself. For nowhere in the Gospels is it maintained that the essence, substance or powers of Jesus were in any way equivalent to those of the Father, or that a Trinity existed of God the Father, God the Son, and God the Holy Spirit, or that the Son had come to earth to wipe out the inherited corruption of mankind ever since the Original Sin supposedly committed by Adam and Eve—a doctrine we looked for in vain in the Gospels. Neither have we found any commands for asceticism, for celibacy, for withdrawing from the world behind the walls of monasteries and nunneries, or for a physical conformity to certain customs, rituals and sacraments as necessary for salvation, such as the baptism of infants who understand nothing of what is taking place, and the drinking of wine and the eating of bread to ingest the actual body and blood of the Christ. As Shaykh Ahmad and Siyyid Kazim have taught us in this school, such physical actions portrayed in the Gospels are symbols of a spiritual attachment to the teachings and commands of the Prophet. The meaning intended by the use of the bread and wine at the Last Supper, the Master has declared, is that the disciples and other believers must continue to "drink in" his words, the very water or lifeblood of their existence, and to constantly "eat" of the body of his doctrines and guidance.

" 'Neither did we find in the Gospels that a fallen angel, Lucifer or Satan, the symbol of temptation, was the source of all evil in the world, and since the days of Adam could be blamed for man's corruption, his immorality, and the "demons" of disease or disbelief. On the contrary, Jesus declared that "every good thing is of God, and every evil thing is of yourselves"—a statement that wickedness and atrocities are man-made, are a yielding to the greed for power and worldly fame, to the lure of riches and earthly possessions and the passions and pull of the self and the flesh. And much to our surprise we found no record in the Gospels that Jesus gave any special consideration to his mother Mary as the Divine Mother of the Son of God, nor any statement that she must be accorded the exalted station she now commands in the Church—indeed the cult of the Virgin is in some areas a far more powerful force in the lives of the people than her Son, depicted almost as an afterthought as an infant tucked away in a cradle. But let Mulla Yusuf quote from the Gospels in refutation of the general Christian view of the Christ as on a par and of one substance with God the Father.'

"Mulla Yusuf promptly produced some slips of paper from a pocket of his cloak. 'There are many statements of the Christ which declare his difference from the Father. He chides the disciples for praising his own goodness, for example, by replying "Why callest thou me good? There is none good but One, that is God." And he states that "My doctrine is not mine, but His who sent me," that "I can of my own will do nothing; as I hear I judge, as I seek not my own will but the will of the Father," that "the words I speak unto you, I speak not of myself, but the Father who dwelleth in me, He doeth the works." And he likewise told his disciples that they must rejoice at his coming ascension to the heavens of God's Will, for in that place he is honored by the Father, who is "greater than I."

" 'Surely these are the words of a Messenger of God as we teach in this school. If such are the words of God Himself walking upon the earth, as some Christians believe, it is strange language indeed for the Almighty to employ. In fact Jesus states that "no one has seen God at any time; you have neither heard His voice nor seen His shape," which proclaims once again that the oneness of God and his Messenger is a spiritual oneness—"I and the Father are one"—that the Father links himself to the pure soul of the Messenger and guides him in His message to mankind. In this way He can be said to be "dwelling" within the Prophet, but it cannot be construed as the Deity Itself in human form. In this connection Jesus refers on many occasions to the Prophethood of Moses, warning the people of Israel that if they truly believed in Moses they would likewise believe in his own station, for he "spoke of me." Like all the Prophets of God we find that the Christ looked backward to extol the one who preceded him, and in both open and symbolic language he points to another yet to come. He himself denies knowing when that future appearance will take place, saying that "about that day and that hour no one knoweth, not the angels in heaven, but the Father alone." Those who followed these clear teachings of Jesus—the Nazarene Christians of Palestine—were later declared heretical by the Roman Church, and Paul's now familiar doctrines became the basis of Christian theology.' "

JULIA: May I suggest that we postpone the remainder of Mustafa's account of this library meeting and resume with some equally telling points when we meet again in two weeks. The subject we are dealing with is inexhaustible, but the quotes brought forward by the Shaykhi scholars are proof enough that the present Church beliefs on the rank of the Christ are not based upon the teachings of the Gospels. Mulla Yusuf might have added that the Apostle Peter was dethroned as the chosen Rock upon which the pure teachings should have been built, and his influence was replaced by a mixture of Hellenistic philosophy, of pagan beliefs and rituals, and of elements of Judaism without the Laws of Moses—the Pauline doctrine of Justification by faith in Jesus alone and no longer by the works of the Law. Christianity became the Message of the Christ on the Cross, the Message of the forgiveness of one's sins by this act, a Message which absolves the world of making the sacrificial efforts toward perfection which the Gospels declare is the aim of man's existence.

But why, you may wonder, does all this really matter today, at a time when we have stated so emphatically that all the religions of the past have lost their former authority to affect any positive changes for a new order in the world? For what my opinion is worth, I can only say that the Christian Church, in its persistent claim to uniqueness and infallible knowledge, will hold firm for a long period of time against any invasion of its fundamental doctrines, and if we wish to establish that a new Prophet and a new Revelation for our day has actually appeared in the Middle East we must muster as much Scriptural ammunition as we can find. This is one of the ways, in my view, that all men and women of spiritual intelligence and good will may gain the knowledge and understanding that will lead them in the end to respond to the new Spirit of Truth in the world.

One of these truths, of course, is that Jesus, far from annulling the Laws of Moses, explicitly reaffirmed the Ten Commandments and added to their dimensions. He stated that he came not to abrogate the works of the Law, but declared of those who believed in his mission that "The works that I do shall he do also, and greater works than these shall he do." And finally we have his admonition to "Think not that I am come to destroy the Law and the prophets; I am not come to destroy but to fulfil." And he adds that "Whosoever shall break one of these least commandments, and shall teach men so, shall be called least in the kingdom of heaven; but whosoever shall do and teach them, the same shall be called great in the kingdom of heaven."

Surely the downgrading of the Laws of religion in the doctrines of the Christian Church has contributed greatly to the centuries-old religious strife in the Western world. Indeed, such lawlessness can be summed up in another statement of the Christ to those who gathered about him in Israel that "This people draweth nigh unto me with their mouths and honoreth me with their lips; but their hearts are far from me. And in vain do they worship me, teaching for doctrines the commandments of men." This is the case as well in every extant religion on earth, as anyone is able to observe. But again, let us lighten our discussion and make way for any comments before we take to the sideboard. Reverend Ahearn, are you in accord with what has been brought forward here tonight?

REVEREND AHEARN: I am indeed, Julia. And I have watched the faces of our friends for any signs of a glazed eye and can report that their attention has been total as usual. We are blessed with a group whose intelligence, whether spiritually oriented or not, is unlikely to toss aside the rare experience we are having in these meetings in probing into matters of such primary importance to the present state of the world. And we are doubly blessed that Don and Madilyn are now aligned with you and Ham in your championship of the new faith. As for the rest of us, we will no doubt fall into line when the time arrives for the great changes, both gradual and catastrophic, that are bound to come upon the earth—they are quite inevitable, in my opinion, and with the knowledge passed on to us by our wise and discerning hosts we should have no trouble in knowing where to turn for the necessary answers. For the present I look forward to a further analysis of the Gospels by our Shaykhi scholars, and indeed to any and all information available to us in these meetings.

HELEN: I am utterly astonished, Julia, at what I've been hearing in this house as you and Ham have continued to open up avenues to religious knowledge hitherto unknown to me. I admit that my concentration on Marxist studies has screened out many segments of world history that are based on religious faith—a general condition that is sadly compounded in every classroom from grammar school through the college years. Even the departments of religion in most of our

American universities are forced to downplay the religious motivations for so many historical actions and decisions of our former governments in this country, partly, I suppose, for fear of disturbing the sacrosanct separation of church and state. The ultimate separation, of course, is in the Soviet Union and other communist countries, but in certain aspects we, too, seem to have carried the original intent of our founding fathers, in providing us with the proper checks and balances, to an almost total blackout of religious history.

It is all the more surprising, then, that physicists such as Philip should have opened their minds on their own initiative to what may lie beyond the veil of our physical senses, over and beyond the particles and waves of their orthodox colleagues. They seem to have shown the unusual ability in our day to combine the mathematical science of physics with the understanding of mystical and symbolic thought. If the older religions continue to lose strength everywhere, and Julia's new faith follows the usual pattern of a slow and difficult development toward a full-blown world religion, perhaps the deeper thinkers among our scientists, like our friend Philip here, will come around to the recognition that a Higher Intelligence is an absolute necessity to account for the organization and the cyclical behavior of a fantastic universe such as we have discussed here, and will be the first to persuade the world that the Prophets and their religions have been right all along.

PHILIP: I thank you for the kudos, Helen. And may I suggest a positive thought that may appear to our group as somewhat out of line, but which has occurred to me on several occasions. The very act in the Soviet Union of wiping out the old and in my opinion obsolete religions of the past, may very well have paved the way for the eventual renewal of faith in the communist lands without the superstitions and outmoded doctrines which originally brought about their downfall in the wake of Marxism. It is interesting that we look upon such nations as evil and monstrous because of their atheistic views and their ambitions to spread the doctrines of their own system—admittedly an oppressive and inefficient form of government—while we ignore the fact that the Laws of God as we have understood them in the past have long been absent from our own culture in the West, and that our vaunted democratic structure, hailed as the answer to all the ills of the world, is in actuality far from a true democracy. Can anyone deny that our own land at the present day is a place where money is paramount, and where such inequalities as racial barriers and sexism, and the problems of poverty, illiteracy, corruption, criminality and the overall pollution of our country combine to nullify the human rights and personal safety of our citizens?

REVEREND AHEARN: I agree that these are factual matters, Philip, and if these conditions are not corrected within a reasonable time we shall be in as deep trouble spiritually and physically as those whom we judge with such disdain. Consider that we point a finger at the Soviets for the widespread blight of alcoholism in that nation and blame it on the system, while in Europe—in Switzerland, Holland, France, free Germany and the Scandinavian countries, for example, as well as in our own country and in Japan—the problem of alcohol or drugs is never mentioned in connection with the form of government or the errors of elected or appointed officials. We must face the fact that such one-sided judgment has been pandemic in the world for centuries and that our species has consistently criticized other races or nations for the things it tolerates in its own backyard. This pointing of the finger has been most often motivated in the past, it seems, by religious differences, but in the case of communism we have found a prized objective in the first full-blown atheistic system known to the world. One way or another, however, those who hurl the stones of judgment against other peoples on our planet are rarely able to accept a pebble of criticism in return.

JULIA: I think it needs reiterating that religion itself and atheism per se are not the basic causes of our difficulties, but only man himself, as the Christ declared. As our scholars in Karbila have pointed out, the evils and worldly ambitions are within ourselves, and unless we transform our minds and emotions before another century goes by it is quite possible that our so-called civilization will descend into a sort of animalism, defined as a preoccupation with physical appetites. In our own species this would undoubtedly entail a sharp reanimation of racial hatreds, the increase of ill-health, both physical and mental, the augmentation of the horrors of drugs and the homes broken by alcohol—a substance now categorized as a powerful drug by the medical world—as well as the expansion of sexual abuse, of criminality far beyond what we see today, and the final impotence of the world's governments to hold off the multiplication of deadly weapons by the Godless merchants of applied science.

Having said all this—the worst possible scenario—let me also say, as Reverend Ahearn has rightly brought to our attention, that the potential of America for a vital transformation, once we are fully awakened to our many deficiencies, far exceeds the rest of the world, and will return this country in the end to its former position as a beacon for enlightenment and civilized living. My guess is that we must go through a fairly long period as yet to regain our equilibrium in this country and that the years between now and the first half of the twenty-first century will perhaps quite literally bring us to our knees.

GEORGINA: I think we must all concur in that, or risk a permanent decline of our place in the world. It will of course involve a change of consciousness on the part of the individuals who make up this nation, and we have had a most wonderful example of such a change in the lives of friends we have known very well—Madilyn and Don. I, for one, am looking forward to hearing more of their experience in Chicago—an extremely active group in the new faith there, Madilyn informs me, composed of adults of every former religion or no religion at all, and a large number of youth. It is the youth in this country, above all, who need our attention, for any further "lost generations" will hold us back from the national transition we so desperately need.

JULIA: The importance of youth in religion is something we should take up in our next meeting. The further findings of our young scholars in the Shaykhi school are on the agenda as well, and as usual your input is expected and will continually be regarded as significant to our major theme—the rejuvenation of the planet through a new Revelation from the East. We have but two more opportunities during this academic year to express ourselves here, but we hope for a following series when our various commitments are out of the way. At that time, with our introductory discussions behind us, we will proffer for your estimation the powerful Revelations of the two Prophets of God who have brought to this planet, as healing Physicians from the world of the Will of God, the solutions to the problems and distortions of the apocalyptic period known in the Christian West as the Latter Days.

This has been another concentrated session, friends, and you are quite ready, I'm sure, for the Adams' special recipe for raspberry mousse. Enjoy yourselves and relax your minds. We will try in the next two meetings to bring you to the Declaration of the Promised Qaim, an event that not only shook the religious life of the Persians but, combined with the further Advent of the One whom that Herald Prophet had warned would soon be made manifest, has been a cause in that land for continuing persecution and the most cruel and oppressive treatment.

V   Light Amidst the Darkness

JULIA: I believe that we have established so far that human beings, both individual and in the aggregate, exhibit crippling blind spots in relation to religion and have done so since time immemorial. But the time has come when we must recognize that religion is evolutionary like everything else, and allow our minds to adapt to this fact. Jesus, and even Paul himself, asserted in so many words that religion evolves—that spiritual milk is given to man in his infancy and during the transformational periods of his development—that spiritual meat must await his intellectual maturity. But whether milk or meat there has never been a lack of guidance for any society on earth, a guidance designed, as we have stressed in our discussions, to suit the mental capacity of the day and the place in which it was given. As men are prone to retain their past habits of thought, it is not surprising that long-held and immature theologies are still with us in the twentieth century. It has been well and simply said by the German theologian Heinz Zahrnt that "There is nothing for which we need God's forgiveness so much as our theology."

PHILIP: Science itself has been guilty of many errors, but by and large there exists a notable difference between the rigid attitudes of religious believers and those who choose to call themselves scientists—or more exactly, physicists and mathematicians, whose interest is as equally concerned as religion, though on a different level, with the workings and the meaning of the universe. Religion should take science as a guide in the manner in which scientists look upon the past achievements of their long-deceased predecessors and former colleagues as evolutionary, as something on which to build. It is true that many scientists have balked at accepting the theories and experiments that have changed the paradigms of their former Newtonian conceptions, but in general the scientific communities around the world have incorporated these findings in their own work, and go on from there. The experts in applied science, who produce most of our technological output for commercial purposes, still utilize Newtonian principles, but this does not prevent the majority from acknowledging the basic discoveries of atomic and sub-atomic physics.

As we are finding out here, an openminded scholarship is the answer in both science and religion. Surely a scholarly analysis, such as Julia has presented to us through members of the Shaykhi school, should long ago have persuaded the great faiths of the world to come together in spite of their contradictions, for the basic similarities and connections between them, as well as with the mysticism of the Far East, far outweigh the internal divergence to be found in all the major beliefs of mankind. The cyclical religions build upon one another as the sciences do, but unlike the latter they are blinded by dogmatic partisanship, and traditionally have torn one another apart. They should take as a model what is happening in science. We observe today that mathematicians, biologists, physicists, ecologists, cosmologists and so on will gather together in scientific conferences and listen intently as one or another of their colleagues presents the latest findings in their own fields. A unification of science, to be sure, is still in its infancy, but this increasing meeting of the minds should nevertheless serve as an excellent example for those deeply divided religions whose members continue to believe only in their own past.

HELEN: That is all very well, Philip, and we can have no argument with you on that score. But may I call to your attention that most scientists, applied or otherwise, are nevertheless guilty of reducing religion to a rank considerably below their own studies. And the subsequent technology that results from such studies, lacking the ethics and value systems of religion, is not only adding to the belief that material progress is endless, but is causing more problems than we can handle. At the same time, along with atheists and agnostics, most scientists in Western societies scoff at any belief in the paranormal or in any life in those unseen dimensions which they themselves have discovered through their proceedings in the new physics. And yet we are learning here that not one of the Founders of religion has failed to assure us that supernatural conditions and an afterlife are not only factual, but are the very reason for their appearance and their teachings on earth. I am compelled to agree with Julia that a further step is necessary to bring our world into harmony—that unless both science and religion put their heads together and find some common ground, we'll continue to be divided by what we have conceded are the two most important influences in our lives.

PHILIP: You are quite right, my dear. I become more convinced of it as our meetings proceed. A scientific religion seems a contradiction in terms, but I can only repeat the statement of the great Einstein that "Religion without science is blind, and science without religion is lame." And a very wise scientist, who took his own advice, H. J. B. Haldane, maintained that "The wise man regulates his conduct by the theories of both religion and science." Admittedly this is a difficult combination to achieve for the average scientist in Western society, entailing the crucial leap into faith demanded by the Founders and practitioners of every religion. Unaccustomed to taking things on faith—though an honest scientist will concede that we do—and understandably put off by the superstitions and animosities of traditional religion, the scientific world in general agrees with the majority of humanists that the days of religious faith to ensure one's development are over, that man and nature alone are responsible for the future of the human species.

On the other hand the religions maintain that the scientists ignore the basic values of a man's life, are the primary cause of materialism, and give only lip-service, if at all, to the obvious achievements due solely to religious faith. When the barriers between the two will come down no one knows, but that they eventually will I am quite convinced, for true religion and true science are of one piece. I can only recall at this point the astute counsel of that giant intellect, Thomas Jefferson, in the early years of the nineteenth century, to "follow the truth, wherever it might lead." It seems that Julia's scholars in the Shaykhi school adhered to such a view, and in doing so they managed to combine a scientific approach to religion while retaining their strong faith in the ongoing system of the Prophets of God.

JULIA: I could not have said it better, Philip. The continuation of Mustafa's account of the library meeting on the Christian Scriptures is even more surprising. You will recall their scholarly findings that the statements of Jesus and the theological doctrines of St. Paul are not in accord, and many quotes from the former were brought forward to demonstrate this fact. This was not done in the spirit of criticism, but only to ascertain the truth. Ham, will you do the honors, please? The translation of the journal, as I have mentioned, was done by Doctor Varqa, who informed us that the Scriptures of other religions had long been translated into Persian for the members of the school.

HAM: "Siyyid Husayn-i-Yazdi," Mustafa writes, "asked a pertinent question at this point in relation to the extraordinary conversion of Saul of Tarsus. 'Is it not possible,' he said, 'that Saul was deliberately chosen by the risen Christ to establish a Christianity more acceptable to the Gentiles and to put a stop to the persecutions by Saul's sect of the Pharisees, whose influence, along with that of the Sadducees, had caused many seekers to abandon the teachings of Jesus and discredit his disciples? Saul himself maintained that after his blinding experience on the road to Damascus he was personally taught by the spirit of the Christ—that in his mission, as he later declared, he had become "all things to all people." The Gospels do say that Jesus directed his disciples to take his teachings to "all nations," a directive that referred in those days, I presume, to the lands surrounding Palestine. And there can be no doubt that the proven intensity and religious zeal of the former persecutor of the early Christians, his literacy and his knowledge of Hellenic customs and beliefs, would be assets of the greatest value to whatever he now perceived as the mission and rank of Jesus of Nazareth.

" 'All we know for certain,' the Siyyid went on, "is that the faith was then brought into line, through Paul's travels and apostolic letters, with the Messianic expectations of the Jews, and in time incorporated the rituals and beliefs of the Gentiles in pagan lands. Few Christians understand the remarkable concordance with pagan beliefs that found their way into the early churches in Asia Minor, Greece and Rome, nor do they realize that a final break was made with the church in Israel, which clung to the teachings of the Apostle Peter and the early disciples, who knew the Christ well. I confess that the primary place given to St. Paul's theology, even to the present day and in spite of the contradictions in the Gospels, has been difficult for me to comprehend, for I have not heard of any contemporary replacement of a Prophet's own teachings in any other religion.'

"Mulla Mahmud now spoke up with some added comments on these contradictions. 'The mystery is compounded when we read in Matthew 15:24 that Jesus at first refused to treat the daughter of a pagan woman from the north, saying that he was "sent to the lost sheep of Israel, and to them alone." And in 15:10 we find that the Christ sent his disciples on the road with certain instructions, among them that they should not follow the way to the Gentile lands but to take his teachings to the people of Israel, to the Jews. Such drastic contradictions are impossible to settle after two thousand years, except to conjecture, as a number of scholars have done, that in the case of both Paul and the Gospels certain tamperings took place to further the beliefs of various scribes one way or the other. Some of the Hadith sayings contain the accusation that a number of passages in the Old and New Testaments had been altered by copyists for their own religious purposes, and Jeremiah complained bitterly that his people no longer knew in their proper form the authoritative laws of Moses, for "How can we say," he laments, "that we are wise, and have the Word of the Lord, when scribes with their lying pens have falsified it?" Whatever the case, it has now become obvious that we need a new infusion of the truth, as Shaykh Ahmad and Siyyid Kazim have consistently upheld in this school.'

" 'It was puzzling to discover likewise,' Mulla Yusuf said, 'that neither the Gospel of St. Mark nor that of St. John makes any mention of the Virgin Birth, nor, for that matter, does St. Paul. I understand that such Virgin Births were a part of the Gentile beliefs in various lands in connection with a number of centuries-old Savior Gods, their Sky Fathers and Goddess Mothers, many of whose cults were still flourishing in the days of the Christ. In particular the widespread cult of the God Mithras remained as a rival of Christianity well into the fourth century A.D. It is a subject that needs some elucidation, and I hope that Mulla Husayn, who is in possession of a number of books from liberal theological centers in Europe, will enlighten us further on the matter. The Master has had these books translated into both Persian and

Arabic, and they show us quite clearly the startling similarities between the cults of the Savior Gods of paganism and the rituals and beliefs of the churches that developed in pagan lands.'

"Mulla Ali now leaned forward to bring up another aspect of the teachings in the Gospels. 'Before Mulla Husayn speaks, may I comment that many in his day looked upon the miracles of Jesus as proof of his divine status as the Son of God, the Jewish World Messiah. But he did not wish to be known as a miracle worker, advising several of the Jews who received physical healing at his hands to go about their business and to say nothing of what had occurred. Shaykh Ahmad was adamant that most of the reported healings of the Christ were spiritual and not physical, that blindness was spiritual blindness, that raising the dead was awakening a person who was spiritually moribund—"let the dead bury the dead" explains the symbology of many such passages in the Gospels. And yet the outstanding reason for the canonization of a saint in the Roman church is based upon the requisite miracles performed by him in the name of Christ, and this includes the saintly women as well. The Christian believers I am acquainted with have tried to persuade me that the proofs of Jesus' singular powers as the Son of God have been his walking on the water, turning water into wine, increasing a small number of loaves and fishes to feed a multitude, and such spectacular actions as the ousting of demons from the mentally ill into a passing group of swine, who then raced hysterically to drown themselves in the sea. Above all they cite his bodily resurrection from the tomb and his appearance to the disciples in his physical form. The Master has taught us that equally miraculous things are related of Krishna and the Buddha, of Moses and Zoroaster, and of other Founders of religion, but that the most remarkable miracle of all is that the very appearance of these

Manifestations in history has brought about a new and unique civilization to the world. We expect that the Qaim and the Qayyúm, after the Advent of the latter Prophet, will follow the same pattern as the rest.'

"The youthful Muhammad-Ali of Barfarush now turned to Shaykh Hasan, respectfully requesting permission to speak. 'We are fortunate in Islam,' he said, 'that the persons who took down the words of the Qoran directly from the mouth of the Prophet on any material available were seventh century Arabians whose inherited capabilities for such transmission were due to the many centuries of story-telling and desert poetry by their forefathers. Any internal contradictions to be found were changes made by the Prophet himself according to an alteration in the circumstances, and not to the whims of those who listened to his words. We can therefore believe in Muhammad's statements of reverence for the religions preceding his own, and his declaration that the Holy Bible was a Book of God, that the Jews and Christians must be respected for their beliefs, and tolerance and friendship displayed in their favor at all times.

" 'As for St. Paul, in spite of his exclusive and incorrect view of the Christ, we must acknowledge that his moral laws and his pastoral admonitions to the early churches cannot be surpassed in any other Scriptural Writ, and surely his teachings on charity or the love of one's fellow man are superior to all other expressions of this divine emotion in their eloquence and spiritual wisdom. Our scholarship in this school is indeed necessary to establish the fact that God's descent into history is a never-ending process, but we seek the truth with compassion as bidden by the Master, while recognizing with a clear perception the man-made misconceptions of the past religions, including our own.'

" 'Muhammad-Ali, as usual,' Shaykh Hasan observed, 'has shown his loving kindness toward all alike, and he speaks with authority and composure in one of such tender years. I might add at this point that the Gospels quote Jesus as saying that "No one cometh to the Father except through me," that his teachings were "the Way, the Truth and the Life"—a declaration which appears to be the strongest kind of support for the Christian belief in Jesus as the sole and everlasting representative of God's Will to man. When I inquired from Siyyid Kazim as to the meaning of this he replied that these statements were quite correct within a certain context—that during the Manifestation of a Prophet of God his teachings constitute the Way, the Truth and the Life for the period of his own Dispensation. It is God's purpose that a new and diverse civilization should be established according to the words and the teachings of the current Messenger He has sent to earth. During this period or Dispensation, no one, as the Christ declared, can better win the approval of the Father than through the guidance given to the world at that time.

" 'Unfortunately we cannot hope to persuade the Christians that every word of the literal interpretations of their Scriptures is not the pure and infallible truth for all time. A start has been made in Europe by certain philosophers and theologians, as Mulla Yusuf has mentioned, to alert the Christian world to the pagan accruals that for centuries have been a large part of the customs and beliefs of the Western churches. Mulla Husayn can best present these findings, which will add to our teachings in this school that the Christ, depicted by St. Paul as the Son of God and the sole Savior for all mankind, is in fact, as he himself declared, "a Prophet without honor in his own country." It is now evident from the recent disclosures looking toward Christian reform in Europe that the deification of the Christ, and many of the rituals and customs of the church down to the present day, were borrowed in their basic essentials not from the teachings in the Gospels, nor from those of Moses or the Israelites in the Old Testament, but from the lands surrounding Palestine. It should be remembered also that the doctrines of the early churches outside of Israel were spread during those crucial days by the pagan languages of Greece and Rome.'

"Mulla Husayn leaned forward to speak, his well-known erudition commanding the concentrated attention of the members of our circle. 'I approach this subject,' he said, 'from the standpoint of certain liberalized Christians who reverence the truth rather than a stubborn adherence to the dogmas of the church, both in their own denominations and in the church in Rome. They blame the deterioration of Christianity on the very things we have heard in this discussion—the contradictions and the many extraneous accretions on the part of the early churches in Asia Minor, as well as the present developments in Western science and rational thought. Indeed, the worship of Reason, enthroned in the so-called Enlightenment of the eighteenth century in Europe, has finally eroded the vital influence of religion everywhere, for so many centuries the one great power that has civilized a great part of the world, both East and West.

" 'But reason and science have their purposes as well as religion, and neither one nor the other should be put aside, for they create a balance for all the many attributes of human life. In that context we produce the following findings by Christian scholars themselves in the interest of spiritual truth and scientific research. Such knowledge can only enhance our belief in this school that rationality and religious faith must go hand in hand, that when this process is eventually achieved the intellectual and religious life of the world will be finally transformed.

" 'During the days of Jesus and Paul, as we have already heard, there existed in the pagan lands surrounding Palestine several long-established cults of Savior Gods and their Virgin

Mothers, the sons and wives of a Sky Father in the heavens who bestowed upon his sons the rule of the earth. A widespread recipient of such worship was the Savior God Mithras, who was "King of Kings, Lord of Lords, and Governor of the world, whose existence is everlasting." Parallel beliefs had existed in the Near and Middle East for many centuries—Dumuzi-Tammuz in Sumeria, Osiris in Egypt, Apollo in Greece, and Attis in Asia Minor, for example, with their own variations and interpretations.

" 'As for Mithras, he was adopted by the Persians from his original home as a primary deity in Mesopotamia, and was made a subsidiary god to the Zoroastrian Creator Ahura Mazda. From there his worship spread to Greece, to Rome, to Spain, to the northern areas of the European continent and as far afield in opposite directions as Britain and the Indus Valley. Surely it is not a difficult task to link the pagan figures of Mithras, his heavenly Father and his Virgin Mother to the triad of God the Father, God the Son and the Virgin Mary—the latter now bodily enthroned by the Roman church as the Queen of Heaven.

" 'And how many Christians are aware that the god Mithras, just before his cyclical death and earthly resurrection, held a farewell communion of bread and wine with his initiates—a sanctified meal that preceded his descent into the lower regions to aid the lost souls there before ascending to a throne in heaven? And how many know that the concepts of redemption, salvation, grace and eternity were already existent in these pagan religions, that the followers of Mithras used the sign of blessing on the forehead, were attired in flowing robes like those of the Roman church, and wore a headdress now known as the mitre from the name of that powerful Sun God? Mithras' sacred day was Sun Day, as it is in Christianity. In addition, the date of his annual rebirth was December twenty-fifth, now known as Christmas Day in the church, and his resurrection occurred, as it does with the Christ, at the time of the spring equinox. As late as Louis XIV in France the monarch was known as the "Sun King" and even at the present day the Emperor of Japan, "the land of the rising sun," is acclaimed by his people as a god-man, a descendant of the Mother Goddess Amaterasu. We might go around the world to present examples of these lingering pagan beliefs, but surely this is enough to convince us that the most exclusive of all the religions has little proof to offer that its otherwise influential faith is the unadulterated teaching of the Prophet Jesus. It does prove to us nevertheless that religious beliefs have consistently crossed the lines from one faith to another, and upholds the teachings of Shaykh Ahmad that the continuity and the similarities of belief throughout the lifetime of the human species cannot be denied.' "

JULIA: Mustafa goes on to record a further investigation into the two Testaments and the Book of Revelation, and if time allows we will present some telling passages that look toward the appearance of a Messianic figure, a new Word of God, whose teachings will coincide with the prophesied time of troubles in the latter days, when both political and spiritual peace, through the Will of God, will finally be established, when swords must be turned into plowshares and debilitating warfare must cease between men.

But there is one further discussion by our scholars which will aid us to envision the way in which we should approach the baffling statements in many of the Scriptures of the past— in this instance the apparent intoxication of the Prophet Noah, purportedly after the Flood in Mesopotamia. That a Prophet so lauded in the days anterior to the Flood should be later described as lying drunken in his tent is an epithet so scurrilous that it is a far more serious vilification than the criticisms directed toward Muhammad or any other Prophet. If Prophets are beings of perfect obedience to the Will of God, the pure vessels of His Revelations, what are we to make of this accusation of inebriation? This is far more than the criticism of the Christ as a wine-bibber and a glutton because of his democratic habit of sitting and eating with the second-class citizens among the Jews. In the case of Noah we have a different situation altogether—the literal reading of a Prophet's name, as in the downfall of Adam, without the help of the scientific discipline of archaeology and a research into the lives and customs of the ancient peoples of the Fertile Crescent after the Flood.

I will sum up the explanation of our Shaykhi scholars and leave it to you as to whether or not it clarifies the heated controversy, subsequent to the Flood, between Noah and his sons, Ham, Shem, and Japheth. It has already been brought to our attention that the Adam in Genesis who fell into sin, and has therefore been blamed for our openness to the evil ways of the fallen Lucifer or Satan, is not the Prophet Adam, who taught the primitive peoples of the early neolithic era in the antediluvian Fertile Crescent the knowledge of what was good and what was not good in the eyes of the One God. The people of this earliest beginning of man's civilization in what we have come to know as the Adamic life-wave of prophetic religions, were known in those days as Adam after their all-wise religious leader and Educator, manifested on earth for that purpose after many thousands of years of man's physical development, his primitive superstitions and his animistic beliefs, both on the European continent and elsewhere. The lingering remains of the Ice Age had finally disappeared and the warming of the earth at that period had made the Fertile Crescent an ideal setting for the first recorded Manifestation from God to man.

It was the people of Adam, then, who fell away from the teachings of the Prophet, giving rise to the church dogma of Original Sin on the part of the "first man." Following in the footsteps of these Adamic people Genesis reports the record of the semi-civilized tribes of Cain and Abel, the "sons" of Adam's teachings, who were tillers of the soil and shepherds, as this first book of the Bible states. Their quarrel is well-known by those who are students of the Scriptures, and the tribe of Cain moved away, no doubt in shame, to the "east of Eden."

We also learn from this allegory that the tribes who came after them—Seth, Jared, Enoch, Methusaleh, Lamech and so on—existed for long periods of time in the Fertile Crescent. The extended lives of these names suggest that these tribes, following in the wake of our first-known Prophet of God, carried on the civilizing process initiated by him, and that the names themselves represent the religious leaders of these tribes whose teachings lived on for an era of unknown duration. This list of developing peoples, before the time of Noah, appears to us today as garbled nonsense, but if we comprehend the symbolic and allegorical language in these ancient records, as found in all the Scriptures of the world, any number of interesting discoveries can be made, often with the aid of the increasing scientific knowledge of the history and movements of early man.

Now I do not pretend that the exact number of years in such records has any historical reality, but as I have said, their great length suggests to the seeker of truth the viability of approaching such accounts with the method I have outlined. This type of analysis, taught by Shaykh Ahmad to the scholars of the Shaykhi school, brought them to the conclusion that the Prophet Noah himself, who appeared in Mesopotamia before the Flood, was in no way involved in the episode reported in Genesis 9:1 to 9:29. In fact it is not difficult to see that the records with which we are dealing here, three hundred and fifty years after the Flood according to "Noah's" recorded age at that latter time, refer to the eponymous name of a tribe of Noachic believers whose religious "sons," Ham, Shem and Japheth, eventually took off in all directions to settle in other areas of the Near and Middle East and the Mediterranean.

The story reads, as you may recall, that before their departure Ham found his father Noah lying drunken in his tent, tattled to his brothers Shem and Japheth, and earned for himself and his descendants the curse of the elder Noah. The scene is played out as if a number of single persons were involved, and this is not unusual in many of the ancient documents under the scrutiny of scholars and theologians. The consensus seems to be, as reported by Mustafa in the journal, that the drunkenness of Noah can be explained in a very mundane manner. Like many of the tribes before and after the Flood these Mesopotamian peoples spent a large portion of their time attending to their vineyards and the making of wine, and the tribe of Noah—farmers and vintners in the later neolithic period following the Flood—became addicted to their own product, and often lay intoxicated and naked in their tents. So much for this type of exegesis, only approximate at best. But I find it a great help in the classroom when either historical or allegorical circumstances need to be understood.

REVEREND AHEARN: I have read a number of books on the deep spiritual meanings beneath the surface in Genesis, and I advise everyone to do so. But I have not yet run across an explanation of the strange behavior of the post-diluvian Noah, a bizarre account that most of us, I presume, have overlooked. On the other hand, some of my agnostic and atheistic friends have utilized such passages to downgrade the power of religion in general, and seem to take pleasure in bringing up the age-old criticisms of the Founders themselves. It is amazing to me that one can still hear or read that Muhammad's visionary revelations and subsequent delivery of the Qoran—a book admitted to be without peer in the Arabic language by a man unable to read or write, and containing teachings and laws exactly suited to the people of his day—were not only self-contrived but undoubtedly due to epileptic convulsions. In addition to these scornful contentions it is maintained that he accomplished purely by the sword and a clever tongue his self-appointed mission of eliminating idolatry—surely a magnificent achievement one way or the other—and that after his fiftieth year he was given over to womanizing with a houseful of wives. But if one looks closely at the full story of Muhammad's life from his early youth to the day of his death, a picture emerges of a healthy, virtuous, trustworthy and compassionate man, a chosen Messenger very much like his predecessor Moses and the latter's deputy Joshua in Palestine, who, like Muhammad, were equipped with the forces necessary to subdue the enemies who stood in the way of a newly ordained faith.

As for Moses himself, let me recall for you that he was known in Egypt as a murderer, for he killed a man for viciously attacking a fellow-Hebrew in that land before his Prophethood. This act, along with his wiping out in the wilderness of Sinai of the unregenerate backsliders who had persisted in their former idolatrous worship of the Golden Calf of Canaan, is another cause for finger-pointing by the atheists. But can these retributive acts of Moses, necessary for the success of his mission, compare in the end with the bringing of the Ten Commandments from Mount Sinai, and causing the eventual establishment of one of the most prolific civilizations known to the world? All the way through Jewish history the people of this widespread faith—scattered as they are in every quarter of the globe—can be regarded as among the most talented and productive people in any culture they have adopted. The present state of Israel, admittedly, is a different matter, necessarily engaged with all its secular energy in maintaining its homeland as a sovereign entity. Israel and its enemies are outstanding examples of the Biblical warning that cries will be raised in the latter days for "peace, peace," and there will be no peace.

HAM: Doctor Varqa pointed out to us that none of the Prophets has promised political peace to the world, with one exception, the Qayyúm, and this revelatory promise will take considerable time to establish after thousands of years of ethnic and nationalistic turmoil. The obvious readjustments needed to overcome our present state of political national-ism, as well as eliminate the hatreds and contempt of our racialism and religious prejudice, will postpone for many years a final peace, both political and spiritual, on a planetary scale. But certain prophetic statements have been made in the new faith—that political peace between the most advanced of the world's nations will begin its binding force around the end of the present century, that the countries of Europe will be united as one economic unit, and that communism, due to the bankruptcy of its atheistic system, will have lost its power to sustain a dictatorship in the face of a growing demand for democratic and economic reforms.

There seems to be ample hope, my friends, that the Qayyúm, the Christ of our age as his followers maintain, and as Julia and I have come to believe, will be known in time as the "Prince of Peace" promised to the world by Isaiah's visions of the future. This latter-day Prophet, his laws coming forth from the mountain of the Lord, was expected by Isaiah to carry upon his shoulders the governance of all mankind, during which time a planetary peace, due to his powerful spiritual teachings and his counsels of justice, would be established. The Will of the Lord of Hosts, Isaiah declared, would bring this supreme event to fruition, and in this long-looked-for apocalyptic Day of God the nations would turn to that mountain in all matters of importance to the world and to the moral behavior of mankind. Justice and Unity above all, Doctor Varqa said, are the guiding motives for the laws of the Qayyúm, and the peoples of the world, after a chaotic period of indifference to his Advent, will be helpless to prevent the prophesied Day of Judgment.

JULIA: We must realize that some of the things for which the Prophets are criticized are due to this quality of Justice, for all of them are endowed with this primary attribute as well as with love and compassion. At the same time the Prophets have a human side in addition to their divine aspects or they would be unable to function during their missions on earth. Those who have looked upon the Christ as "meek and mild," for example, must counterbalance this view with his angry overturning of the money tables in the Temple—and surely his criticism of a "generation of vipers" is scarcely in keeping with the innocuous description of a "gentle Jesus" so often praised in the Christian hymns. Prophets are centers of divine power, and they possess the God-given ability to use the circumstances available to them to express their absolute authority when the occasion warrants. Once this is understood the various religions should recognize that the Founders are endowed with the spiritual endorsement to do what they personally will to do in forwarding the faith they have come to earth to establish. The drastic actions of Moses in the wilderness, of our Father Abraham in Canaan and Muhammad in Arabia, should be appraised in this light, including any mundane behavior involving a Prophet of God. But this independence applies, we must understand, to his physical actions and not to the Revelation itself, which is solely due to the Will of God.

REVEREND AHEARN: The story of Abraham in Genesis, the first biographical account of its kind in the Old Testament, is a very human story indeed, and brings to vivid life not only his own trials and vicissitudes in the path of God, but those of his immediate family and descendants. Following Julia's mention of Abraham's connection with Islam through his son Ismael, I looked further into the claims of the Muslims, and found in various accounts that this ancestral Prophet had not only visited the Hijaz in Arabia from the idolatrous city of Ur in Mesopotamia and had taught there the belief in One God, but had also repaired the ancient ruins of the original Kaaba in Mecca which the Muslims maintain was first erected by the Prophet Adam, who appears to have traveled rather extensively as well. And they likewise maintain that Abraham visited Ismael later from Canaan, that during this sojourn the two together dedicated the idolatrous cube once more to the glory of God, embellished it with the famous Black Stone that had fallen from the heavens, and had prayed that idolatry would someday disappear from that land. Whether or not they traveled further south to Arabia Felix, as a few of the writings maintain, there have been no Sabean records found there to verify this claim.

GEORGINA: Apropos of the subject of Scriptural criticism, I recall my indignation, as a Catholic, when some writings I had run across depicted the Christ as a charismatic rabbi deluded by the conviction of his early return to earth before a generation or so had elapsed—a misreading, as already suggested here, of the word generation. In discussing this recently with Reverend Ahearn he presented a possible clue on the element of time by pointing out that a thousand years is declared in the Bible to be a Day in the eye of the Creator, and therefore of the Prophets. One might conjecture, then, that when the Book of Revelation given to St. John announces that the Christ is returning "soon" or "quickly" it meant what it said in this time context, that these cyclical life-spans of religion appear to the Prophets as of far less duration than they do to our human minds. And we should note in this connection that if the Prophets are equal in their status in spite of the difference or potency of their missions, then the same "Holy Spirit" can be said to return in any one of them, and the Christ's reappearance in the Day of Muhammad and in the Glory of the Father at the time of the end is a valid conclusion, no matter in what body this Spirit may manifest itself on earth. In all such matters as this, the Reverend felt very strongly, he said, that there are layers of esoteric meanings behind the outer statements in Scriptural Writ, and that we have a right to speculate on their hidden import no matter how far afield we may go.

JULIA: I have occasionally opened up such discussion in the classroom, Georgina, and it makes for very lively, very provocative exchanges. But things sometimes get out of hand in such sessions, for the pupils of today find it difficult to sustain an interest in metaphysical affairs and prefer to pinpoint attention on the peccadilloes and sexual behavior of certain figures in the world's Scriptures—the favorite pastime in our culture of name-calling, no matter the recipient, sacred or profane. If one of the pupils, for example, points out with some disdain that Muhammad married a nine-year-old child in Medina who later became his favorite wife and companion in his household, another voice will respond to put him down and retort that Solomon, after all, had eight hundred wives, that David did away with the husband of Bathsheba in order to possess her for himself, and that incidents of incest and adultery are openly recorded in various Scriptures.

This type of classroom interchange, of course, is academically out of order, but it allows me nevertheless to bring out the fact that many such occurrences in the past are in keeping with certain customs of the time, as in the case of Muhammad's protective marriage to Ayesha, the daughter of his closest companion, Abu Bakr, who became the first Caliph after the Prophet's death. And when a member of the class accused

Zoroaster of taking the drug haoma to further his visions of other dimensions and his revelatory relationship with the One God, Ahura Mazda, I was able to state emphatically that there is no proof whatever that he made any personal use of such a drug, and without any record in religious history or in the Zoroastrian Scriptures themselves the accusation is worthless. As for the misbehavior of Abraham's incestuous nephew Lot and his daughters, of King David and Bathsheba, of the people of Sodom and Gomorrah and many other profligate wrongdoers recorded in the Scriptures of one religion or another, their waywardness is obviously a lesson in immorality and is not intended as idle gossip or scandal. I tell my pupils that their critical attitude toward such past behavior should be directed instead to deploring the corruption and immoral conduct of the generation to which they and their peers belong.

On several occasions I have stated my belief that a new world faith is in the making, a faith that is eminently suited to the days in which we live. But a disinterested silence, and the possibility of being accused of proselytizing in the classroom, have kept me so far from putting its unifying theology and principles on the class agenda. These young people, brought up in a materialistic, humanistic culture, find it impossible to imagine that any religious faith can ever again take possession of the minds and hearts of the people in our modern technological civilization in the West. I have no doubt, however, that in time the increasingly dangerous aspects of a changing world will bring them around to another point of view. Don tells me that there arc already groups of declared young believers in our schools and colleges, actively spreading the principles of the new faith. This is still a drop in the bucket in our educational system, but as everyone is aware, there is always a starting point for anything new in the world.

MADILYN: In the nineteenth century Matthew Arnold wrote, with his usual insight, that "We appear to be wandering between two worlds, one dead, the other powerless to be born." Arnold was an eminent poet, critic and educator, as we all know, who died in 1888 before word of the new faith had reached his ears in England, or he might very well have hailed it as a breakthrough to the future. In that same year Sarvepali Radhakrishnan was born in India, was later knighted for his intellectual achievements and statesmanship, and as Julia has noted, presided as President of India from 1962 to 1967. As one of the most advanced of the modern thinkers in the Eastern hemisphere his written words are a startling confirmation of much that we have heard and said in these meetings, and reflect, I believe, a possible and even probable return to the hopes and dreams of the Romance poets in Europe, whose vision of a world of harmony and brotherhood had faded into insignificance. Radhakrishnan's declaration, though short, is so telling in its orientation toward a new age of religious unification that I have brought it with me this evening to share with you.

"We cannot afford," he wrote, "to waiver in our determination that the whole of humanity should be a united people, whose Muslim, Christian, Jew, Buddhist and Hindu would stand together by a common devotion, not to something behind but to something ahead, not to a racial past or a geographical location but to a great dream of a world society with a universal religion of which the historical faiths are but branches"—the branches, I would add, of a planetary tree. Many such images of unity are being presented today by thoughtful writers, and one of them is particularly apt in our modern civilization—the comparison of our planet to a spaceship whose crew must work together in harmony and friendship in order to prevent the possibility of ultimate catastrophe. Such images, poetical, religious or technological, are arising with increasing fervor in the second half of the twentieth century, but so far the sovereign nations pay little attention to such perceptions, and appear more fearful of a unified world and a shared world government than of a nuclear war or some other devastating blow to the human race.

DON: Surely the world can take our United States as a prime example of unification, brought about by the foresight of our founding fathers and those who followed in their footsteps. In the early days of our country, two hundred years ago, our Presidents were statesmen—in particular, in my estimation, Washington, Jefferson, Madison and Monroe—Virginians every one. I am not faulting the following Presidents by this choice but we all have our favorite characters in government, and mine appear to be four of the first Presidents who laid the basic foundation for our American democracy. These were men of great religious faith, and though I paid little heed to this in the past I recently discovered a statement by James Madison, the acknowledged "master builder of the Constitution," that reflects the sentiments in those early days which have long been absent in both our government and in ourselves. "We have staked the whole future of American civilization," he said, "not upon the powers of government, far from it. We have staked the future of all our political institutions upon the capacity of each and all of us to govern ourselves, to control ourselves, to sustain ourselves according to the Ten Commandments of God." Such statements did not mean much to me until our recent visit to Chicago, but since that time, as you are all aware, I am quite a different man.

HAM: We haven't forgotten, Don, that you brought up the subject of the place of youth in religion. It appears to have been true in the past that a disproportionate number of the younger members of a declining or corrupt society, less addicted perhaps to established religious beliefs, are at-tracted to the teachings of a new Prophet, and in many cases have carried the heaviest burdens of persecution and martyr-dom. This does not mean, as we have already pointed out, that persons more advanced in years are not equally prepared to spread a new faith and to give up their lives in the process. This is eminently true in the global religion we have been discussing here, as is clearly evident in the wide range of believers in all segments of society in Persia and in other cultures around the world, rich and poor alike.

REVEREND AHEARN: We might add, Ham, that the Founders of the world's faiths, without exception, began their missions in the springtime of their lives. Jesus was thirty or less when he began his teaching in Israel, and was cruelly put to death three years later. Moses, Zoroaster, Muhammad, Krishna and the Buddha were all young men when they were chosen as creative vehicles for establishing a new religion and a new civilization. Our present cultures tend to forget the influence and achievements of youth in the past history of the world. We see nothing today that parallels the capabilities of figures in their early years such as King David, for example, who captured and rebuilt Jerusalem and wrote the immortal Psalms. One can point to Alexander the Great and the world of the young Greeks, to the Pharaohs of Egypt and the creative genius of their younger subjects, to the youthful Emperors and Kings of many nations and a host of their representatives in the prime of life engaged in politics, in building great cities, in artistic endeavors and literature, and in the study of science, religion and philosophy.

On the contrary, as we have all agreed, our young people, even beyond their college years, remain immature in com-parison, are largely disinterested in government, in ethical matters or religion, make no effort to learn of other cultures or civilizations, and dwell in general on their future security and their own personal happiness. They should take to heart the statement of Nathaniel Hawthorne that "Happiness in this world, if it comes at all, is incidental. Make it the object of pursuit and it leads us on a wild-goose chase, and is never attained."

HAM: All the more power, then, to the young people of today who are turning their backs on our money culture, and those among them, according to the Hellers, who are joining the faith in increasing numbers and departing for foreign lands to spread the word. Unfortunately, those whose goal in life is hedonism—the principle that pleasure and personal liberty are the highest goals to be found in this earthly existence—are unimpressed by these young people, perceiving them as members of a cult or followers of a "false prophet"—a designation to which the Christ, including that of a blasphemer and political rebel, was himself subject in the land of his birth. But there is a way, Jesus declared, to discover the truth of this matter. A true claimant to Prophethood will prove by his fruits—that is, the fruits for mankind following upon the application of his teachings—that he is indeed a manifestation of spiritual grace and not, as Jesus expressed it, a "wolf in sheep's clothing." He also warned that many impostors would attempt to mislead the world, claiming that they were the very person of the Christ returned to earth, using his name and saying "I am he." We know that this has been the case through many centuries since the Crucifixion, and that all such claimants have come to naught. No true Prophet, the Founder of a great religion, has claimed to be a former Manifestation returned to earth in person, and all have had distinctive names and personalities. And surely the abundant fruits of the civilizations produced on earth by their very appearance cannot possibly be credited to what Jesus has delineated as a "wolf in sheep's clothing."

JULIA: It is, of course, some time before these fruits are observable. All the Prophets have had to await their final recognition, and this can vary according to the state of the people and the amount of hostility in the clergy and the government. Consider that the mention of Jesus in the writings of his day amounted to little more than a few lines by the Jewish historian Josephus and the Romans Tacitus and Suetonius, referring to a man known to some as the Christos or Messiah who had preached a new faith to the Jews and was crucified. In fact the great majority of the people knew little of Jesus' life and teachings for three hundred years or more, at which time the Emperor Constantine in Byzantium—the new Roman capital on the Bosphorus—converted to the faith for political purposes and made it the state religion.

In the light of the continuity of the great Semitic religions, such an eventual recognition, in one way or another, was bound to take place. For Christianity did not arise in a vacuum of primitive superstition but sprang directly from the Old Testament of the Jews, just as Islam followed in the footsteps of both Judaism and the New Testament. These religions were therefore, in this sense, one continuous faith, and were destined by the Will of God to flourish as a dynamic and creative force, in each case, for at least a thousand years. Although all of them may seem to us to be opposed, they were revealed to reform a declining faith in their own area, or in the case of Islam to rejuvenate a diverse and idolatrous people with a distinctive and wholly dissimilar history.

Now you might very well ask in this connection if there have been any failures in the missions of the Prophets. The only record we have come across can be found in the Qoran, where we learn in statements by Muhammad that the Prophets Hud and Salih preached in vain to the idol-ridden people of Yemen and the Hadramaut coast of southern Arabia, who successfully resisted, along with stubborn pockets of Sabeans, Jews and Christians, the attempts of these Manifestations to transform the deterioration of the once-flourishing cultures in this area. Whatever the actual case, the Qoran and the history of this region both record that the rapidly declining civilization of Arabia Felix during this period was subject to massive calamities, to the bursting of a great dam and prolonged droughts, and to a consequent desiccation of the whole coast.

We might mention again at this juncture that one of the titles of Muhammad is "The Seal of the Prophets." The belief of most Muslims that their own Prophet is the last in the line of the major Founders of the great prophetic religions is more appropriate than the world is yet able to comprehend. The theological explanation for this title must wait for another time and, God willing, we shall later address this subject with the aid of the Revelations of the Qaim and the Qayyúm. In our final meeting in two weeks we shall once more refer to Mustafa's journal as we approach the Hour of the Declaration in Shiraz of the Herald Prophet, that shining light who falls between the past religious Dispensations and those of the future.

HAM: We have received a notice, by the way, that the books we ordered on the new faith will arrive here in three or four weeks. They will be obtainable in this house by any of you who wish to pursue a continuing and detailed knowledge of what we have introduced to you in our discussions. And once again we thank you, one and all, for your willing participation in a most exceptional, and, I believe, unprecedented coming together of academic minds. You have made it possible for Julia and me to redeem our great debt to Doctor Varqa in a most unexpected and inspiring way, and to pass on to you, as friends who are both intelligent and intellectual, our firm belief that the future civilization of the world is in the creative hands of a planetary Prophet of God. You have done this without major objections, and without causing us possible embarrassment for our acceptance of the new faith with unreserved enthusiasm. And for all this, dear friends, I repeat once again that we are more than grateful to each and every one of you.

As for refreshments tonight, Reverend Ahearn and I decided some days ago to relieve the ladies of kitchen duty. He has brought us a home-baked carrot cake with raisins and nuts and all sorts of unspecified ingredients, while I have endeavored to produce some French ice cream to accompany this masterpiece. Coffee as always—and if any of you wishes to add to the calories there is hot chocolate available in the kitchen.

VI   Darkness Into Dawn

HAM: Before we settle down to a final meeting tonight, Julia and I must share with you an important fact that has come to our attention through our goods friends Madilyn and Don. In the past week they have passed on to us a number of recent scholarly studies on the episodes connected with the search, the finding, the claims, and the subsequent development of the Herald Prophet's introductory mission in Persia. They are somewhat different in certain aspects from what has been generally accepted in the past. But this in no way lessens the dramatic thrust of the prophesied Day of Resurrection in May of 1844.

The fullest account that has come down to us concerning the history of the early years of the faith was not undertaken until 1888 by an ardent and dedicated believer, Muhammad-i-Zarandi, known as Nabil. A rich storehouse of material, a great deal of it compiled from second-hand sources emotionally involved in the unique events taking place in Persia and the holy cities in Iraq, this remarkable volume has comprised for the faith a Bible of unorthodox occurrences from the time of the Forerunners Shaykh Ahmad and Siyyid Kazim to the execution of the Herald Prophet in Tabriz in 1850 and the barbaric persecution of his remaining followers in Persia in the next three years.

This abundant source material, incomparable in its coverage and spiritual dedication, has stood alone in the faith as the fixed and definitive text of its initial events from the birth of Shaykh Ahmad in 1753 to the departure from Persia in

1853 of most of the believers still alive for the city of Baghdad. There in this Ottoman city they joined their former leader, Mirza Husayn-Ali of Nur and Tehran, who was exiled to Baghdad in that year by the Qajars and the Persian ulama for his open and consistent upholding of the Cause of the Herald. From later accounts we learn of the trials and tribulations of these residual believers in Baghdad, their disorganization and internal divisions in spite of the strong leadership of Husayn-Ali, the highly respected son of a one-time wealthy landowner and minister of the court, Mirza Buzurg of Nur in Mazindaran. Ten years later, in 1863, due to the wise maneuvers and spiritual influence of Husayn-Ali, esteemed by Persians and Iraqis alike for his judgment and advice, and loved by all who knew him, the mission of the Herald was vindicated and the faith assumed the name by which it is now known the world over.

The Hellers have informed us that writings previous to the history compiled by Nabil are being discovered in increasing numbers by dedicated and high-caliber scholars within the faith. Some are contradictory in accounts as expected, others are filled with legendary and mythical material derived from past beliefs, including those of other religions, and a good many have passed from hand to hand, supposedly corrected or amended, or altered to suit the ideas of the author. A number of these sources are still in private hands in Iran and Iraq, and have now become available for inspection. Altogether these hitherto unexamined writings have permitted the members of the faith to incorporate new possibilities of historic fact, and we must now take them into consideration.

Although Doctor Varqa's martyrdom precluded his knowledge of such recent studies, and therefore our own awareness, he did point out to us that the writings of Mirza Jani and his brother Mirza Sabeh of Kashan, and that portion of Mustafa's journal written in Shiraz in the summer of 1844, following the Declaration, differed in a number of aspects from the generally accepted account of this long-awaited Day. The affiliation of these writers with the Shaykhi school, their companionship with key members of the Siyyid's inner circle, and their sensitivity to the high degree of Messianic spirit then sweeping the Shia world, should indicate, I believe, that these contemporary and in some cases eyewitness accounts of the search and finding of the Promised One of Islam are as near to the actual happenings of that highly confused time as one is able to extract from conflicting reports. The journal in particular, we believe, will aid us in understanding the subsequent four years of speculation as to the true status of the charismatic young Shia whose claims aroused Persia and Iraq to an extravagant display of excitement, both negative and positive.

JULIA: In the past two centuries the world's faiths have undergone what has been scornfully designated by some as the "higher criticism," a process of exegesis that attempts to purify the various Scriptures of their obvious errors and contradictions, and interpret them from a more rational standpoint. But such scorn is no longer in fashion, and as Ham has indicated we should welcome whatever emerges from a scholarly and detailed search for the truth. This in no way pertains to the written words of the Twin Prophets of the new faith, the first Scriptures in the handwriting of the Founders themselves or of their chosen amanuenses. We may properly apply such methods, however, to certain physical events which recent discoveries have brought to our attention. To allow our thoughts to become static on the details of a faith so new in the world would confine us to the same rigidities found in every religion in the past. In order, therefore, to present to you what Ham and I consider a fairly accurate account of the Declaration and its aftermath in Shiraz—an account that is echoed recently in newly discovered writings—we will turn once again to Mustafa's journal. But first, in order to aid us in comprehending the status claimed by a young Shia merchant of Shiraz and Bushihr in 1844, we need to go back to the late spring of 1841 in Karbila, following Mustafa's report on the library meeting on the Christian faith.

The year 1257, or 1841, in spite of a general downturn in the textile and mercantile enterprises in Persia due to Western competition, was a busy time for the new shop in Karbila, and entries in the journal, except for one strange episode in the classroom of the school and its consequences, consisted in the main of the ongoing disturbances against the rule of the Turks. Mustafa takes note of the fact that during the times of pilgrimage, when the holy city was crowded beyond its capacity, the agitation was increased to such an extent that the members of the school kept discreetly to themselves, and that he himself locked the front door of the shop and dealt only with his trusted clientele, most of them well-to-do Persians in the town.

Doctor Varqa had informed us that Mustafa's grandfather and his uncles, Mirza Jani and Mirza Sabeh, were among those who had made a considerable fortune as merchants, were well-known in Baghdad and the holy cities, as well as in the business centers of Persia and as far to the east as India and Afghanistan, factors that undoubtedly contributed to the flourishing of the new family enterprise in Karbila. Like others of the mercantile class whose wealth had prevented them from feeling the pinch in the world of trade, this was a family, the ancestors of Doctor Varqa, who epitomized the general honesty, the moral integrity, and the mutual trust of the merchants of Persia. The Prophet Muhammad himself was a highly successful merchant in his younger years, a fact that was no doubt instrumental in establishing this particular class as the most respectable and respected of the otherwise corruptible subjects of the Qajars.

But let me go directly to an unusual entry in the journal, for we believe that Mustafa, level-headed and dedicated to the path of truth as he saw it, can best evoke for us the approaching signs of the Advent of the Qaim, the Herald Prophet of the Qayyúm.

"During the days of pilgrimage in 1257," he writes, "my shop was visited via the back door by a total stranger, who declared that he was a merchant from Persia and wished to see the goods that I had put on display. I was so taken with his courteous manner and the charm of his personality that I deserted my other client altogether, deeming the young man, obviously a Siyyid by his dress and turban, to be a member of an elite family in Persia and possibly connected with the ruling aristocracy, some of whom were in trade. Quietly he appraised the merchandise on view, pronouncing the goods as superior in both quality and price. He then purchased a bolt of lavendar silk—a rare commodity in the tightness of the present market—and thanking me warmly, and apologizing to my client, he departed with a final word which surprised me. 'I shall see you again in the Master's classroom,' he said, 'where perhaps you will note what occurs there. And I will gladly speak to the proper people of the excellence of your merchandise.'

"The magnetic attraction of that young Siyyid, his poise and his winning smile, lingered in my memory until the following week, when I found time to attend a lecture at the school. I settled myself in the back row, hoping to locate his presence there, if indeed he was a part-time pupil of Siyyid Kazim during pilgrimages to the holy city. I saw no one who remotely resembled him, and prepared to take my usual notes on the lecture, a stirring exhortation once more on our duty to recognize the Qaim at his appearance. Perhaps a half-hour or so elapsed when a movement at the doorway from the courtyard caused me to glance at the figure who was quietly entering the room. With a start I realized that the young merchant from Persia, in some astonishing way, had kept his word to me on the very day of my attendance, and was now seating himself not four feet away to my left where I was able to observe him with careful attention.

"The very appearance of that young Siyyid stirred me once again to a strong feeling of anticipation, as if he were somehow different in degree and rank from the rest of us. Indeed I felt that he intended for me to receive this impression, but just why or for what purpose I could not possibly imagine. I have often thought that my sensitivity to certain mystical aspects behind the surface of one's ordinary comprehension was inclined to carry me beyond the limits of reality, but we were taught in the school that this was a trait to be developed, and I make no excuses for certain conclusion that I shall present in this journal. One must balance the rational mind with the undeniable occurrences which have no rational explanation, and I shall not hold back when such an event takes place.

"I do not hesitate, therefore, to vouch for what happened next in that room. And I hereby report that suddenly the Master ceased speaking, looked toward the rear of the room, and rose from his seat on the platform. Now I had heard that a reading of minds was a skill accepted by the Sufis and other unorthodox and esoteric branches of Islam but I had never been present on such an occasion. I can only say that the Master then returned to his seat, briefly completed his exhortation, and dismissed the class. Meanwhile the young merchant had turned to me with a smile as if he wished me to remember this moment and to carefully observe his appearance once more. He need not have been concerned, for his face I shall never forget—delicately handsome, aristocratic, paler than most Persians, with dark eyes communicative of some hidden knowledge which left me desirous of learning more of his background. Was he a person known in Karbila, I wondered, or perhaps a former acquaintance of Siyyid Kazim, a Shaykhi believer in one of the city centers in Persia? No one else in the classroom except Shaykh Hasan-i-Zunuzi, who had taken a seat at the side of the room, had taken any notice of his arrival or early departure. This seemed a sign to me that his comings and goings at the school were known to the regular scholars and were not a cause for wonderment or curiosity.

"As we gathered for conversation in the courtyard, Shaykh Hasan approached me and drew me aside to a shady bench, away from the rest of the pupils. The Shaykh, as a close companion of the Master, was privy to most of the happenings behind the scenes of the school's daily curricula, and it was obvious that he wished to discuss something of importance in the wake of the sudden dismissal of the class.

" 'Mulla Mustafa,' he said, 'I may be speaking out of turn on a certain matter in relation to the Master and the young personage who appeared today in the classroom. I request that you do not spread to the pupils in this school what I am about to tell you. This young man has visited the holy city in the past and has not only sat among the pupils from time to time at the lectures but has been seen by me visiting the Siyyid in his residence. I have not until recently been involved with him personally, nor have most of the pupils, and in fact he speaks very seldom aside from exchanging friendly greetings with the younger scholars. As the Master has not only encouraged you to take notes within the school, but has embraced your family as trusted believers in his message, I am about to suggest that you put down for posterity the following event, which has left me uncertain as to what to believe.

" 'First of all I must confess to you that I have been one of those who have thought in the past that Siyyid Kazim, with whom I have worked so closely for so long, might himself be the Promised One of Islam. When I dared to express on a recent occasion the conjecture on the part of a number of the Shaykhi scholars to this effect, including myself, he replied almost angrily that this was not only incorrect but a blasphemous thought that should have no place in the school. He reminded me that Shaykh Ahmad emphatically stated that neither of the founders of the school would be alive to witness the Advent, a fact that he himself had passed on to the pupils on numerous occasions, exhorting them to set out in search of the Qaim at his own demise. He was, he said sternly, but one of the privileged Forerunners of a new Dispensation, a verity that should long have been thoroughly understood by the scholars of the school. I felt properly rebuked, and asked to be forgiven for entertaining such a view—it was due to his great wisdom and intuitive knowledge, I said, that we had dared to think of him in these terms. I was duly pardoned, but a subsequent occurrence brought forcibly to my attention that he had not forgotten these errant conjectures, as complimentary as they might have seemed to one who did not possess the Master's spiritual gifts.

" 'Before I tell you of this strange occurrence,' the Shaykh continued, 'I must point out to you that a long-held Shia doctrine, as well as our own Shaykhi belief, pertains to a series of Babs or Gates to the Promised One, whose spiritual attainments have raised them to the elevated rank of keeping alive on earth a connection with the Qaim—that Holy Soul whom the orthodox Shias perceive as the Hidden Imam, the last of the Imams of the House of Muhammad. Surely you yourself have been taught in Qum this doctrine of successive Gates over the past one thousand years, sometimes three or four at a time, and you have no doubt heard it said that Shaykh Ahmad and Siyyid Kazim are considered by many Shaykhi believers to be the Babs or Gates to the Final Days and the coming Apocalypse. Such theological constructions are deeply ingrained in the minds of a great majority of Shias, and in my estimation should not be ignored as the Advent approaches. The general population is much more likely to accept the claims of a new Gate than the final appearance of the Promised One himself.

" 'You must also be aware, Mustafa, that although this school denies that a Hidden Imam from the past will arise from certain fabled cities in planes surrounding the earth, we nevertheless concur in the overall Messianic belief that a Promised One, the Qaim, will arise within the faith of Islam. According to the Shaykhi teachings this prophesied spiritual leader has already been born into the world and is alive somewhere in Persia, his identity and whereabouts still unknown and his person unrecognized. The role of the Qaim in our Shaykhi doctrine is not to rule either Islam or the world in a new Dispensation, as the orthodox Shias believe, but to herald the coming Manifestation of the true Lord of the New Age, the Qayyúm, the return of the Holy Spirit in its most potent form, whose mission would unify the peoples of the earth. These conflicting doctrines will no doubt play a crucial part in the early days of the mission of the Qaim. No one knows how the Cause of God will work itself out in this respect, but we must be prepared for any number of unexpected contingencies.'

" 'I have often heard these various doctrines being discussed in Kashan,' I replied, 'but such complicated beliefs have in times past been incomprehensible to me. I am deeply grateful for all you are telling me and I shall duly record your explanations for future remembrance. They will not see the light of day until after the Advent, of that I assure you.'

"By now the pupils had dispersed to their houses or to study in the classrooms and the Shaykh relaxed against the trunk of a tree behind the bench. 'A few days ago, at an early hour,' he informed me, 'I was sent for by the Master as he was about to leave his residence. He merely remarked that a special person who had sat in the classroom on several occasions in the past had returned to Karbila as a pilgrim, and he wished me to accompany him to visit the young man in his present quarters. No name or any other information was given to me, and the Master was silent as we walked to a small house not far from the school. At the door we were met by a youth of about twenty-one-or-two, obviously a Siyyid, whose face seemed familiar to me, and as he embraced the Master and greeted me warmly I recalled that I had seen him recently in the classroom and entering the Master's residence. Although Siyyid Kazim returned his embrace as if he were an old friend, he remained strangely silent as we were led to the second floor.

" 'The following half-hour was astonishing to me. Scarcely a word was exchanged in that upper room, which was filled with the fragrance of flowers placed in large vases on the rich Persian carpet that covered the floor. The setting was beautiful beyond compare, and I felt as though Paradise had descended upon us as the young Siyyid bowed his head in a brief prayer and then chanted in the most mellow tones the rewards recorded in the Hadith for those who looked forward to the Hour of Resurrection and a New Day. While the chanting permeated my being, I recalled that I had seen this same youth in the past week standing at the entrance of the Shrine of Imam Husayn, so profoundly absorbed in realms of communication beyond one's average understanding that he attracted groups of onlookers amazed at his spiritual concentration and the copious tears that poured from his eyes.

" 'This youth, Mustafa, is the same young Siyyid who sat beside you a short time ago in the classroom, when you and I witnessed a most unusual communication between the Master and the back row, and it may be that a silent interchange was likewise taking place in that upper room. Above all I was struck by the unprecedented humility exhibited by the Master toward our host, making the point, I am now convinced, that if he himself were the Promised One, his position of superiority during this visit would have been amply displayed.

" 'There is no doubt, however, that our young host was in total charge of proceedings. This was amply evident when he poured a delicious drink into a silver chalice—a type of metal cup forbidden to the clergy of Islam for reasons I no longer recall—while he quoted a verse from the Qoran which seemed to me to be a symbolic message of the coming Apocalypse—"A drink of a pure beverage shall their Lord give them." The Master drank from that forbidden cup, and I, of course, did likewise, which struck me anew that this young Siyyid from Persia was in some mysterious way superior in rank to our beloved teacher. Shortly afterward he rose and led us to the doorway below, bidding us farewell with appreciation for our visit and bestowing upon us two beautifully wrapped gifts with such warmth and benevolence in his manner that for a moment I felt I had reached that plane described in the Qoran where "all is peace and all secure," a place without care or worldly concern.

" 'The Master continued his silence as we returned to the residence, satisfied, I am sure, that neither I, nor any other member of the school, could any longer consider him a candidate for the sacred rank of the Qaim. The actual status of our host on that strangely ambiguous visit, however, remained an enigma to me. Since that time I have prayed diligently for enlightenment, and it has come to me, in keeping with all I have said here, that the striking charisma and obvious independence of that young visitor could only be reasonably explained if one's mind could entertain an exciting thought—that this mysterious youth, only partially known to any of us, could very well be one of the appointed Gates for these Messianic days, or, as I now suspect, the sole Gate delineated in Islamic prophecy as the Fourth Support, the final Gate to the imminent Advent of the Promised One. As the Master has stated repeatedly that he will not be alive for the Declaration of the Hour, I can only presume that his untiring proclamation of the coming Apocalypse has earned him the great bounty of knowing and receiving assurance of the future from the immediate representative of the unknown Qaim.'

"Shaykh Hasan's stirring recital," the journal goes on, "left me overwhelmed with joy. For I now felt certain that the captivating personality who had been in my shop, had conversed with me, and had shown me his personal attention in the classroom, could be none other than that Fourth Support, the Gate to that Holy Soul who was even now, as taught by Siyyid Kazim, alive somewhere in Persia. There and then, on that bench in the courtyard, I vowed to devote my journal henceforth to following the life and movements of that chosen Gate whose mission in time would herald the Manifestation of the Promised One of Islam, the Qaim. As for the Qaim himself, he in turn, according to the teachings of the Shaykhi school, would be the Herald Prophet of another Manifestation still to come. The Gate, the Qaim and the Qayyúm—it seemed to me quite clear at this point as to how the Hour of Resurrection in the year 1260 would lead into the final Dispensation of a Universal Prophet."

JULIA: We have here an interesting conclusion on the part of two enquiring minds in the aftermath of their close contact with a highly unusual visitor in Karbila. The conclusion should occasion no surprise in a milieu of numerous and complicated beliefs that would not prove themselves until the prophesied Hour, three years in the future. But Mustafa, true to his resolve, made every effort to unearth the information he hoped to gather on the young Siyyid's background. He learned from other merchants in Karbila that his name was Ali-Muhammad, that his father had passed away when he was a child, and that during his adolescence his uncles, well-known and respected in Shiraz, and with business branches in various locations in Persia and elsewhere, had put him in charge of their office in Bushihr. He was known there, these sources said, for his deep religious commitment to the words of the Qoran and the sayings of the Prophet and the Imams, and had often been seen standing for hours in prayer and meditation in the mosque in that port town or on his own rooftop, unmindful, summer or winter, of the heat or the cold.

Mustafa eventually learned that when the Siyyid departed from Karbila after visiting the shrines of the Shia Imams in each holy city, he returned to Shiraz, where he married a cousin, the young daughter of a grand-uncle, whose descent, like that of her husband, came directly from the grandson of the Prophet, Imam Husayn. Later still Mustafa was told that a son was born of that union who died in his infancy, and that Ali-Muhammad shared with his mother, his wife and an Ethiopian servant a small house in the merchants' quarter of the city. There he lived peacefully, engaged in business with his three uncles, known and respected for his careful book-keeping and his moral stance in all matters pertaining to family life and religion. But try as he might, Mustafa was unable to glean any information on the Siyyid's possible relationship to the Messianic expectations of the Shaykhis.

As Siyyid Kazim showed no inclination whatever to discuss any further details of this young man, Mustafa and Shaykh Hasan were obliged to turn to other matters, and during the next two to three years the brief reports in the journal were unproductive of any further knowledge of Ali-Muhammad. Mustafa produced his own observations, however, on the Turkish attack on Karbila in January of 1843, when he was forced to take refuge at the school. The details of that attack are horrendous, and Ham has given us a glimpse of its cruelties and monstrous abominations, which included the ravishing of the town's women by the Turkish troops. It left the city in partial ruins and completely subdued. Siyyid Ibrahim, in the nick of time, had absented himself from Karbila and taken off for Qazvin, and Haji Kirman Khan and his friends were safely established in a new Shaykhi school in Kirman.

Siyyid Kazim and his pupils, on the other hand, aware that only a short time remained for God's judgment on Islam, rode out the storm of that brutal attack in heroic service to hundreds of terrified and wounded Persians who fled to the Master's residence and into the classrooms, many to die there for lack of food, water, and the help of a doctor. The Zillus-Sultán, adhering to Najib Pasha's advice, gathered the exiled members of the royal family and most of the wealthy Persians within the confines of his house and courtyard in the center of the town, leaving the servants, the owners of small shops, the laborers and those foolhardy enough to face the soldiers, to receive the brunt of the attack. The commander of the troops, apparently superstitious of the possible results of murdering the Persian ulama, ordered the soldiers to spare this class along with the royals. Except for the looting and the vandalism of the houses of the clergy and those of the rich, and the days without proper food or the water for daily ablutions, these privileged classes were spared the gun and the sword. In doing so the Ottoman Sunnis hoped to put off any attempt by the army of Muhammad Shah to retaliate, but they need not have been concerned, for the Shah had taken to his bed with a bad case of gout, and Mirza Aqasi was wise enough to foresee a losing battle for a troublesome, rebellious town across the border.

HAM: As we have agreed before the tapes were on to prolong our last meeting in order that Julia and I may present the essential details of the Declaration in 1844, and as time is flying as usual, we must take you forward now to late January of that prophesied year, when the first stirrings of the search for the Qaim began in the Shaykhi school. You will recall that after three years away during which he had brought into the fold many converts to the coming Advent, Mulla Husayn returned to a chastened Karbila and found to his overwhelming grief that his beloved Master had passed away three weeks before his arrival. Eulogies and consolations had come from every side at this unexpected event, and although the Siyyid had warned repeatedly that he would not be alive to witness the Advent of the Qaim, the stunning loss of his leadership, and the lack of any successor named by the Master, had left the school and the Siyyid's family in a state of temporary paralysis.

As the days went by, Mulla Husayn, deploring amidst his grief the lack of action by his companions, made one final effort to persuade them to depart on their search for the Promised One, but to no avail. Resolving to carry out the mandate alone if necessary, he enlisted his brother and cousin to accompany him to the ancient mosque in Kufa—a place sacred to the Shias not far from Karbila—to pray there for guidance for the customary forty days and nights. According to Mustafa this move by Mulla Husayn was a positive action of leadership which soon had its effect on a number of Husayn's close companions, who proceeded to follow him to the mosque. Within a short time this aroused a number of other believers to join them in Kufa, a long-ago encampment of the fourth Caliph, the Imam Ali, the son-in-law and cousin of the Prophet, whose shrine in Najaf was a major point of pilgrimage. In the precincts of that ancient mosque, now almost in ruins, they were hopeful that their prayers and fasting would point them in the right direction to search for the Qaim.

Madilyn has informed us that recent scholars have estimated the number collected at the mosque as forty or more, but that approximately half that many had gradually returned to Karbila, as yet unready to start out for a destination still undisclosed by Mulla Husayn or by any personal visions or dreams in answer to their prayers. The issue of the numbers and their movements is still unclear, but I have no doubt that additional studies on such matters will bring further details to light. In this connection there is a saying of Muhammad that "The ink of the scholar is more precious than the blood of the martyr." For martyrs can die for any number of false and misleading reasons, religious or political, while the pen of a good scholar is utilized in the search for truth.

Neither Julia nor I maintains that Mustafa, caught in the midst of these happenings, is devoid of errors engendered by understandable emotional responses, but we feel confident that his journal can serve us well in depicting a fairly balanced view of events. Where he is unable to obtain the actual facts, he says so, but we can receive from this source as approximate a picture of reality as can be hoped for in the natural confusion that accompanies contemporary developments.

"Word has filtered back to Karbila," he writes, "that at least twenty or more members of the school have taken off from Kufa on the road south to Basra, but whether together in one group I have been unable to ascertain. There is some intimation that Mulla Husayn and his relatives, and perhaps several others, intend to take a trading vessel from the city of Basra on the waterway of the lower Euphrates to the port of Bushihr, and decide there what their next move will be. As for me, I shall no longer be attending the lectures, for older Shaykhi scholars, in particular Mirza Gawthar and Mirza

Muhit, have taken over the classrooms, and show quite clearly that their interest lies in obtaining control of the school and not in the search for the Qaim. The Master's family is still in the residence, and both his sons, I understand, are hopeful of retaining family influence in the school, but just what will occur in this matter is hard to foresee.

"Ten days after the Siyyid's death the poetess Qurratul-Ayn arrived from Qazvin to meet with her mentor and correspondent for the first time, and the word is that she was devastated to find him no longer alive. Although I have not seen her as yet—she has been for over a month in the family residence—those who have called upon her tell me her beauty is incomparable and the eloquence of her language and the lyrical power of her speaking voice cannot be adequately described. She is taking a house with her sister Mardiyyih in Karbila, I was told, to carry on the teachings of the Master, and a younger sister's husband, Muhammad-Ali of Qazvin, and his brother Hadi, for some time enrolled in the school, have joined the group on their way to Persia.

"I have thought in the past week that I might leave the shop in the care of my bookkeeper and attempt to join the companions in Bushihr, or wherever they may have gone from there. I am anxious to report in the journal this most important occurrence in the life of Islam, and to follow the fortunes of those members of the school whom I have come to know well in the past three years. But I must first obtain permission from my family in Kashan, and perhaps I will write to this effect in a few days. Fate will decide—but how can I remain in Karbila when so much is at stake in this prophesied year? I shall pray at the shrine of Imam Husayn, and hope for the very best outcome."

JULIA: Our young scholar was as good as his written word. He prayed ardently at the shrine of the Prophet's grandson, and in an unusually short time received permission from his uncle Mirza Jani, who stated that he himself intended to join the group as soon as the Promised One was found, as he intended to write a history of the faith at a later time. Mustafa then took off on the road to Basra and joined a caravan for Bushihr on the last day of April. His inquiries in that latter port produced little of the group's present whereabouts, but certain Shaykhis in the town had recalled that a number of Mullas and others from the school in Karbila had been seen praying in the mosque, and when approached had said they were on their way to Shiraz to communicate with the many Shaykhis in that city, from where they would probably go on to Kirman to consult with Haji Karim Khan on the latest status of the new school in relation to the Advent. The group had rested for a time in Bushihr, these sources said, in preparation for the upward climb to Shiraz, and they should arrive in that city around the twentieth or twenty-first of May.

"I decided to go on to Shiraz," the journal continues, "and I hired a well-traveled mule, hoping that I would reach there before the group moved on. Halfway up that rugged road I caught up with several of the friends, exhausted from the heat and lagging behind several others, who, they told me, were trailing behind Mulla Husayn and his two relatives. As it turned out, Husayn, his brother and his cousin, and those who were close behind them, arrived in Shiraz three days before the rest of us, who had slowed our climb because of the injury to the leg of one of our companions. We finally reached the Allah-u-Akbar gate on the afternoon of May twenty-fourth. Wearily we paused to look down from that famed mountain pass on the cypress-dotted plain of the city of the poets, but which, as we had heard on the road to our dismay, was no longer the serene and peaceful site of its storied past and was now under the rule of a corrupt and arrogant governor from Tehran incapable of controlling the lutis and the brigands who infested its streets. We decided to keep together for safety, and made our way to the main mosque where we hoped to find both lodgings and those who preceded us.

"Imagine our joy to find Mulla Husayn seated in that mosque, surrounded by a large group of listeners as he expounded the teachings of the Shaykhi school. The Mullas Ali, Mahmud, Yusuf, Ahmad and Jalil, as well as the brother-in-law of Qurratul-Ayn and his brother Hadi, were sitting in that group. The rest of us, now joining them in the mosque, consisted of Siyyid Husayn from Yazd, Shaykh Said from Bombay, an Indian, Mulla Baqir of Tabriz, Mirza Muhammad-Rawdi of Yazd, Mulla Khuda-Baksh of Quchan, and Mulla Hasan of Bajistan. Counting the two relatives of Mulla Husayn, there were now fifteen of us, not including myself, who had followed in the footsteps of Mulla Husayn. Mulla Muhammad-Ali of Barfarush was nowhere to be seen, and we were told that he had either remained behind in Kufa for further prayers or had gone to visit his family in the north.

"We had no sooner hailed our fellow Shaykhis from the school than they rose from the crowd around Mulla Husayn and led us aside, their faces a study in dismay. Three days and nights had now gone by since their arrival, they said, and Husayn had shown no intention whatever of questioning the Shaykhis of Shiraz on their possible knowledge of the whereabouts of the Promised One. And stranger still, since their first night at the mosque he had made no mention of going on to Kirman, and had settled down to deliver the lectures he was now engaged upon. As his two relatives were equally nonplussed by this behavior, Mulla Ali had finally requested them to confront Mulla Husayn as to the meaning of his unexplained cessation of the search. He had merely replied that he had his reasons for the present course of action, that he would soon bring these reasons to light, and that he asked meanwhile for their patience and their prayers. But some were anxious to go on to Kirman, and were prepared to do so without Husayn. In spite of their impatience the calming words of Mulla Ali persuaded them to cease complaining, and to remain for several more days in Shiraz.

"The next morning—on May twenty-fifth—I saw Mulla Husayn and Mulla Ali in the mosque in what appeared to be a profound conversation. I learned later that Husayn was explaining to his closest companion the purpose of his strange behavior, and was giving Ali instructions to pass on to the rest of the group. At the time I sensed that something most important must have occurred, that a disclosure of some sort was about to be made. As things have turned out, I do not hesitate to report the contents of that conversation, which Mulla Ali—aware of my historical motivation in connection with the journal—was finally persuaded to share with me.

"Husayn had told him, he said, that there was a person in the city who had made an astonishing claim which, in the past three days, he had been struggling to persuade himself was worth a longer stay in Shiraz. He asked the indulgence of Ali and the rest of the companions, saying that the matter rested on his shoulders alone. He then proceeded to partially outline what had taken place in those last three days, requesting that Ali say nothing as yet of what had occurred.

" 'On my first day in the city, on May twenty-first,' Ali reported Mulla Husayn as saying, 'I was approached in my cell at the mosque by Siyyid Ali-Muhammad, with whom I had traveled to Najaf to visit the shrine of Imam Ali in the spring of 1257, just before I departed for Isfahan and Mashad. I was glad to see him, and in fact had planned to call upon him to discuss our possible movements. He welcomed me warmly to the city, and invited me to partake of his hospitality at his home in the merchants' quarters on the following evening. The others would surely understand, he said, that our former acquaintance justified a renewed conversation on Shaykhi affairs. He would send his Ethiopian servant to accompany me before the evening prayers.

" 'I cannot at this present time give you the full details of our exchanges during that first evening and ensuing night, though I long to do so. For three days and nights I have kept my counsel, and for three nights I have returned secretly to that house, where Ali-Muhammad presented to me additional proof of his vast knowledge of the Messianic expectations of the Shias and the way in which the Shaykhis depart from the Muslim clergy of both divisions of Islam. He declared that he himself was an unknown participant in the coming Apocalypse, but that shortly his own mission would become apparent to the world. Meanwhile he induced me to establish a lecture course, which he himself has attended, and to say nothing of what had occurred between us.

" 'But today he said to me in the mosque that my companions should be told to fast and pray in their cells, that they may be led to recognize him as the Gate to the coming Lord of the New Age, the Manifestation whom God, in due time, would overshadow for the resurrection of mankind. He has intimated that his mission did not entirely coincide with the expectations of either the orthodox sects of Islam or the members of the Shaykhi school, a fact that would soon become apparent. And there was a logical reason, he said, for withholding the full extent of his claims during the initial period of his mission, as otherwise many lives would quickly be snuffed out by the government and the orthodox ulama, who had recently pronounced the teachings of Siyyid Kazim a dangerous heresy. As for my Shaykhi companions, he assured me that for those who believed in his present claims there was no question that God, in His mysterious way, would, in the words of the Qoran, "unlock further the door of His mercy." ' "

HAM: On the very night after this disclosure, according to the journal, Mulla Ali had gone to Mulla Husayn's room in a state of excitement, and had found him poring over a number of separate pages covered with exquisite calligraphic writing—an example, as he was soon aware, of the most refined, the most perfect art of penmanship. Ali, who had just had a remarkable experience as he prayed in his cell, demanded to know by whom it was written. Husayn refused to discuss the meaning of the papers, when suddenly Ali burst into tears, declaring that he had just had an overpowering vision as he prayed in his cell—that a brilliant shaft of white light had led him to a house in the merchant's quarter of the city, a place he would instantly recognize if he were able to find his way there. Composing himself, he stated his conviction that in that house there dwelt the Hidden One himself, the one whom they sought, the Qaim, the Promised One of Islam. The vision assured him that God had endowed the soul of the Qaim with the power to lead the world into the consummate faith of "Him whom God will make manifest," the Qayyúm, the Lord of the New Age.

The journal tells us that Mulla Husayn clasped the hands of his close friend at this joyous news, and informed him that he was the first to discover the truth by spiritual means, as the Master had exhorted them to do. "I shall take you to that house tomorrow," he said, "and you will have the opportunity, as I have had, of recognizing the claims of that charismatic young merchant whose revelatory proofs, an example of which I have brought here to this room, are now, in my estimation, irrefutable and complete. I am only regretful for my early hesitation—indeed I deplore the three days and nights I have put off my wholehearted acceptance of the claims that were put before me on the evening and night of May twenty-second and twenty-third. In my desire to be certain of my final conclusions I have spent precious time in futile discussion, however polite—a circumstance I put down to the many contentious years I spent in my younger days as a pupil in the curséd madrasas of the orthodox ulama in Khurasan. But this is no excuse, and I have been properly rebuked for it. It is my hope that the rest of our companions will undergo the same enlightenment as you have been granted in so short a time. Meanwhile conceal your knowledge until this occurs, and give thanks for the great bounty of recognizing our new Lord and Master, Ali-Muhammad, the Gate to the Qayyúm himself. What now remains is that one by one we must all be actively enrolled by him in the coming Cause of God."

JULIA: Suffice to say that over a period of two months or more the rest of the group in Shiraz were led by one means or another—by dreams, visions, or in some intuitive or esoteric manner—to recognize the person of the young Siyyid as the Qaim, the immediate stepping-stone to the Apocalypse prophesied in all the Scriptures of the world. As one by one they were taken into the presence of Ali-Muhammad, now known to these devoted Shaykhi scholars as the Bab, each of them was enrolled as a Letter of the Living, until sixteen members of the school, including Mulla Husayn, had declared themselves as disciples of the Herald or the Gate of "Him whom God will make manifest." The Bab informed them that he was awaiting the impending arrival in Shiraz of a final Letter, and that he had already added the name of Qurratul-Ayn, now teaching in Karbila, as number seventeen. Although they had never met, the poetess' brother-in-law had carried with him a letter and a poem written by her in praise of the coming Lordship of the Qaim, his knowledge and purity, and his God-given mission in the Cause of the reformation of Islam. As the only woman among the Letters of the Living, Qurratul-Ayn was honored for all time for her devotion to the teachings of Shaykh Ahmad and Siyyid

Kazim and her total dedication to the Cause of the Herald Prophet. The Bab accounted himself, he told his disciples, as number nineteen, a magic number in the future faith of both the Qaim and the Qayyúm.

The last of the seventeen disciples to arrive in Shiraz, dusty and travel-weary, was Muhammad-Ali of Barfarush. Shortly after entering the city he accosted Mulla Husayn on the street and demanded that he be taken to the presence of his Lord without delay. When Husayn objected, saying that he must first recognize the identity of the Bab through fasting and prayer, Muhammad-Ali pointed to a figure walking ahead of them on the street, and replied with quiet assurance, "I know him by his gait, for I have walked and talked with him in a dream. It is Ali-Muhammad, the Qaim, your Lord and mine. Introduce me to him without further delay." At that moment, the journal informs us, the Bab turned and gestured to Husayn. "Let him approach," he said, "for he and I have already been in contact through the spiritual world. He who is the last to arrive shall not be the least in this Cause."

I presume that all these paranormal occurrences would not go over at all well in the scientifically oriented cultures of our Western hemisphere. But if I may pause for a few moments I would like to quote from a book I have here with which most of us are fairly well acquainted, "The Varieties of Religious Experience" by a brilliant intellect, William James, whom many of our Western thinkers regard as the foremost of American psychologists and philosophers, and whose additional interests in esoteric matters—the phenomena of paranormal and psychic events, including a wide range of so-called supernatural happenings—has given him a unique position as an outstanding scholar, writer and lecturer. Georgina has already mentioned his study of the various levels of consciousness, and I will read his final conclusion on the subject.

"Our normal waking consciousness, rational consciousness as we call it," he writes, "is but one special type of consciousness, whilst all about it, parted by the filmiest of screens, there lie potential forms of consciousness entirely different. We may go through life without suspecting their existence; but apply the requisite stimulus, and at a touch they are there in all their completeness. No account of the universe in its totality can be final which leaves these other forms of consciousness quite disregarded. How to regard them is the question. At any rate, they forbid our premature closing of accounts with reality."

Such statements as this, which include the recognition of the powerful force and amazing results of profound prayer and meditation, have been made with equal conviction by Professor F. W. H. Myers in England, by the psychiatrist Carl Jung, and by many others in our Western world undeterred by the totally material view of the constitution of man. I find them particularly encouraging as we attempt to understand the lives and missions of the Prophets, and in this instance the recorded history in Shiraz of Ali-Muhammad the Bab and the Letters of the Living.

HAM: It is a moot question among certain historians, Doctor Varqa said in Tehran, as to whether or not Ali-Muhammad, during the initial period of his claims, fully realized his own true status as a Prophet of God in his own right. If he was aware of this fact, he appears to have utilized for the public at large, until his trial in Tabriz in 1848, the accepted Shia custom of taquiya, the prudent dissimulation of one's true knowledge and beliefs when the lives of others, including one's own, are at stake. Whatever the case, the complexities of the Declaration in Shiraz in 1844, the doctor said, were not yet completely understood, but he believed that Mustafa's later interview with Mulla Husayn would give us as close an approximation to the actual events of May twenty-second and twenty-third as contemporary sources were able to produce.

You will wonder why we have put off for so long that all-important Declaration on the night of May twenty-third. We have wanted first of all for you to absorb as many of the intricate ramifications of the Muslim beliefs and expectations as we were able to pass on to you, and secondly to end our last evening together with a Revelation that originated a religion which now embraces millions of people around the globe. If you will withhold any comments until I have read from the journal, you will, I believe, receive some answers as to how a new Revelation, in this case as witnessed and received by Mulla Husayn, can change the course of religious history. In view of our desire to give you a full exposition of the Declaration and its aftermath in Shiraz, your previous consent to a more prolonged evening for this final meeting has been most welcome.

Mustafa begins his account with gratitude to Mulla Husayn for the unexpected bounty of hearing from his own lips the details of three days and nights of wavering indecision in wholly accepting the claims of Ali-Muhammad. During Husayn's recital, he writes, he was fortunate in being able to envision the figure of the charismatic young Siyyid who had come to his shop in Karbila, and into whose presence he had not yet been led in Shiraz.

" 'On the late afternoon of May twenty-second,' Mulla Husayn reported to me, 'I was guided by the Ethiopian servant Mubarak to a modest house whose small courtyard was embellished by a flourishing orange tree, planted and carefully tended, the servant said, by the Master himself. My first impression was one of surprise at the humble environment of the Siyyid, whose aristocratic bearing and majestic carriage had caused me to image his surroundings as reflecting the wealth of the merchants of Shiraz. But I would soon discover that my host's physical habitation in no way reflected the spiritual wealth I would soon encounter in that house.

" 'Ali-Muhammad was awaiting me in his personal chambers on the second floor. He came forward to greet me in his usual gracious manner, and immediately turned his attention to our preparation for the sunset prayers. He himself poured the water for my ablutions, after which he called for the samovar, and made some tea. His quiet assurance in caring for my comfort had put me at ease, and I resolved to question him about the object of our search, for it seemed to me at that moment that God might have led me to this house for some helpful information on the possible whereabouts of the Promised One. As we stood together in prayer I supplicated that unknown Hidden Qaim to grant me the bounty of discovering the place where he awaited the loyal followers of Siyyid Kazim.

" 'Our prayers were prolonged until sometime after sunset, when my host bade me be seated to converse with him on the present state of Shaykhi affairs. Since the death of Siyyid Kazim, he said, no appointed successor had come forward to claim his place. Whom did I and my companions consider to be the leader, beside myself, in carrying on the teachings of the Shaykhi school?

" ' "Our true leader," I told him, "has been described to us by Siyyid Kazim on many occasions. The leader is the Promised One of Islam himself. When he is found we will lay at his feet every resource at our command to aid him in his mission as the Herald Prophet of the Qayyúm. We are already aware of his attributes and the signs that will assure us of his Lordship over the coming transitional period of reformation and renewal of the Muslim faith."

" ' "And just what," my host replied, "are the details of these features as outlined for you by Siyyid Kazim?"

" ' "He is descended from the House of the Prophet through the Imam Husayn," I told him. "He is in his mid-twenties, of medium height, and has no bodily deficiencies of any kind. His knowledge is not dependent on the learning of ordinary men, and he does not indulge in the useless customs of the Muslim majority, such as smoking or the idle conjectures of the clergy in their religious schools, those worthless madrasas of the orthodox. Surely you must have heard the Master extolling his virtues, which Shaykh Ahmad had gleaned from his many years of study of the prophecies contained in the Hadith."

" 'There was a long pause while Ali Muhammad poured for us another cup of tea. As he stood at the samovar he suddenly turned to me, and in ringing tones he declared to me, "Behold, Mulla Husayn, these signs you have listed can all be applied to my own person," and one by one he proceeded to point out that his physical, mental and spiritual attributes coincided perfectly with the statements of Siyyid Kazim.

" 'I was not only surprised at this turn of events, but seriously disturbed at these observations, deeming them inappropriate from a usually circumspect descendant of the Prophet. I answered him politely, but my manner indicated that to compare oneself with such a Holy Soul was a strange departure from the usual course of religious discussion. I began to laud with great emphasis the powers and the vast knowledge of the prophesied Qaim, while my host gazed at me with uncritical eyes, quite undisturbed by my obvious concern over his bold comparison. Under the spell of that steady gaze I was suddenly seized by remorse for my lack of both courtesy and humility, and vowed that if my host again referred to this subject I would immediately produce a treatise I had written and which I carried in my robe, a systematic exposition depicting my inability to understand the meaning of certain abstruse allusions in the commentaries of Shaykh Ahmad and Siyyid Kazim.

" 'I had no sooner decided upon this course of action than my host once again asked me to note his resemblance to Siyyid Kazim's description. I felt it was now urgent for me to produce the treatise and to carefully observe the extent of his knowledge on these esoteric matters. Imagine my astonishment when he scarcely glanced at the contents, and proceeded to give me a full and satisfactory account of its symbolic meanings. He then went on to advance certain truths which he maintained were totally unknown to the orthodox ulama, who thought themselves the last word in spiritual understanding and religious scholarship. Only by turning to himself as the Herald of "Him Whom God will make manifest," could the world of Islam, the creation of his ancestor Muhammad through the Will of God, obtain the true picture of coming events.

" 'Observing my amazement he proceeded to place a large supply of paper and a pen on the low table beside him, declaring that now was the time to unveil the hidden significance and purpose of the Surih of Joseph in the Qoran. Picking up his pen he began to write with such rapidity and to chant in such melodious tones that I was utterly astounded at what was taking place before me. The extraordinary revelatory verses, streaming continuously from his pen, were of such import on the glorious rank and uniqueness of "Him Whom God will make manifest" that had I not been in a state of mental numbness and confusion they would have persuaded me then and there of the claims he had put forward to be the prophesied Herald and Gateway to that Great Being yet to declare himself.

" 'When at last he put down his pen, he glanced at the clock on the wall. "It is now two hours and eleven minutes after sunset," he said. "In the days to come this night, this very hour, will be celebrated the world over as one of the great moments of religious history. My delivery tonight of the first chapter of the new Revelation, as yet incomplete, will be known as the Qayyúmul-Asma, the Mother Book of that coming Dispensation prophesied by Muhammad and by all the living religions of the world. I am aware of your bewilderment, and though I should by all rights in this matter rebuke you for your hesitation and for the tests you have put before me, you are here as an honored guest, and we shall spend further time tonight, and in other meetings as well, to put your mind at rest on my mission of preparing Islam and the world at large for the great Apocalypse which is even now impinging upon the lives of all mankind."

" 'We were served by Mubarak at this point with a most delicious meal, which soon brought me to my senses. It was the fourth hour after sunset when Ali-Muhammad once again took up his pen and began revealing further verses of the Qayyúmul-Asma. The night seemed to slip away as I sat enthralled by his voice and the words that poured from that magic pen. On several occasions, overcome by these happenings, I made an effort to receive permission to return to the mosque, but my host demurred, saying that I must first reassert my equilibrium or whoever saw or spoke to me would surely think that I had lost my mind. As the dawn approached he requested that I say nothing of his identity until such time as eighteen destined believers were enrolled in his Cause. We parted company with further meetings in view, and you have already taken note of what occurred in the next three days. Now that I have totally capitulated to the claims of Ali-Muhammad, and the Letters of the Living are equally aware of his true status as the Qaim, we can only conjecture that his decision to be known only as the Bab, the Gate to a coming Manifestation, at least for the foreseeable future, is a means of delaying his own martyrdom as well as that of his followers until the teachings of a coming Apocalypse have been spread throughout the land. Meanwhile the signs and attributes of his God-given endowments as a Prophet of God are as evident to us as the noonday sun.'"

JULIA: We sincerely regret at this juncture that there is no time in this last meeting to carry the story of the Bab and his disciples through the many vicissitudes, the successes and failures, the loyalties and enmities of the people of Persia, and to give you the full details of the truly incredible life of the one whom the Qayyúm would later eulogize as a youth who, and I quote, "Though young and tender of age, and though the Cause He revealed was contrary to the desire of all the peoples of the earth… yet He arose and steadfastly proclaimed it… He was afraid of no one; He was regardless of consequences. Could such a thing be made manifest except through the power of a divine Revelation, and the potency of God's invincible Will?…" And He further states of the Bab:

"In His Book, which he hath entitled Qayyúmul-Asma… He prophesied His own martyrdom. In it is this passage: 'O Thou Remnant of God!'—that is, the Qayyúm—'I have sacrificed myself wholly for Thee; I have accepted curses for Thy sake; and I have yearned for naught but martyrdom in the path of Thy love. Sufficient Witness unto me is God, the Exalted, the Protector, the Ancient of Days.' "

The Bab often proclaimed that the glory of God and His Messengers is far above that which His creatures on earth declare of Them. As for those whose names have become familiar to us as disciples of that sacrificial youth, we can do no better than to quote a portion of the inspirational words from their young Lord to the Eighteen Letters of the Living, twelve of whom courageously and with the utmost dedication laid down their lives in his path. Warning them of the dangers, the calamities, the storms and afflictions they were about to undergo, he wrote as follows:

"I am preparing you for the Advent of a mighty Day . . . The secret of the Day that is to come is now concealed. It can neither be divulged nor estimated..." He urged them to "Scatter throughout the length and breadth of this land, and, with steadfast feet and sanctified hearts, prepare the way for His coming. Heed not your weaknesses and frailty," he exhorted them, but "fix your gaze upon the invincible power of the Lord, your God, the Almighty. Has He not, in past days, caused Abraham, in spite of His seeming helplessness, to triumph over the forces of Nimrod? Has He not enabled Moses, whose staff was his only companion, to vanquish Pharaoh and his hosts? Has He not established the ascendancy of Jesus, poor and lowly as He was in the eyes of men, over the combined forces of the Jewish people? Has He not subjected the barbarous and militant tribes of Arabia to the holy and transforming discipline of Muhammad, His prophet? Arise in His name, put your trust wholly in Him, and be assured of ultimate victory."

There is more, much more in that letter to stir the emotions as the Bab addressed the humble pupils of Siyyid Kazim as "my beloved friends." He tells them to ponder the words of Jesus as he sent his disciples forth to propagate the Cause of God, and almost verbatim he repeats certain phrases of Jesus in the Gospels to strengthen their spiritual resolve. Indeed there were many believers among the unorthodox sects who later maintained that the Bab was the long-expected return of the Christ to herald the coming of the Holy Spirit in the glory of the Father—a claim that was never made by the Herald Prophet himself. On the contrary, his whole mission was devoted to that Great Figure who was yet to appear—a mission during which he hoped, and initially believed, that the religion of the Shias would be transformed in advance of that second Advent. But the immediate goals of that mission, partially due to the heightened militancy of the Babis in the face of the unspeakable persecutions of the government and the clergy, were unattained. The Bab was imprisoned four years later in the province of Adjerbaijan, and eventually executed in Tabriz in the month of July in 1850.

HAM: It appeared at that time that the turbulent lives and the sacrifices of the Bab and his followers had finally ended in total defeat. At his trial in Tabriz in 1848, the Bab was badgered and insulted from start to finish as an "immature and unlettered wretch." When asked toward the end of these disgraceful proceedings to state his claims in unequivocal terms, and he broke at last his stoic reception of the taunts of the mujtahids of Tabriz to finally declare calmly but unmistakably that he himself was the Promised Qaim, the cries of hostility in that court can well be imagined. As they turned away from him, assured now of a final death sentence for this blasphemous youth, he repeated in emphatic tones, "I am, I am, I am that Promised One, the One whose name you have invoked for a thousand years, at whose mention you have risen, whose Revelation you have prayed God to hasten." This only served to cause an increased clamor and additional epithets from the furious ulama, one of whom then attacked him as a "perverted and contemptible follower of Satan." At this point the Bab rose from his seat, and without further ado walked quietly from the room.

This was not the end of the matter. The leading mujtahids of Tabriz, unable to persuade all of the members of this inquisition to sign his death warrant, were reduced by necessity to returning the Bab to his second place of incarceration in Adjerbaijan, the castle fortress of Chiriq, expected by the government in Tehran to be a more astringent punishment than his former nine-month imprisonment in the mountain fortress of Maku to the north. The village of Maku, with its stark and forbidding fortress clinging to the craggy mountainside above it, was adjacent to the Turkish and Armenian borders, and had always been obedient to the strict orders of Mirza Aqasi, who was born near that village of immigrant parents from Armenia. The Prime Minister therefore expected that the troublemaker from Shiraz would soon fade from the memory of the people. On the contrary the usually inflexible warden of the fortress, a Kurd and a Sunni, shortly capitulated to the charm of his prisoner and to the startling Revelations, so akin to the verses of the Qoran, that streamed from his pen. As a result a constant flow of visitors from near and far had been allowed by this smitten Kurd to enter the fortress or to stand and receive the revelatory words from an open window above them. The situation was so manifestly opposed to the anticipations of the court and the orthodox ulama that many disbelievers were now willing to acknowledge the Bab's charismatic powers in alleviating the restrictions of an isolated confinement.

Affairs at Maku, from the standpoint of the Prime Minister, rapidly went from bad to worse. Siyyid Husayn of Yazd and his brother Hasan had been permitted by the warden to join the Bab within the fortress, and Siyyid Husayn now became his amanuensis, while his brother Hasan was allowed to do the shopping in the town. Eventually Shaykh Hasan-i-Zunuzi, waiting patiently in the mosque on the outskirts of the town, was given permission to visit the Bab at will, and he too took up the duties of recording the increasing flow of the Bab's writings. It was here that the Persian Bayan first saw the light of day, the Book that is deemed the major Revelation of the Bab, along with the Arabic Bayan produced later in the castle of Chiriq.

The laxness and permissiveness at Maku and the spiritual surrender of the populace had so angered Mirza Aqasi that he determined to impose a far stricter confinement on the persistent youth who had now become the nemesis of his court career. As the leniency continued in spite of his warnings, he grasped at the timely request of the Russian Ambassador to remove the Bab from the area of Maku. Fearing that a revolution might be brewing in the region between Persia and Russia, the Ambassador petitioned the Persian court to remove the prisoner—a disturbing element in such a volatile location—and Chiriq was agreed upon as amenable to strict orders from Tehran.

At this crucial time, in July of 1848, Muhammad-Shah was showing signs of such debilitating illness that his former tutor, increasingly afraid of the loss of his only link to power, was hopeful that his present intended destruction of the activities of the Bab and his followers would offset the final deprivation of his fading authority at court. But only three weeks after the change of incarceration, Aqasi became so alarmed by the totally unanticipated continuation of visitors to the Bab at Chiriq—where the warden, a Kurdish chieftain married to a sister of the Shah, and considered a harsh and unbending disciplinarian, had himself succumbed to the spiritual influence of the Bab—that a now thoroughly frightened Minister, deprived of any aid from a suddenly dying monarch, decided upon ordering a trial at Tabriz, hoping that his urgent request for a death warrant would bring this aggravating movement to an end. You have had a partial view of the utter mockery in that court of all the civilized norms of justice and interrogation.

Present at this contemptuous tribunal was the seventeen-year-old Crown Prince, Naziri'd-Din Mirza, now Governor of Adjerbaijan. He appears to have contributed little to the proceedings, but Mustafa's journal implies that he too disagreed on imposing a death sentence on a true descendant of the Prophet, no matter how overweening his claims. In their angry frustration the leading ulama involved in that shameful trial decided to subject the Bab to the painful rigors of the bastinado, and this was inflicted personally by the Shaykhul-Islam, the government-appointed religious leader of Tabriz.

The Bab was subsequently examined by a well-known physician in the city for painful swellings to his legs and feet, and to the misplaced gashes on his delicate face. At the same time the doctor was asked to report to the Shah as to the mental condition of the young Siyyid—whether he was sound of mind or could properly be considered a madman. Doctor Cormick, an Englishman, wrote to the Shah—among other words of respect for his uncomplaining patient—that "his whole look and deportment went far to dispose me in his favor," and that he would recommend to the monarch that the prisoner's life be spared and his punishment made easier to endure. One can well imagine at this point the renewed desperation of an increasingly agitated Prime Minister in Tehran.

Upon the return of the Bab to the fortress of Chiriq in August of 1848, he proceeded to compose a letter to Mirza Aqasi, dwelling on the evils of his rule and prophesying his complete downfall. It was not delivered until after the death of the Shah on September fourth of 1848, and by that time the fallen Minister had found himself hounded from pillar to post, his pleas for aid ignored by his former victims and his sycophants at court, who, rich and poor alike, had turned their backs on this pathetic figure of a man. Destitute and in miserable health, the life of this pitiful creature came to an end a year later in one of the sanctuary shrines in Iraq.

JULIA: Friends, we are well aware that we must bring our story of the Bab to an end here tonight, however episodic, and can only suggest again that you fill in the gaps when the books arrive—you will find there many events that I am quite sure are capable of shaking one's Western complacency on religious matters, and will aid at the same time in opening one's mind to those transcendental forms of consciousness which we have already discussed in these meetings. The apparently unnatural occurrences resulting from these higher states of mental activity are generally relegated to the realms of imagination, hallucinatory delusions, a wide range of mental disorders, and even, in certain cases, to the illusory scenes produced by a clever magician. But I would like to leave you with a final episode in relation to the Bab which has no ready explanation, scientific or otherwise—an event attested to by thousands of spectators in the barracks square of Tabriz, consisting in general of enemies of the faith.

After the death of Muhammad-Shah, a new Prime Minister, Mirza Taqi Khan, had come to power under Nasiri'd-Din Shah, the new monarch. Though a different character from Aqasi, and considered a capable and loyal minister of the Shah, he began his rule with an iron hand, determined to eliminate any disturbing elements that arose in the land. By July of 1850 the Bab's two-year imprisonment in Chiriq had shown no abatement in the crowds of visitors or the laxity of the warden, and the patience of Taqi Khan had finally come to an end. Deputizing his brother to carry out his wishes, he ordered the execution of the Bab to take place without delay in the barracks square in Tabriz.

There was a youth in Tabriz, a relative of Shaykh Hasan-i-Zunuzi, who had been a devoted and impassioned follower of the Bab. His disparaging stepfather had finally confined him to the house to prevent his further visits to Chiriq, and had padlocked the door of his room. While praying constantly to be released, this young devotee, Muhammad-Ali-i-Zunuzi, experienced fleeting visions of the Bab standing before him and declaring with a look of happiness that his martyrdom was at hand. Within a few days this fated youth became aware that a large crowd of jeering citizens were pouring through the street outside the house, and rushing to the door of his room, and finding the padlock inexplicably loosened, he ran into the street, where a throng of excited people, men and women alike, were at that moment showing their perverted delight at the sight of the Bab, with a rope about his neck, being led in ignominious display by the orders of the brother of Mirza Taqi Khan.

Aroused by this dreadful sight Muhammad-Ali, in his struggle to reach the Bab, pushed aside those who stood in his way, and succeeding in his determination he knelt at the feet of his Lord, requesting in a rush of words that he be allowed to share in the martyrdom about to take place. When the Bab immediately gave his promise to this effect, Muhammad-Ali followed him to the barracks square, defying all efforts of his friends and relatives in the crowd to dissuade him from this suicidal course. Angered with his persistence, the footmen in charge put him in a cell next to the Bab, and notified the authorities of his intransigent behavior.

The next morning the death warrant was signed by the hostile spiritual leaders of the city, a warrant which included as well the execution at the same time of a disobedient and run-away youth, who insisted that he be put to death by the side of his Lord and Master, the Promised One of Islam. On the ninth of July, in the bright noonday sun, no less than ten thousand spectators were jammed on the ground and on the rooftops surrounding the barracks, awaiting a public show that would soon turn into a striking spectacle so incredible that to this day the citizens of Tabriz, descendants of believers and unbelievers alike, speak of that day with wonder and endless speculation. I can do no better than to quote for the last time the words of Mustafa, a visitor to the Bab at Chiriq, and a spectator in the barracks so shaken by the death decree of the Promised Qaim that his pen could not conceal his personal grief or the dreadful shock of that doomsday event.

"I had found a place," he writes, "as close to the wall of the barracks as they would allow me to stand, wishing to gaze once again at that beautiful face. Shaken with emotion I was scarcely able to stay on my feet, and the tears streamed from my eyes, blurring the preparations taking place on that forbidding wall. Soon the Bab, followed by that consecrated youth, Muhammad-Ali-i-Zunuzi, were brought into the square from the cells they had occupied in the barracks, the Bab calm and collected in his usual manner and his young disciple smiling in anticipation of joining his beloved Lord in Paradise. For a moment I was struck with envy of that youth, and I realized that my unrestrained emotions were quite out of order in the face of the two figures who stood so serenely before that silent crowd, quite prepared to give their lives for the Cause of God. An Armenian Christian regiment of seven hundred and fifty rifles were now in place, ready to carry out the orders of their commander. Imagine my surprise when this Christian officer stepped forward and approached the Bab. He seemed to be asking for forgiveness for the act he had been called upon to perform, and apparently receiving the absolution he had hoped for, he stepped back to take command of his men. My heart was about to burst with the awful anticipation of witnessing the impending event, for nothing and no one except God Himself could now save our Lord from earthly extinction.

"Two ropes had been suspended from a strong nail on the wall of the barracks, and the Bab and his disciple were now lifted up to hang entwined by the ropes before the gaze of a hushed crowd of onlookers, divided at this climactic moment by their individual emotions. The head of the young martyr of Tabriz lay on the breast of the Bab, awaiting with his Master the volleys of seven hundred and fifty rifles stationed in three files, each to fire in turn on two defenseless bodies, when two well-placed bullets could easily have accomplished the termination of their lives. Unable to face that agonizing moment I buried my face in my hands, ardently praying that this criminal murder would quickly come to an end. As the third volley finally sounded I opened my eyes to a scene filled with smoke and confusion. I could discern only Muhammad-Ali standing at the base of the wall, his body unhurt and the ropes severed and in shreds. The Bab was nowhere to be seen, and the cries that went up from that crowd I shall never forget, for surely it was nothing less in many eyes than a miracle, as I myself believed.

"The Bab was soon found in the cell he had formerly occupied, engaged in an animated conversation with Siyyid Husayn, his amanuensis and secretary—a conversation previously interrupted by the footman who had led him into the square to be shot. This poor lackey, still standing by the door of the cell, was so awestruck by what had occurred, that on being told by the Bab that he had now completed what he had to say to Siyyid Husayn and to return him to the square, suddenly rushed into the street, refusing to carry out his allotted task. At the same time Sam Khan, the commander of the Christian regiment, declared he had done his duty and would not repeat his assault on an obviously innocent man. Another regiment was called to the scene, and the two figures suspended once again from the wall. Although I was unable to hear every word that the Bab now addressed to the crowd, once more awaiting his momentary death, I have since been told that he spoke as follows:

" 'O wayward generation! Had you believed in me, each one of you would have followed the example of this youth who stands in rank above most of you, and would willingly have sacrificed himself in my path. The day will come when you will have recognized me; that day I shall cease to be with you.'

"Immediately the guns resounded once again and the bodies of the Bab and his companion were riddled by the bullets. The face of the Bab was almost unmarred, and there was a smile on his lips which seemed to reflect the happiness he had recently expressed at his approaching release from the earth. That night and the next day I spent with Siyyid

Husayn, unabashedly displaying our grief at the loss of the Manifestation in our midst. Meanwhile several loyal friends in Tabriz and from Tehran were intent upon retrieving the two entwined bodies, thrown in careless abandon beside the moat outside the city. Guards had been posted there to prevent the believers from making this attempt, but in the dead of night the weary sentinels fell into a sleep so deep that the rescue of the sacred remains took place without bloodshed on either side. The bodies were taken to a silk factory by a devoted Babi, and from there, enclosed in a case especially constructed to preserve those holy remains for future burial, it was carried to Tehran, where it was understood that the Babi leader, Mirza Husayn-Ali of Nur, would have the last word on their final disposition. The guards at the moat had blamed the disappearance of the bodies on marauding animals, and the self-righteous ulama of Tabriz declared from their pulpits that this was the end of the matter, as it was prophesied that the body of the Promised One would be preserved from all beasts of prey and all creeping things, and the truth of the false claims of that deluded young Siyyid had now been established."

JULIA: I must end this recital with the proven historical retributions that befell the major enemies of the Bab. We have already mentioned the abject circumstances in which Mirza Aqasi was forced to spend his final days, and Muhammad-Shah, who had submissively agreed with him that he should not meet with the Bab, was carried off at forty-five by a combination of painful diseases. The governor of Shiraz, Husayn Khan, was relieved of his post for his cruel activities and incompetence, and spent the remainder of his life in poverty and shame. The Prime Minister of Nasiri'd-Din Shah, Mirza Taqi Khan, embroiled in the intrigues of the new court, was not only deprived of his former honors, but fled the capital in disgrace, and was pursued by court enemies who opened his veins and left him to bleed to death.

There were many others in high places who had contributed in great measure to the waves of persecution and horror that swept over the land both before and after the execution. The death-dealing Mayor of Tehran, who had caused the decapitation of seven of the leading citizens of Tehran—including the guardian uncle of the Bab who had moved there to be nearer to his nephew—was himself tortured and strangled by his enemies at court. The Shaykhul-Islam of Tabriz, who had inflicted the bastinado on the Bab at the time of his trial, was stricken with an agonizing paralysis of the limbs, and was shunned by his former underlings. The brother of Mirza Taqi Khan, who had presided over the execution in Tabriz, was imprisoned in unspeakable conditions, where he suffered intensely and soon died. Other persons in privileged places fell suddenly from grace, and still others found themselves unable to achieve their ambitious plans for power in the government or in the ranks of the clergy.

We might consider, if we wish to do so, that all these strange reversals from the former prominence of these people were due to pure coincidence, especially in a land where such changes of fortune often took place, and I leave that to your own opinions. But I cannot resist adding that the extraordinary pinpointing of these particular individuals descended likewise upon the second regiment of soldiers whose volleys had taken the life of the Bab. Although they might appear to be innocent of any savage intent, they too might have refused to deal the final blow as did the regiment under Sam Khan. Whatever the cause, two hundred and fifty soldiers and their officers of the second regiment were wiped out by the collapsing of a wall in a sudden and violent earthquake. The remaining five hundred, in a mutiny against the government, met the same fate as the Bab and his young disciple. They were executed by three volleys of bullets by another regiment, their dead bodies pierced by bayonets and lances, and left exposed in the same manner as their former victims.

You will wonder why I choose to enumerate these ubiquitous historical events in ending our tragic story of the Bab. I cannot possibly eliminate these happenings, for they have become as much a part of the new faith as the records of atonement in the other religions of the world. Indeed, the chaos that ensued in Persia after the death of the Bab was not only confined to the hostile individuals in the government and among the ulama, but appeared in the unprecedented and devastating occurrences in nature, which caused prolonged suffering for many years to the people of Persia. Severe dust storms, such as the one that arose in the area of the barracks on July ninth of 1850, continued to darken the skies for days at a time in Tabriz, and were followed by major earthquakes in both that city and Shiraz. Epidemics of cholera and other diseases, and sudden death from unknown causes, are recorded in the annals of this stricken land, as well as famine and starvation in areas formerly abundant with food. Such contemporary records by Persian and other historians are quite apart from any reference to the death of the Bab, but all agreed that the people at this time of calamity suffered "the like of which had never been known." Perhaps we can put all this down to the remarkable interconnection between any and all occurrences in the universe, a subject which has already been discussed here. I simply give you the facts as they occurred, and again you must appraise them in whatever way they appear to you.

A final comment on these periods of chaotic turbulence before and after the appearance of a Manifestation. Doctor Varqa pointed out that disorder appears to intensify until the new teachings are adopted and a new civilization established. We see this chaos in its worst forms today in Ireland, in Lebanon, in Iran, in Israel and its neighbors, and in fact in all areas of the globe, and it can only be described, from the standpoint of the usual up-and-down patterns of earthly life, as approaching the borders of madness. Indeed the Qayyúm has revealed to the world that the evolution of mankind proceeds in forward and backward steps, in cycles of unifying consolidation and opposing periods of violent disturbance and discord—that progress is not a straightforward linear process, but nevertheless tends always to a higher level than before. This is a learning process in the interests of evolution, surely, which eventually brings the lagging and rigid minds of the human species to recognize that such backwardness and disorder redounds to the detriment of themselves and of all mankind. When we finally appraise the world's history with this understanding, a new approach to our problems will begin to eliminate the past modes of thinking which have brought about our distorted swings on the way to maturity.

PHILIP: What you have just said is quite astounding, Julia. Perhaps you are unaware of the fact, but your statements are wholly in keeping with the most recent paradigm, the latest cause for excitement in the world of science. I have already expressed this non-linear behavior in the Chinese concept of yin and yang and vice versa, but discoveries in physics have carried this ancient concept to a new level of understanding as to how the universe operates as a unitary whole, responding to events, either positive or negative, which impinge upon the atomic structure behind the material world. This most recent, and startling, paradigm stems from the study of chaotic turbulence in nature—in weather patterns, in the ups and downs and the randomness of almost every area of activity and movement in the material world, including the behavior and diseases of the human body. Just as we have mentioned that a sneeze will affect all the atoms of the universe, the scientists engaged in the study of chaos have propounded what they have called the Butterfly Effect—that the movement of the wings of this tiny creation can change the weather halfway across the world by disturbing the air currents and causing a sudden and unexpected condition of chaos—a tornado, a hurricane or an unpredictable storm.

All of this will no doubt appear to the world at large as pure poppycock, and I have hesitated so far to introduce the subject in its latest form. But Julia's observations have induced me to bring it up, especially as she has declared that a revelatory teaching in the new faith has testified to both order and disorder in the universe. And our brightest minds in our scientific laboratories now assure us, as she too intimates, that there is a basic order in the universe which underlies the cyclical disorders, that the chaotic behavior we observe in this world will sooner or later return to a former position of relative stability—the hurricane will die down, the earthquake will cease, the flood will dry up, the stock market will stabilize, the war will end, and the chaos in the wake of a Founder of a new religion will eventually give way to a Golden Age in a new and diverse civilization.

This is a complex subject, friends, but let me assure you that the linear concept of evolution presented to the world by Newton and Descartes, and supposedly proven by Darwin, is no longer tenable. We should now understand that the way the universe works is not like a giant clock going steadily forward in one direction, but is more like a great sun-dial, whose ever-changing lights and shadows reflect the recurring cycles of our earthly history—cycles presided over by the orderly outpouring of the life-giving sun, which represents for us the balancing force behind the disorder in the world. How the scientists have come to the final conclusion of the order behind the chaos is a complicated procedure, but you can find the still-developing story of this marvelous paradigm in the latest scientific books and journals. I have been moved to bring this up at our last meeting to give you what I perceive as a great leap forward toward the unification of religion and science, for by this recent declaration in both areas we can readily see that these two basic divisions in the life of mankind are speaking at last with the same voice.

HAM: What you are saying, Philip, is music to my ears. The burden of holding back on the teachings of the Qayyúm has weighed heavily on both Julia and me, for they fully pertain to the world in which we now live. But the life of this great Prophet presents a series of dramatic events that in our estimation should stand apart in their vast significance, both in relation to the introductory mission of the Bab and to the prophesied continuity of the Qayyúm's role as a planetary Manifestation. We can only bring forcefully to your attention at this present time that this Greatest Name, the Promised One of all religions, has bestowed upon our stricken planet the healing solutions for our worldwide problems, personal and otherwise.

REVEREND AHEARN: I am sure that Madilyn will recall the words of the poet Robert Brook, which express succinctly the same sentiments which Julia and Ham have consistently held forth for us here. "Behind the night," he writes, "somewhere afar . . . there lies some white tremendous daybreak." It is my opinion that "somewhere afar" is a likely time element for a whole new system to be established on this earth, for the world is so politicized that any Prophet for our present day must deal not only with spiritual matters but with the whole realm of political activity—in other words, as Isaiah prophesied, the future Messiah must carry upon his shoulders the government of the world, an obligation which includes the economics of the whole planet, now in such chaotic disarray everywhere. The Christian religion of the past two thousand years has little specific advice to offer on these matters. The Christ advised the people of his day to "render unto Caesar that which is Caesar's, and unto God that which is God's," a command that is quite to the point, but since God has been almost eliminated in our day in favor of Caesar, and no active relationship exists today between church and state as upheld by government law in the West, we are desperately in need of counseling from the one great Source that has the power to bring about a new and advanced civilization for both East and West.

MADILYN: This may come about, actually, sooner than one might expect. Indeed this new system is functioning worldwide today among millions of members of the new faith, regardless of the perilous state of the world. In this respect the Bab wrote of his own appearance as follows: "O Hour of the Dawn! Ere the resplendent glory of the Divine Luminary sheddeth its radiance through the Dayspring of this Gate, call thou to mind that the appointed Day of God will indeed be at hand in less than the twinkling of an eye." Emphatically reiterating the principle of progressive revelation as the God-given system for the evolution of mankind, he reveals that all the Prophets of God since the time of Adam have looked forward to this Day of Redemption, and have spoken of the final spiritualization of man. The purpose underlying his own Revelation, he writes, "has been to announce the advent of the Faith of Him whom God will make manifest." And every faith in its turn, he tells us, together with all the Revelations preceding it, prepared the way for the Revelation that was still to follow. "The process of the rise and the setting of the Sun of Truth," he assures us, "will thus indefinitely continue—a process that hath no beginning and will have no end . . . Well is it with him who in every Dispensation recognizeth the Purpose of God for that Dispensation, and is not deprived therefrom by turning his gaze to the past."

JULIA: The clock tells me it is time to bring things to a close. Let us take away with us the prophecy and the promise of the Qayyúm to the two hundred nations and territories of our planet undergoing the death pangs of their obsolete systems and the birth pangs of a new and unified civilization.

"Beseech ye the one true God," He addresses mankind, "to grant that all men may be graciously assisted to fulfil that which is acceptable in Our sight. Soon will the present day order be rolled up, and a new one spread out in its stead. Verily, thy Lord speaketh the truth, and is the Knower of things unseen."

Along with this spiritual food, dear friends, we are blessed tonight with a tempting variety of refreshments from the ladies of the Unitarian church. Thanks to Reverend Ahearn they are now aware of a new Name to place among the Founders of our world religions. Enjoy yourselves as we "break bread" for our last evening together—and Ham and I give you our final thanks, each and every one, for the unflagging attention and the wise and pertinent contributions you have bestowed upon us in this house.

One last word before we come to the close of our final meeting. Madilyn will recognize these four lines from the visionary poetry of Lord Tennyson, who clearly foresaw the future Parliament of Man:

> "Our little systems have their day;
> They have their day and cease to be:
> They are but broken lights of Thee,
> And Thou, O Lord, art more than they."

But I wish to leave you with the thought that these systems of Tennyson's poem, applicable to the Dispensations of the past, have nevertheless been preparatory for a Day that shall not be followed by night—a Day presided over by a Universal Prophet under whose spiritual guidance a line of succeeding Prophets will appear on earth approximately every one thousand years. Bringing with them progressive Revelations of the knowledge of the universe and its Creator, these subsidiary Prophets of God will forward the evolutionary process toward the total spiritualization of mankind. The Dispensation of this great planetary Prophet is thus a culminating Day to all that has gone before it in the life of the human species as we know it, a Day which the Bab has described for us in these revelatory words:

"Better is it for a person to write down but one of His verses than to transcribe the whole of the Bayan and all the books that have been written in the Dispensation of the Bayan. For everything shall be set aside except His Writings, which will endure until the following Revelation. And should anyone inscribe with true faith but one letter of that Revelation, his recompense would be greater than for transcribing all the heavenly Writings of the past and all that has been written during previous Dispensations. Likewise, continue thou to ascend through one Revelation after another, knowing that thy progress in the knowledge of God shall never come to an end, even as it can have no beginning."

Epilogue
by Professor Hamilton Adams

Almost five years have now passed by since the foregoing dialogues took place in our home. Because of our busy lives and the various commitments of our colleagues, the tapes remained untouched on a closet shelf until July of this year, when Julia and I found time to edit the contents for possible publication. We had not forgotten for a moment that the tapes were there to be reviewed, and have always hoped for further discussions that would carry us forward to the more recent happenings in a rapidly changing world.

In this first presentation of discussions on matters that Julia and I felt were of paramount importance to our present world, we decided to leave my own Introduction and Julia's Islamic Prelude as they were first written, and we have not altered the basic comments or opinions of our colleagues except to join certain of their statements together, as I have already observed in my Preface to the dialogues. But I must note that so much of further historical importance has taken place in the past five years, some foreshadowed in the present book, that any renewal of our dialogues must now incorporate events of such import the world over that no amount of imagination could possibly have foreseen them in our initial meetings as occurring before the twentieth century had come to an end.

We are delighted, therefore, that our original group—with the exception of our good friends Philip and Helen, who finally decided to marry and are now teaching in an eastern university—have shown a definite desire to come together once again for another round of talks. In the beginning of the fall semester two new members of the faculty—Professor of Economics Stanley Crozier, formerly of the University of Beirut in Lebanon, and Nora Strawbridge, a newly appointed Professor of Journalism—were told of our former meetings and have mentioned their interest in joining our reassembled group. Professor Strawbridge has spent many years in reporting the important happenings in the Near and Middle East, and on her last assignment escaped from the dangerous regime of the Ceausescu family in Rumania. The addition of these two colleagues would add greatly to our understanding of the incredible turn-about in the nations of communist Eastern Europe, in Latin America, in Africa, and behind the scenes in China, areas of upheaval that both professors have dealt with in their writings.

Professor Strawbridge has expressed her opinion that a prolonged period of social unrest, often violent in nature, will run parallel to the obvious forces of unification and new and startling alliances now unfolding in the world, and both she and Professor Crozier seem to agree that a major problem everywhere lies in the ever-increasing distortions in the world's financial institutions and money exchanges, the lack of balance in the currencies of the different nations, and the whole field of economics in relation to the rich and the poor. Such world-wide distortions, they believe, as severe as they already are, will continue to plague one country after another, and along with the problem of divergent religions and philosophical beliefs will offset the recent gains in the downfall of communism and the unification of parts of Europe. In their talks with Professor Heller, who has recently published a successful book on the ignorance of the Western world in its lack of knowledge and understanding of other peoples, their cultures and their religions—the result, he maintains, of our defective educational system—our new colleagues have expressed an interest in discussing the principles of the new faith which he has courageously outlined in his book in spite of Philip's advice.

We are hopeful that in April or May of the coming year we will gather a group together once again to examine the present trends in a wide range of global affairs. For those who will have read our conclusions in Dialogues I, any follow-up discussions should clearly establish that we have correctly foreseen the unavoidable breakdown of the old order of things and the painful and prolonged step-by-step unfoldment, prophesied by the Twin Prophets, of a new world order for mankind.

Julia has insisted that we leave the reader with an all-important fact in connection with the phrase "a new world order." The future order revealed by the planetary Prophet and envisioned by the new faith has no relationship whatever to the so-called "world order" proclaimed by former dictatorial leaders bent on military conquests, nor by present-day political visionaries, however well intended. As for the new world order declared by certain writers as being prepared behind the scenes by conspirators in high places, with plans to establish an autocratic world government that will deliver the resources of the whole planet into their eager hands, it goes without saying that the planetary governing body outlined by the Qayyúm can in no way be compared with such power-hungry mundane plans. The world order we will deal with in Dialogues II, in all its aspects, material and moral, is spiritual in nature, and will mark for the human race not only a final coming of age, but a subsequent upward movement on the great planetary arc of its earthly evolution.

December, 1990

Appendix by the Author

As stated in the Foreword, I am hereby listing a variety of basic books which have made it possible to embark on the background material for Dialogues I. These books do not contain the life of the Qaim nor that of the Qayyúm, whose missions and life histories were introduced to Julia and Hamilton Adams by Doctor Varqa in Tehran. As I have hitherto explained, the details of these lives, other than the information to be found in these initial Dialogues, have been reserved for prospective discussions in the spring months of 1991, and I have postponed the listing of the major volumes, running into many dozens of books, which will lead us into the very heart of the twin Revelations poured out upon the world in the nineteenth century and the subsequent sufferings and final exile of the Universal Prophet as a Prisoner in the Holy Land.

And once again I must emphasize that the scenes and conversations presented as taking place in the Karbila school are fictional, though the settings, the contemporary events, and the contents of the teachings are in keeping with both contemporaneous accounts and the most recent historical findings by scholars in the faith. Mustafa's journal has provided an opportunity to combine these two sources of information, and adheres as closely as possible to the actual facts of an often confusing period in the life of the faith. And finally, where revelatory quotes are presented as coming from either the Qaim or the Qayyúm, they have been taken verbatim from the Writings of the Prophets themselves. On the other hand, the spoken words of the Qaim in Mustafa's journal are fictional but reflect the statements made in the same context in such accounts as The Dawn-Breakers by Nabil and in the contemporary reminiscences of the Herald Prophet's closest companions.

It remains to point out that the journey between Bushihr and Shiraz of a group of sixteen Shaykhi scholars in their search for the Qaim is conjectural, as well as the conversations between Mulla Husayn, Mulla Ali and Mustafa during the days of indecision in Shiraz in respect to the claims of the Bab. Nevertheless, such scenes and conversations, once again, are based on contemporary reports, on accounts in Nabil's narrative, and on recent findings by scholars in the faith.

Acknowledgement of Sources for Dialogues I

1. *Muhammad and the Course of Islam* by H. M. Balyuzi, George Ronald Publishers, Oxford, England, 1976.
2. *Muhammad the Messenger of God* by Betty Kelen, Thomas Nelson Inc., New York, 1975.
3. *The Holy Qoran*, Translation and Commentary by A. Yusuf Ali, The Islamic Center, Washington, D.C., 1978.
4. *The Qoran Interpreted* by Arthur J. Arberry, George Allen and Unwin Ltd., London, 1955.
5. *In the Path of God: Islam and Political Power* by Daniel Pipes, Basic Books, Inc., New York, 1983.
6. *History of Early Iran* by George G. Cameron, University of Chicago, and Greenwood Press, New York, 1968.
7. *History of the Persian Empire* by O. T. Olmstead, University of Chicago Press, 1948.
8. *The Columbia History of the World*, edited by John Garraty and Peter Gay, Harper and Row, New York and London, 1972.

9. *History's Timeline* by Cooke, Kramer and Rowland-Entwistle, Crescent Books, Crown Publishers, New York, 1980.

10. *Crossroads of Civilization (Persia)* by Clyde Irving, Weidenfeld and Nicolson, London, 1979.

11. *Great Religions of Modern Man* (6 volumes), George Braziller Publishers, New York, 1961.

12. *The Nature of Religion* by Robert O. Ballou, Basic Books Inc., New York and London, 1968.

13. *The Varieties of Religious Experience* by William James, Macmillan Publishers, New York and London, 1968.

14. *The Old and New Testaments of the Bible*, King James and New English versions.

15. *Creation* by Gore Vidal, Random House, New York, 1981.

16. *The Tao of Physics* by Fritjof Capra, Bantam Books, New York, 1977.

17. *The New Story of Science* by Robert M. Augros and George Stanciu, Bantam Books, New York and Canada, 1984.

18. *Great Essays in Science*, edited by Martin Gardner, New American Library, New York, 1984.

19. *God and the New Physics* by Paul Davies, Simon and Schuster, New York, 1983.

20. *The Dancing Wu Li Masters* (Physics and Mysticism) by Gary Zukav, Bantam Books, New York and Canada, 1980.

21. *The Global Brain* by Peter Russell, J. B. Tarcher Inc., Los Angeles, 1983.

Fictional Characters in Dialogues I

1. Doctor Varqa of Tehran, fictional descendant of historical characters Mirza Jani and his brother Sabeh of Kashan.
2. Mustafa and his grandfather Mirza Jamal, fictional nephew and father of Mirza Jani and Mirza Sabeh.
3. Professors Julia and Hamilton Adams and their four campus colleagues engaged in the dialogues.
4. The Reverend Ahearn, Unitarian minister, and Madilyn Heller, poetess, wife of Professor Heller, members of the group.
5. Professor Heller's relatives in Chicago, members of the new faith.

Historical Characters

1. The Qaim and the Qayyúm, the Twin Prophets arising in Persia in the nineteenth century.
2. Shaykh Ahmad and Siyyid Kazim, Forerunners of the Qaim, and founders of the Shaykhi school in the holy city of Karbila in Iraq.
3. All the characters in Julia's Prelude on the history of the Muslim religion from its inception in 610 A.D. through the nineteenth century.
4. The Eighteen Letters of the Living, the devoted disciples of the Qaim, the Gate to the Qayyúm. All but one of the Letters (Qurratul-Ayn) are former scholars in the Shaykhi school in Karbila, as named in the text of the dialogues.
5. The monarchs of the Persian court, their families and ministers, and all those mentioned as persecuting the Qaim and the Babi believers in Persia and Iraq.

The abbreviated excerpts from the writings of the Qaim and the Qayyúm in the last chapter have been checked for their correctness by a designated scholar in the faith.

Personal Acknowledgments

And last but not least, I wish to make the following acknowledgments in connection with the writing of this book.

First, my heartfelt thanks to Dolores Springer who did such a wonderful job of computer-typing the manuscript, and gave me valuable advice on rearranging certain phrases and statements to clarify their intended meanings. Her interest in material new to her was a special boon to me, coming as it did from the first reader to encounter Dialogues I.

My sincere appreciation goes as well to Hans Loffel of Fingerprints Graphic Design and Printing, who designed the cover of the book and patiently aided me with the galley proofs, the map and the various adjustments required in transforming a manuscript into a printed book. His help enabled me to complete a final product in record time on my own home soil in Hawaii.

Finally, and to the greatest extent possible, I wish to express my gratitude to my housemate Bernice Caine. Without her kind attentions, the good meals, the many errands and household chores generously provided by her, there would have been no opportunity of my working on the foregoing project. Her verbal encouragement on my presentation of a world view of the basic problems of our day has given me the hope that the Dialogues will coincide, in the not too distant future, with a final recognition that a new order, spiritual in nature, is in the making for all the peoples of our planet.